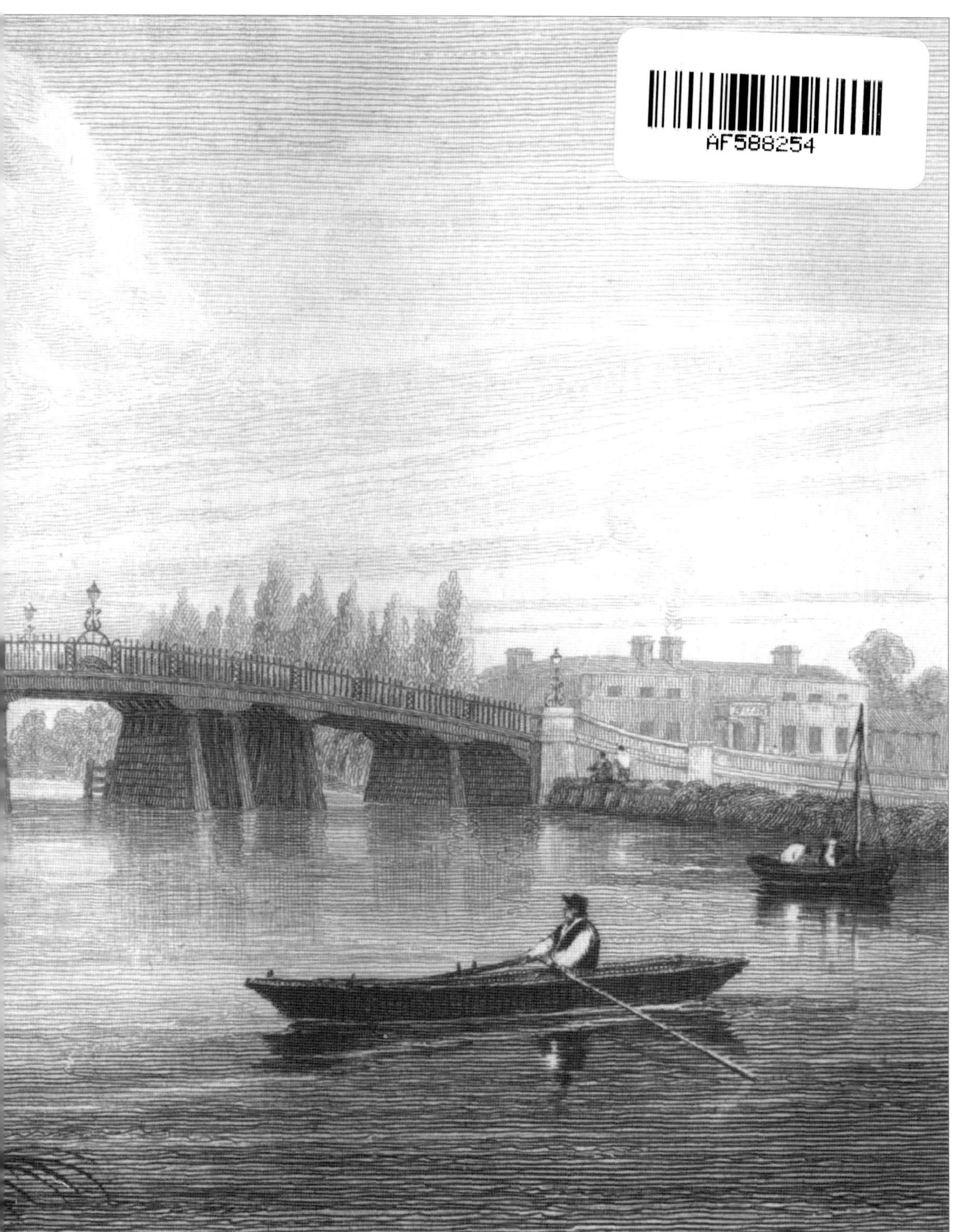

Staines Bridge from *Views on the Thames* by W.B. Cooke and George Cooke.

THE MIDDLE AND LOWER THAMES
FROM SONNING TO TEDDINGTON

A Pictorial History

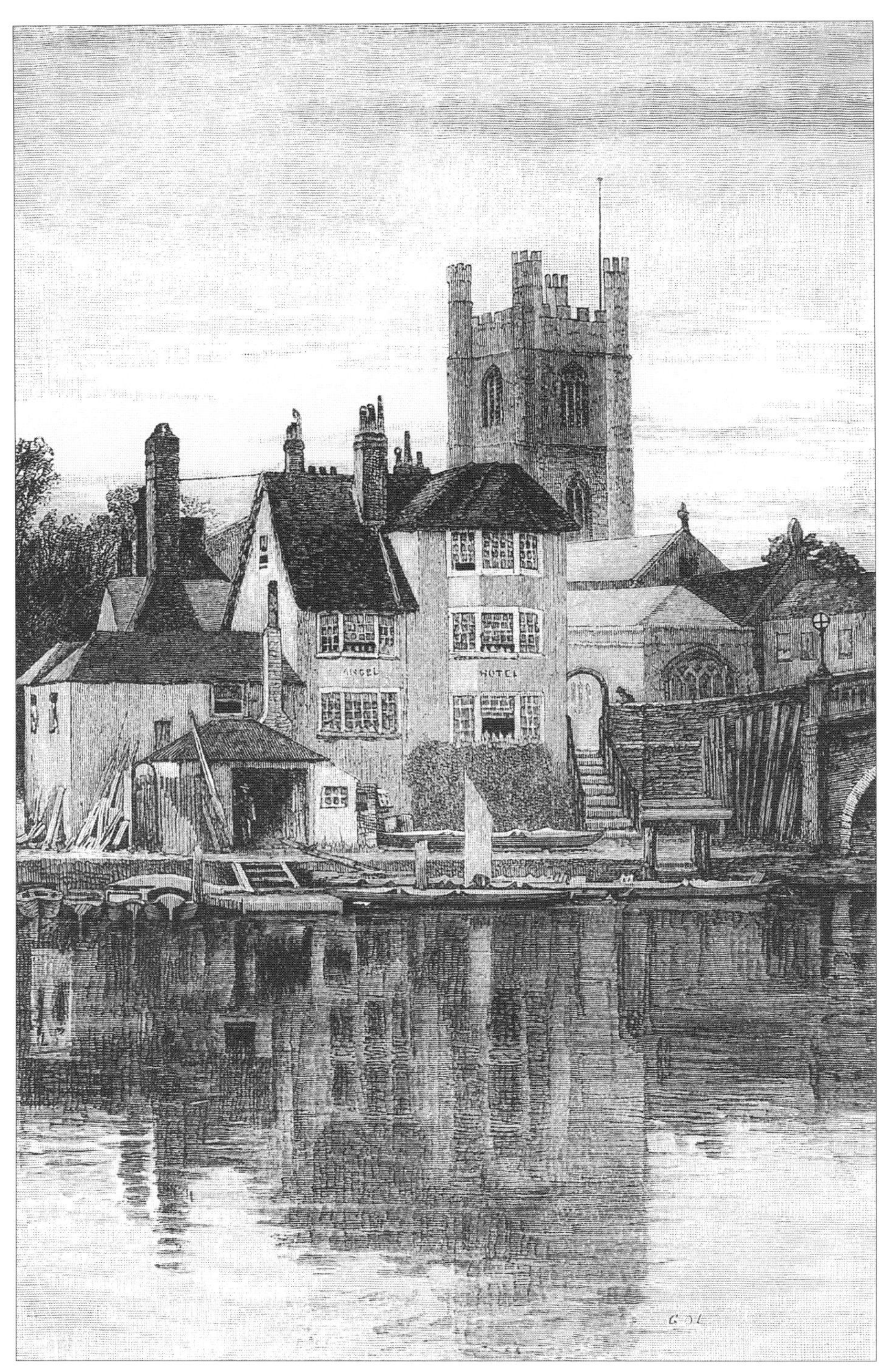

Angel Hotel, Henley-on-Thames, *c.*1880s.

The Middle and Lower Thames
from Sonning to Teddington

A Pictorial History

Josephine Jeremiah

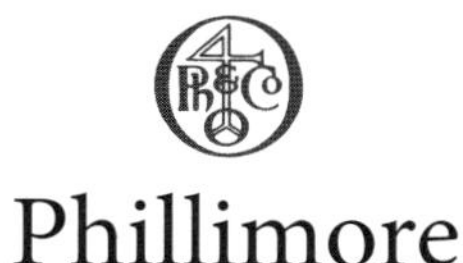

Phillimore

2009

Published by
PHILLIMORE & CO. LTD
Chichester, West Sussex, PO20 2DD, England
www.phillimore.co.uk

ISBN 978-1-86077-583-3

Printed and bound in Great Britain

List of Illustrations

Frontispiece: *Angel Hotel*, Henley-on-Thames, *c.*1880s

Hedsor to Boveney Lock

Windsor to Bell Weir

Staines to Hampton Court Palace

Thames Ditton to Teddington Weir

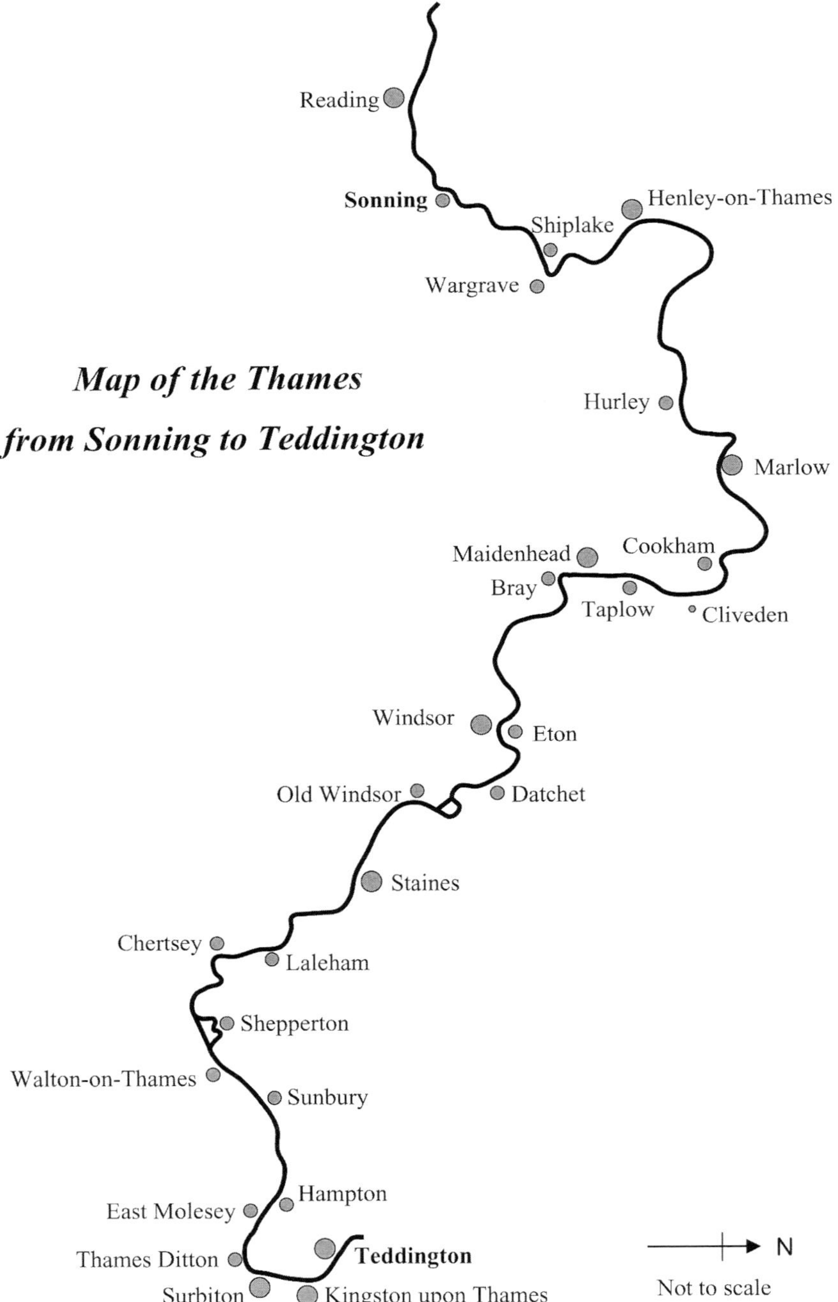
Map of the Thames
from Sonning to Teddington
Reading
Sonning
Shiplake
Henley-on-Thames
Wargrave
Hurley
Marlow
Maidenhead
Cookham
Bray
Taplow
Cliveden
Windsor
Eton
Old Windsor
Datchet
Staines
Chertsey
Laleham
Shepperton
Walton-on-Thames
Sunbury
Hampton
East Molesey
Teddington
Thames Ditton
Surbiton
Kingston upon Thames
N
Not to scale

An Historical Journey

My first experience of boating on the River Thames below Reading was during a trip downriver from Lechlade with my husband, Ian, in a small 16ft-long boat during the summer of 1977. Our destination was Cliveden, but, after mooring there, we took the wrong turning and spent some time wandering in the woods before finding the right path to Cliveden House. Later excursions, in a narrowboat, included cruising down to Teddington and stopping off at well-known places along the way, some of which were familiar from my childhood. I remember happy family outings to Henley-on-Thames, Hampton Court Palace and Windsor. My recollection of Henley is of the town being decorated for the Henley Regatta, while a memory of Hampton Court is of my aunt getting lost in the famous maze there. As a child, I was fascinated by Queen Mary's Dolls' House at Windsor Castle. Little did I think then that, many years later, my thoughts would be centred on these and other places along the 'Royal River'.

Rising in the Gloucestershire Cotswolds, the River Thames flows in a generally easterly direction for 215 miles to the sea. It passes Cricklade, Lechlade and Eynsham before reaching Oxford, after which it flows on past Abingdon, Wallingford and Reading. From Sonning the Thames goes past Henley-on-Thames, renowned for its regatta, to Marlow and then Cookham. Running through spectacular wooded scenery at Cliveden, it passes Maidenhead and flows on to Windsor, celebrated for its castle, and Eton, noted for its college. The river continues past Runnymede, where Magna Carta was signed, and Staines, where the London Stone marked the ancient boundary of London's jurisdiction on the Thames. Flowing past Shepperton and Sunbury, the river reaches Hampton Court Palace and then Kingston upon Thames before arriving at Teddington Lock, below which it becomes tidal.

The upper part of the River Thames was the focus of an historical journey in *The Upper and Middle Thames from Source to Reading* (2007). This second volume, featuring the middle and lower reaches of the non-tidal Thames, is a continuation of the journey in the words and illustrations of 18th- and 19th-century authors and artists and in the postcards of early 20th-century photographers. In the illustrations various pleasure boats are depicted, while some of the earlier aquatints and engravings show sailing barges on the river. River craft at this time included West Country or 'western' barges. According to Peter H. Chaplin, in *The Thames from source to Tideway* (1982),

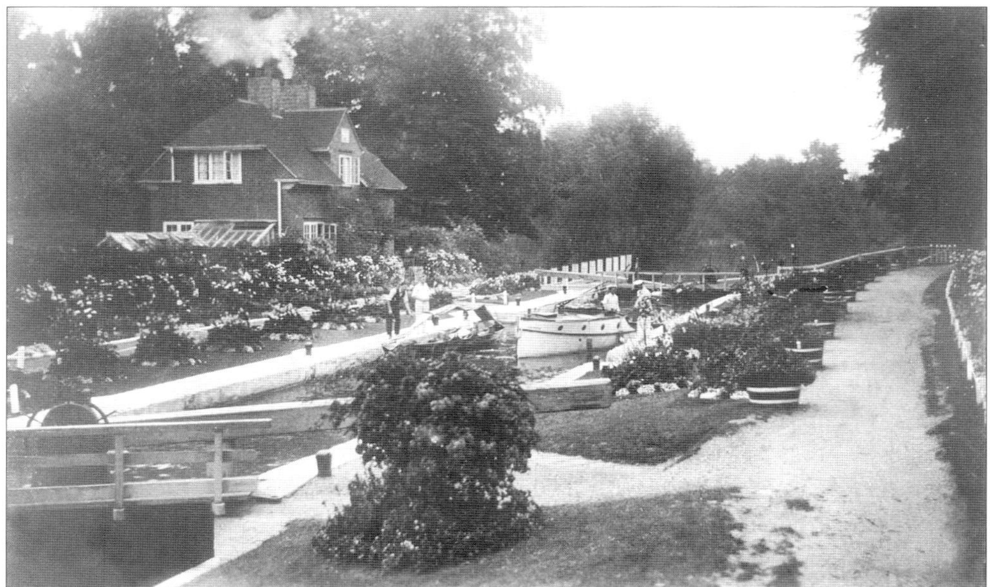

1 Writing in the early 20th century about Sonning Lock, Horace Bamford, in *The Old-World Village of Sonning-on-Thames*, remarked that 'no Lock more charming can be found on Thames side'. He commented that artists such as Holman Hunt and George D. Leslie were well known to the old lock keeper here.

these barges varied from 25 to 200 tons, while E. Paget-Tomlinson, in *Britain's Canal and River Craft* (1979), put their capacity from 40 to 146 tons. They usually bore one sail and were around 80ft in length and 12ft in width. Their central masts could be let down so that the vessels could go under bridges. As the sails did not always supply the necessary propulsion, towlines were fastened to the tops of the masts. In the 18th century, the barges on the river were hauled by gangs of men known as 'halers', but by the 19th century they were towed by horses.

An example of some of the goods carried on the Thames in the late 18th century can be found in *The Universal British Directory of Trade, Commerce and Manufacture* (1791). Concerning Henley-on-Thames it stated, 'A considerable trade is carried on from hence to London in malt, grain, flour and beech-wood'. At Marlow it noted, 'The Thames brings goods hither from the neighbouring towns especially great quantities of meal and malt from High Wycomb and beech from several parts of the county, which abounds with this wood more than any in England.' At this time, a commodity brought upriver from London was coal.

A century later, the River Thames was known more for its pleasure boating and recreational use than for its trading boats. In Victorian times, the attractive scenery and the fishing on the Thames drew many visitors to **Sonning** in Berkshire where a charming riverside walk, bordered by the tall trees of the adjacent Holme Park, was known as Thames Parade. Among those who came to the vicinity was the artist and author George D. Leslie who, in *Our River* (1888), observed, 'The view of the church and bridge from the tow-path is one of the best composed group for a landscape painter I ever saw.' He also wrote about **Sonning Lock** as being 'much celebrated for its roses and bees, which are both cultivated and attended to by Mr. Sadler, the lock-keeper'.

Jerome K. Jerome, the author of *Three Men in a Boat* (1889), described Sonning as 'the most fairy-like little Nook on the whole river'. Visitors to the Thames at Sonning, in Victorian and Edwardian times, may well have agreed with him. Mr and Mrs S.C. Hall, in *The Book of the Thames* (1859), remarked, 'The church and village of SONNING are very simple, but highly picturesque ... many of the cottages are covered with climbing plants — the old honeysuckle, the time-honoured jasmine, and the sweet clematis, mingled with the more recent acquirements of simple florists of humble homes.'

In *A New Map of the River Thames, from Thames Head to London* (1879), Henry Taunt noted, 'At Sonning the river branches out, encircling a group of islands.' In the fifth edition of his book, published in 1886-7, the author commented that a 'pale cold flower' called the snowflake grew on these islands in May. This is the rare wild flower known as 'Summer Snowflake' or 'Loddon Lily'. Its Latin name is *Leucojum aestivum*.

About a mile downriver of Sonning, the unnavigable St Patrick's Stream leaves the river and joins the River Loddon, which flows into the Thames below Shiplake Lock. Referring to another now rare flower, George D. Leslie, in *Our River*, noted, 'In the meadows about the Loddon and the St. Patrick's Stream in the spring time the beautiful fritillary or snake's head can be found growing in great abundance.'

Upstream of the lock, **Shiplake** is situated on a chalk cliff on the Oxfordshire bank. The church of St Peter and St Paul is renowned for its ancient stained-glass windows, which were originally in the Abbey of St Bertin at St Omer. Another claim to fame is that the poet Lord Tennyson was married here in June 1850. George D. Leslie described the scene at **Shiplake Lock** and Mill:

> The Mill is a fine specimen of a Thames mill, having plenty of nice woodwork about it; the lock is at present kept by an old man-of-war's man, who has erected a flagstaff in his garden, and hoists the colours on it in orthodox fashion. Little camping parties are here generally found; the view of the mill from the weir water behind the lock is a good one, and the whole of this water with its eyots will repay inspection.

A different view of the mill was given by Charles G. Harper, in *Thames Valley Villages Vol. II* (1910), who reported, 'Shiplake Mill, once a picturesque feature, is now at this time of writing, a squalid heap of ruins.'

Salter's Guide to the Thames of 1913 mentioned the long camping island beside Shiplake Lock, noting that it was owned by the Corporation of the City of London and that the tents and bungalow there could be hired through the lock keeper. The Thames Conservancy took out a long lease of the island the following year and generations of families have enjoyed this site since.

The next village, **Wargrave**, is downstream on the Berkshire bank. *Dickens's Dictionary of the Thames* (1887) described the village as being 'in the middle of a first-rate fishing district and highly popular among artists'. George D. Leslie made Wargrave his headquarters one particularly bad summer when 'sketching was almost out of the question', though he managed to do plenty of punting. That summer, he painted one side of the signboard of Wargrave's riverside hotel, the *St George and Dragon*, with St George on a white horse, spearing the dragon. His friend, J.E. Hodgson, painted the other side, showing St George 'having vanquished the dragon and dismounted from his horse, quenching his thirst in a large beaker of ale'.

Downriver of Wargrave is the entrance to a side stream only navigable by small craft. This is the Hennerton Backwater, which rejoins the main river after about a mile and a half. *Salter's Guide to the Thames* of 1913 noted that along the part of the Thames parallel to this backwater there was 'a long line of houseboats'. Among these was Mr A.G. Vanderbilt's *Venture*, built by Salter's of Oxford in 1909. According to the guidebook, this was 'perhaps the most luxurious houseboat in the world'.

Henry Taunt commented, 'Below Wargrave our attention is arrested by the beautiful background of hills, with the mansions embosomed among their clothing of woods; and nearing Marsh Lock, the river runs along at the foot of some bold cliffs, forming part of the grounds of Park Place.' Concerning the boathouse belonging to Park Place, it seems that 19th-century writers held differing opinions. Henry Taunt described it as 'a very picturesque boat-house in the Gothic style'. Mr and Mrs S.C. Hall wrote of visitors to **Park Place** landing at the 'very charming' boathouse, which in reality was a furnished dwelling containing 'some fine and severable remarkable, works of Art, — statues, pictures, wood-carvings, and foreign curiosities, — in the examination of which a half an hour may be profitably expended'. However, the American authors Joseph and Elizabeth Robins Pennell, in *The Stream of Pleasure* (1891), went 'past Park Place with its grotesque boat-house, niched and statued' without further reference to the locality.

Before Henley is reached, boaters have to pass through **Marsh Lock**. George D. Leslie observed, 'At Marsh Lock there are two Mills, one on each side, and the opposing currents from these Mills renders the approach to the lock from below always rather difficult.' The author of *Our River* added that Marsh Lock was a terrible one to pass through on Regatta morning. He remarked, 'I shall never forget coming through from Wargrave on one of these occasions. The gates could hardly open on account of the jam of boats against them, everybody as usual wanting to get in first, the ladies being by far the most eager and energetic in their endeavours.'

In the 1879 edition of his Thames book, Henry Taunt commented that there was not much of note in the town of **Henley-on-Thames** besides the bridge and the church, but that it was 'well known to oarsmen, on account of the annual Regatta held here, established in 1839, which may be considered one of the most successful meetings of the kind held in England'. George D. Leslie devoted a number of pages in *Our River* to an account of Henley Regatta during the late 19th century. He set the scene by describing the week before the races began, when along the high roads boats on carts were seen continually arriving and the various crews took up their quarters in the town, hanging their respective flags from the upper windows. The author remarked, 'On the bridge from morn till night a constant string of idlers and rowing men lean on the balustrade, watching the practice or gossiping with each other.'

According to George D. Leslie, when it came to the day before the race, the scene was even more animated:

> Wherever camping is allowed, small tents are seen, with their picturesque inhabitants busy in cooking, and making themselves at home. Great house-boats and steam launches, one after another, are taking up their positions along the appointed line, which, gay with bunting, already stretches down to Phillis Court. There are numbers of small boats and punts with awnings rigged up in them, beneath which parties of two or three make themselves independent of lodgings in the town. The occupants of these boats, and the campers generally, affect picturesque and rather outlandish costumes. Frequently at this time two or three of them are met on foraging expeditions, carrying great stone jugs for beer, or baskets of potatoes and meat.

Early on the morning of the first day's racing, the church bells rang out and numerous boats started arriving, while the early trains brought 'general riff-raff, along with some of the more eager and interested of the spectators', and the élite came by the later trains. The river gradually became covered with boats, which were 'scattered about

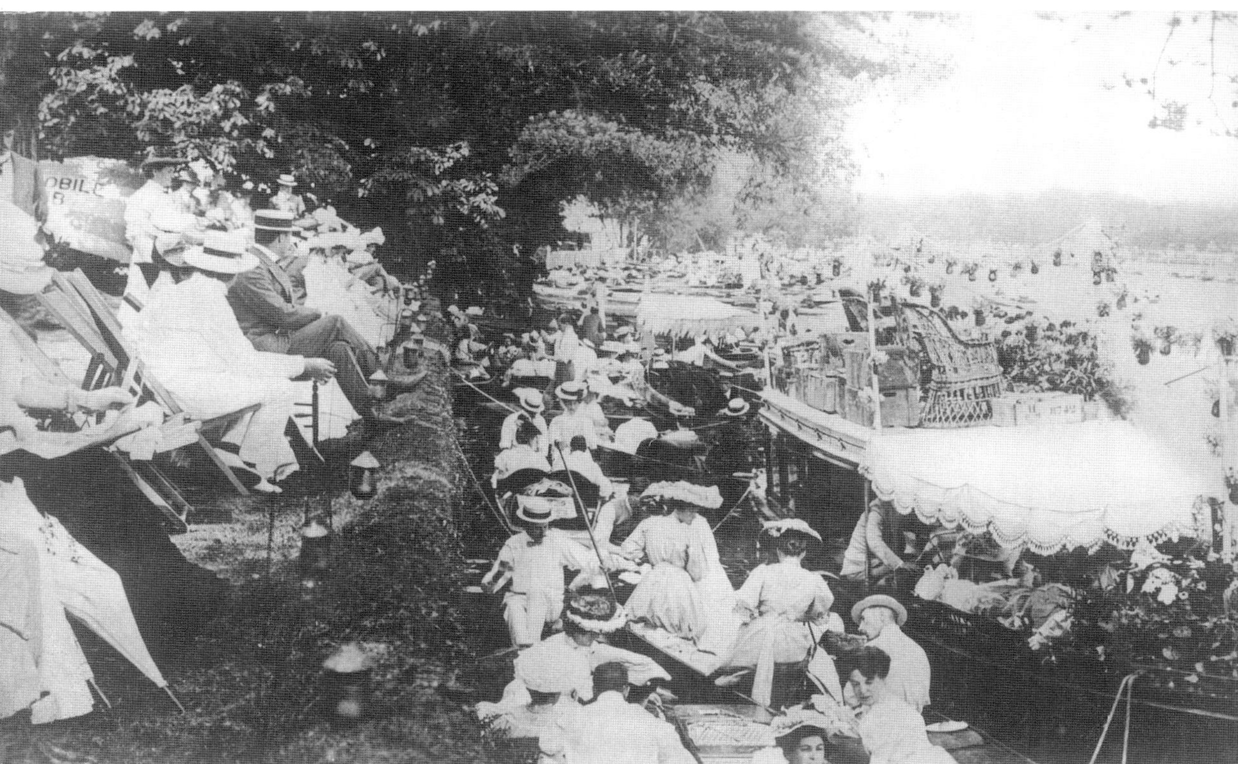

2 Lunchtime, Henley-on-Thames, *c.*1907. In *The Stream of Pleasure*, the Pennells observed that Regatta week was when Englishmen masqueraded 'in gay attire' and Englishwomen became 'symphonies in frills and lace,' and together had picnics 'in house-boats, launches, rowboats, canoes, punts, dinghies, and every kind of boat invented by man'.

in apparently hopeless confusion'. George D. Leslie remarked that 'the Conservancy men row up the stream, clearing the water as they go, and gradually driving, like sheepdogs, the straying herds of boats towards the Oxford shore'. Then the races began and he noted, 'Amidst the roar of cheers and the swell from the umpire's boat the sound of the band is heard playing the well-known air, and the first heat is lost and won.'

Downstream of Henley, the river flows past Fawley Court and **Temple Island**, on which stands an imitation temple built in 1771 as a vista to be seen from Fawley Court. The next lock is **Hambleden Lock**, which was opened in 1773, though a weir had been in existence for hundreds of years here and the mill was mentioned in Domesday. In *The Thames Highway Volume II: Locks and Weirs* (1920), Fred S. Thacker stated that the first lock keeper was Wm. Hall, who was paid 5s. weekly. He mentioned another lock keeper, Caleb Gould, who came to the lock in 1777 and was 92 years old at his death on 30 May 1836. George D. Leslie gave details of this long-lived lock keeper, who 'wore a long coat with lots of buttons' and who 'ate for his supper every night a dish of onion porridge', being 'hale and hearty to the very last'. This lock keeper and his son, Joseph, who came after him, sold bread to the bargemen and others, which was baked in the large oven at the back of the lock house.

There were once two ferries in the vicinity. Fred S. Thacker reported that that the Aston or Hambleden Ferry was a rope ferry in 1785, while George D. Leslie referred to it as 'the horse-ferry where the tow-path changes sides', located where 'a grassy lane leads down to the river from Aston and Remenham Hill'. Henry Taunt advised boaters to land at the ferry for Aston's inn, the *Flower Pot*. There was an advertisement in his book for the hotel at Medmenham Ferry, the next ferry downriver, where the towpath crossed again. This described the *Ferry Hotel*, Medmenham Abbey, as 'The snuggest inn on the river'.

Henry Taunt considered that the ivy-mantled **Medmenham Abbey** with its 'modern antique tower' was 'chosen as the favourite spot for picnicing by persons from Marlow and Maidenhead as well as Henley'. Mentioning Medmenham Abbey's infamous past he wrote, 'During the last century it acquired great notoriety as the meeting-place of a club of *débauchés* of rank and fashion: of their doings it would be unwise to speak, but the motto over the doorway sufficiently shows the class of men.' This motto was 'Fay ce que voudras' or 'Do what you will' and Henry Taunt was referring to the Hell Fire Club associated with Sir Francis Dashwood.

Charles G. Harper, in *Thames Valley Villages Vol. II*, noted that 'the lovely grass-lands over against Medmenham are glorious in June before the hay-harvest' and that one could walk by them along the riverbank to Hurley. The author observed that the ground, rising into chalk cliffs on the Buckinghamshire bank, was topped by the 'great unoccupied house of Danesfield', which was said to have as many windows as the days in the year, and commented that this was the handiwork of Mr R.W. Hudson of 'Hudson's Soap'.

Passing Danesfield House, now a hotel, **Hurley Lock** is soon reached. In the late 16th century and early 17th century, the weir here was known as 'Newlock' or 'New Lock'. The pound lock was opened in 1773, though around sixty years later the

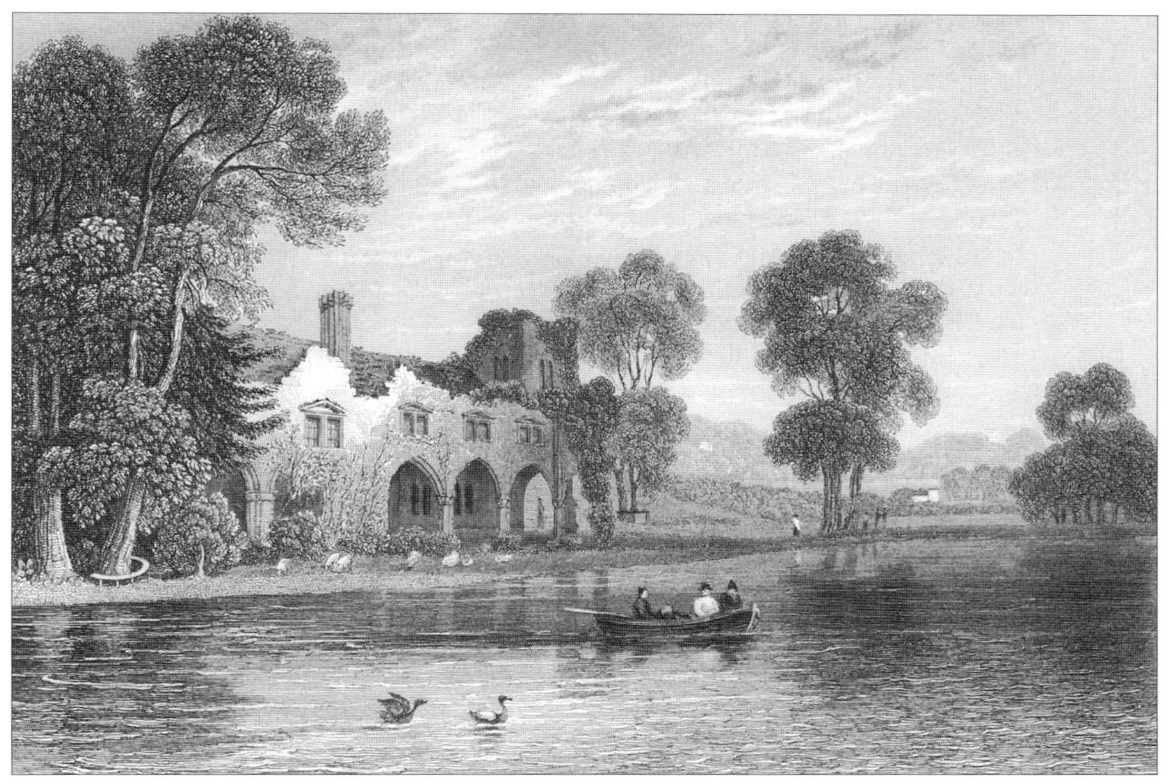

3 An engraving of Medmenham Abbey from *Eighty Picturesque Views of the Thames and Medway*, also known as *Tombleson's Thames*, c.1834 with a description by W.G. Fearnside:

> The abbey house, with its ivy-mantled walls, is an interesting object, and its effect is heightened by the addition of a modern-antique tower, cloisters, and other erections, corresponding with the style of the former building, and executed with great taste; so that when the hand of Time shall have rubbed off the sharp edge of the masonry, and covered it with a verdant mantle of ivy and moss, some future historian may class the modern with the ancient pile.

location was still referred to as 'New-lock wear' by W.G. Fearnside in *Tombleson's Thames*. A century later, it was noted in Ward, Lock & Co.'s *The Thames* that the very extensive weir at Hurley was most picturesque, while the backwaters of the islands were 'among the prettiest on the river'. This locality was a place well-known to campers. In the mid-1930s, there were tea gardens at the lock and the bathing pool was a favourite spot during summer weekends. However, in *Thames Journey* (1949), Paul Gedge observed that there had been changes. He remarked that 20 years previously people could stroll freely on the lower island between the lock cut and the backwater and bathe in the deep pool, but now the bathing pool was fenced off and fees were being charged for admission, while there was a CAMPING PROHIBITED notice in the centre of the island.

Hurley is the name of the nearby village on the Berkshire bank, which Mr and Mrs S.C. Hall described as 'pretty and picturesque'. They added, 'Adjoining Hurley was Lady Place, formerly a priory for Benedictine monks, more recently a stately mansion, but now indicated only by aged garden-walls.' This mansion, the seat of the Lovelace family in the 16th and 17th centuries, was taken down in 1837. The crypt of this house is said to have been the secret meeting place of the nobles who plotted the overthrow of James II, which resulted in William of Orange coming to England in 1688 and subsequently accepting the throne as joint monarch with his wife, Mary.

Opposite Hurley, on the north bank, is **Harleyford Manor**, a red-brick Georgian house originally designed by the 18th-century architect Sir Robert Taylor. James Thorne, in *Rambles by Rivers: The Thames* (1847), described it as 'a large house surrounded with rich grounds, and as it lies embosomed among the trees, looking far better across the river than when close at hand'. George D. Leslie appears to have had the same opinion as he remarked that the house 'itself is ugly enough, though no house on the river has a sweeter situation'. Today, the estate is the home of Harleyford Marina and the setting for timber lodges, which are holiday homes.

Temple Lock comes next. Not far below the lock and weir is **Bisham Abbey**, once the home of the Hoby family. Legend has it that the abbey is haunted by a Lady Hoby who is said to have beaten her son to death for blotting his work with ink. This tale is supported by the discovery of some blotted copybooks of the period during repairs to the building. Today, Bisham Abbey is one of the National Sports Centres in the United Kingdom where training for over 20 different sports and organisations takes place. Bisham Abbey Navigation and Sailing School runs a variety of courses from this venue.

In John and Joshua Boydell's *An History of the River Thames* (1794), William Combes wrote, 'From Bisham abbey the river flows, in one beautiful length of about a mile, to Marlow, between meadows backed by arable uplands to the left, and a line of woods to the right. The spire of the church is seen at some distance, and the bridge on a nearer approach.' He added that the church was 'very ancient and spacious, with a wooden spire' and noted, 'A new bridge of wood, of a pleasing form, was built here in 1789, by a subscription of the neighbourhood; it is painted white, and is no inconsiderable ornament to the river.' When W.G. Fearnside described the location of **Marlow** in *Tombleson's Thames*, a new crossing over the Thames had recently been built. He wrote, 'The stream now flows on in an almost straight line to Marlow, situated on the left, in the midst of marl beds (whence, probably, its name) and passes under the fine iron suspension bridge, which connects with one span, the counties of Bucks and Berks.'

Marlow Bridge is associated with the long-remembered taunt to bargees of 'Who ate puppy-pie under Marlow Bridge?' This came about after the larder of a waterside hostelry was raided once too often by bargemen. In revenge, the innkeeper had a large 'puppy-pie' baked, which, as expected, was stolen by the thieves and consumed with much relish, beneath the bridge, before they knew of its contents.

On the Berkshire side of the bridge is the famous inn called the *Compleat Angler*, which is said to have once had the more modest name of the *Angler*. In *The Book of the Thames*, Mr and Mrs S.C. Hall noted:

> Marlow is the very paradise of the Thames angler ... among the other attractions ... is one of the pleasantest inns remaining in railway-ridden England; with a most kindly and accommodating landlady, who seems, by intuition — and certainly is from long practice — aware of all the ways and wants of brethren of the angle, who are her best, and, indeed, almost her only customers; for her 'hostelry' is not in the town, but a quiet nook close by the bridge on the Berkshire side of the river.

Nearly thirty years later, *Dickens's Dictionary of the Thames* advised ordinary boating parties not to rely on obtaining quarters at the well-known *Compleat Angler* near the bridge without giving considerable previous notice.

Describing the scene at **Marlow Weir**, W.G. Fearnside remarked, 'The Thames here branches out into two channels, one of which, on account of the stream being arrested by Marlow-lock, rushes over the weir to the right, forming a pleasing cascade, and adding much to the highly beautiful features of the surrounding scenery.' Henry Taunt, in the fifth edition of his Thames book, mentioned that the 'grand old weir' had recently been rebuilt with concrete blocks, which he thought may have been better for the stability of the weir, but which did not compare with the falling water of the former structure.

Fred S. Thacker, in *The Thames Highway Volume II: Locks and Weirs*, stated that his earliest note of navigation at Marlow, dating from 1306, was of a winch at Marlow and that there was a reference to it again in 1544. The first pound lock here was opened in

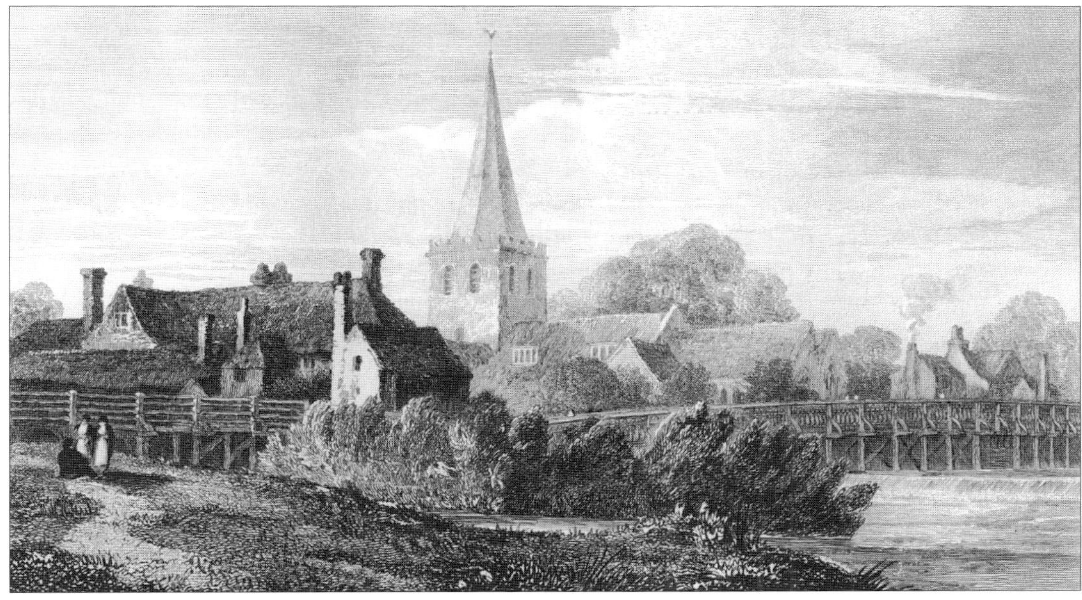

4 The church, bridge and weir at Great Marlow from *Views on the Thames* (1822) by W.B. Cooke and George Cooke. This illustration, drawn by S. Owen and engraved by W.B. Cooke, was first published on 1 October 1814. Replacing a timber structure, this wooden bridge was opened in 1789. It was superseded by the present suspension bridge in 1832. In the same year, the old church, having been affected by floodwater over the years, was rebuilt on higher ground.

1773 and this was replaced by another lock on a new site in 1826. George D. Leslie, in *Our River*, remarked that Marlow Lock and mill were 'very good old-fashioned specimens of their kind', but that the lock was 'a dangerous one to pass, being an old one, with many ragged piles and broken woodwork about its sides'. **Marlow Lock** was rebuilt by the Thames Conservancy in 1927.

Downriver from Marlow Lock, **Quarry Woods**, sloping down to the Thames on the Berkshire bank, were referred to as 'the Marlow walk' by Henry Taunt as they were a favourite location, especially when the trees had their autumn colours. *Dickens's Dictionary of the Thames* commented that the woods were within a ten minutes' saunter from Marlow Bridge and that picturesque walks could be taken by the riverside or over the hill to Cookham Dean. It was also noted that there was no more favourite spot on the river for camping than Quarry Woods.

George D. Leslie stated that Quarry Woods, with the islands in front of them, 'form a magnificent piece of scenery'. The author thought it was almost as fine as Cliveden, downstream, and was inclined to prefer it because of its wildness. He added, 'The eyots and backwaters are very beautiful, but I am sorry to say that since I first knew these woods a house has been built in their very heart, and the steam-launches moored in front considerably mar the otherwise perfect wildness of the place.'

W.G. Fearnside, describing the scene downstream of these hills and woods, observed, 'the heights of *Hedsor* and *Cliefden* are seen in the horizon ... forming a beautiful boundary to the prospect'. He added, 'Before we approach those places, we pass near a large farm-house on the left, called *Coare's*, *Bourne's* or *Bones* End, near which the rivulet *Wyke*, or *Wick*, merges its name and its waters in those of the Thames.' Later in the century, *Dickens's Dictionary of the Thames* dismissed **Bourne End** as being a place of no importance except for being a station on a branch of the Great Western Railway. *Salter's Guide to the Thames* of 1913 commented that the most conspicuous features of Bourne End were the green railway bridge and the boathouses and rafts. The guidebook mentioned sailing craft and racing boats were to be found practising on the wide stretch of the Thames here, as Bourne End was the headquarters of the Upper Thames Sailing Club.

Cookham also had a station on the Wycombe branch of the Great Western Railway, which Henry Taunt noted was five furlongs from Cookham Bridge. In advertisements from the 1879 edition of his Thames book, the *Bell and the Dragon* was promoted as being near the River Thames and ten minutes' walk from the station, while the *King's Arms Hotel* provided 'Dinners and Luncheons to Order, Large Parties Accommodated'. Near the bridge, the *Ferry Hotel*, having been extensively enlarged, offered 'superior accommodation to Anglers, Boating Parties and others visiting this the finest part of the Thames'. At this hotel, boats, punts and canoes were let by the hour, day, week or season 'on reasonable terms'.

According to *Dickens's Dictionary of the Thames*, Cookham stood at the end of what was considered to be the best part of the Thames and, along with Maidenhead, was probably better known by visitors from London than any other location on the river. Today, Cookham is also known for the Spencer Gallery, opened in 1962, which is devoted to the work of artist Sir Stanley Spencer, who was born in the village in 1891.

After Cookham Bridge, the river branches into four channels. One on the left sweeps around to Hedsor Wharf, from which timber and paper were shipped and coal unloaded when it was on the original navigation channel. Another is the lock cut, which, with **Cookham Lock**, was opened on 1 November 1830. The other two branches surround one of the largest islands on the river. **Formosa Island**, covering about fifty acres, can be accessed from Cookham by a footbridge. In *Picturesque Views on the River Thames* (1792), Samuel Ireland noted that Sir George Young had recently finished 'a handsome house' on this island for his 'constant residence'. However, the author observed, 'delightful as the situation may prove in the summer months, the winds and floods, it is to be feared, will render it uncomfortable in the winter season'. Both James Thorne, in *Rambles by Rivers: The Thames*, and *Dickens's Dictionary of the Thames* mentioned the pleasure grounds on the island.

Henry Taunt gave a description of the Thames in this vicinity in *A New Map of the River Thames, from Thames Head to London*:

> Passing down the Cut and through the Lock, we reach the overhanging woods, and turning short round, glide tranquilly along the river at their base; and here the scenery is the grandest on the river, but it is impossible to give any adequate description of it: it must be seen. The mind of everyone is so entranced with its loveliness that details cannot be entered into, but all is summed up in the one expression, 'How beautiful!' Cliveden House is built on the summit of the hill, and the view from its terrace is unequalled. The mansion was first erected by Geo. Villiers, Duke of Buckingham ... Villiers' house was destroyed by fire, and the present mansion — designed by Barry — erected in its place.

Formerly owned by the Duke of Westminster, **Cliveden** became the home of the Astor family in the late 19th century. William Waldorf Astor was a Member of Parliament until he became 2nd Lord Astor on the death of his father. In 1919, his wife, Nancy, became the first woman to take her seat in the House of Commons. Cliveden, now a National Trust property and a prestigious hotel, is remembered for being at the centre of the 'Profumo Affair', a political scandal of the early 1960s.

William Combes wrote of the river continuing its course 'beneath a chain of bold woody hills, which is crowned with Cliefden, a magnificent feature on the highest point, and Taplow-house in a less elevated situation; which, though it possesses not so stately a form, is a more picturesque object'. W.G. Fearnside remarked on the Thames now 'pursuing its unruffled course for some distance in peaceful serenity, beneath the shadowy and refreshing coolness of Cliefden woods'. He added, 'it then arrives at Boulters lock and weir ... On the left we observe Taplow paper-mills. The small village of Taplow lies in Buckinghamshire, removed a short distance from the river.'

In *The Stream of Pleasure*, Joseph and Elizabeth Robins Pennell noted that, between Marlow and Cookham and beneath the steep wooded slopes of Cliveden, 'the name of the smaller boats was legion'. They saw every possible kind of rowing boat, punts, dinghies, sailing boats, canoes and 'even a gondola and two sandolas'. The Pennells

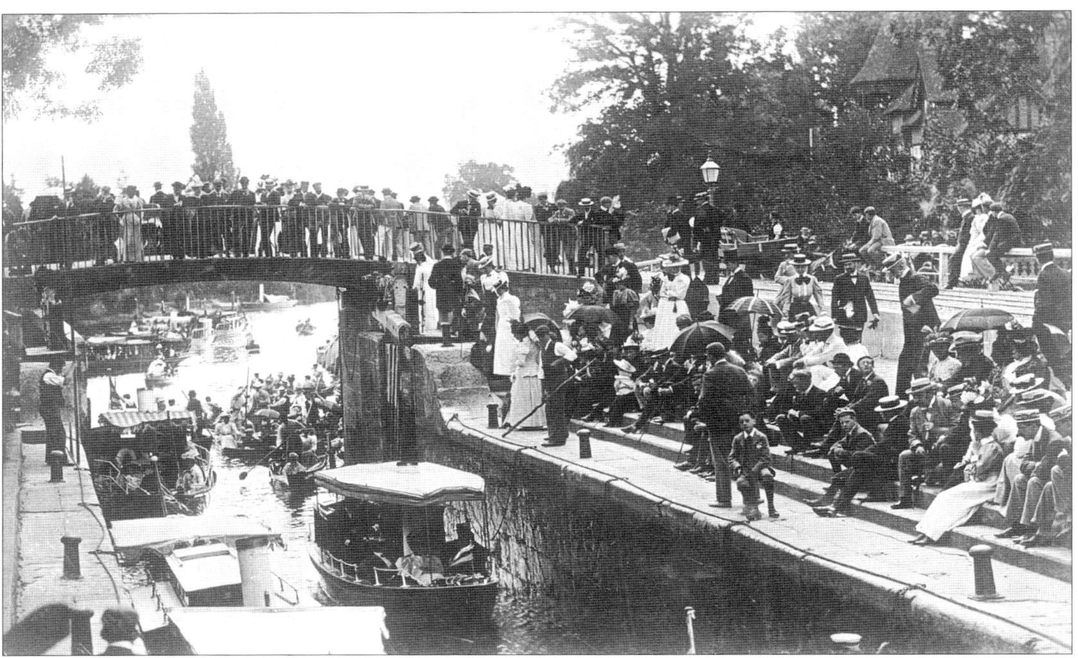

5 A view of Boulter's Lock, looking downstream. Steamers were making their way into the lock watched by many onlookers, while those in smaller craft, below the lock, waited their turn.

had found the locks in this vicinity more crowded than usual with men waiting on the banks with baskets of fruit and flowers, but it was while waiting outside **Boulter's Lock**, on the way back to Cookham, that they found the greatest crowd. When the lock gates opened, out came the boats 'pell-mell, pushing, paddling, poling, steaming' and the Pennells added that there was great scrambling and bumping and brandishing of boathooks. They made their way into the lock as best they could, with the lock keeper helping the slower boats with his boathook, until eventually all were fitted in and there was no space for even one to capsize. It was not only the lock which was crowded. The Pennells commented that both banks were lined with onlookers, as Boulter's Lock on a Sunday afternoon was 'one of the sights of the Thames'.

Henry Taunt's 1879 edition of his Thames book carried a variety of advertisements for places at **Maidenhead** where boats could be hired. At the *Ray Mead* hotel at Boulter's Lock, the steam launch *Undine*, suitable for large or small parties, was available along with 'Pleasure Boats and Punts of every description'. Henry Woodhouse of Bridge Street, a steam launch, boat, canoe and punt builder, had a new 55ft-long steam launch, *Princess Beatrice*, for hire, which was fitted up with every convenience. At Maidenhead Bridge, boat and punt builder Jonathan Bond offered 'Every Description of Pleasure Boats for Sale or Hire'.

Writing about Maidenhead, James Thorne, in *Rambles by Rivers: The Thames*, noted, 'The bridge over the Thames is a very fine one ... but it is far surpassed in grandeur of design by the bridge which, just below it, carries the Great Western Railway over the river, which is probably the finest brick bridge in England.' However, this author was rather disparaging about the town itself, remarking, 'Maidenhead is a market-town of one long street; but there is nothing in it to stay the feet of a rambler.' *Dickens's Dictionary of the Thames* was not very complimentary either, commenting that the town mainly consisted of two streets and was not very important or attractive.

In *Our River*, George D. Leslie described the river scene at Maidenhead:

> The bit of river between the railway and road bridges is familiar to all travellers on the Great Western Railway. A small eyot, formerly much wilder and much prettier, a row of eel-bucks, a pretty little boat-house by the side of the eyot, and two or three steam launches anchored off the coal wharf, form the main features of the scene, backed up by Bridge House and the 'Orkney Arms,' with the stone-bridge between them.

Travellers on the Thames in the 19th century found **Bray**, the next village downstream, worthy of mention. James Thorne observed:

> Passing under the railway bridge, we enter upon a portion of our river that is a perfect contrast to that we have just left. The country on each side is low, and long beds of osiers line the river, only the square tower of Bray church, rising from a clump of large trees before us, at all relieves the way.

George D. Leslie mentioned that 'here the river takes a bend to the left, and on the right you pass an eyot with eel-bucks on one side of it'. Noting that eel-bucks were generally placed in backwaters away from the course of the regular navigation, he added, 'a stage is raised up like a little wooden bridge, on the down-stream side of which a set of square frames like gallows is erected; up these frames the eel-baskets are raised by small wooden windlasses'.

Mr and Mrs S.C. Hall, in *The Book of the Thames*, advised, 'The voyager will surely go ashore at Bray, not only to examine the venerable church, but to speculate concerning that renowned vicar who has obtained a larger share of immortality than any of his predecessors or successors.' They were, of course, referring to the Vicar of Bray, the subject of a well-known folk song, who was said to have adapted his principles, during a period of religious changes, in order to stay in his position as vicar of Bray. Tradition has it that this vicar could have been Simon Aleyne, who held the office during the reign of four monarchs in Tudor times, or Simon Simonds, who was vicar of Bray during the Protectorate and the reigns of the later Stuart monarchs.

Dickens's Dictionary of the Thames noted that visitors to Bray from the river could land at the *George Inn*, while those walking on the Buckinghamshire side of the river could be ferried across if they hailed the opposite shore. Visits to both the church and to Jesus Hospital were recommended.

Downstream of **Bray Lock** is a bridge over the Thames carrying the M4 Motorway, which links London and South Wales. A short distance below the bridge is **Monkey Island**, which featured in 19th-century guidebooks to the Thames. James Thorne remarked that this island was one of the notable things between Bray and Windsor, of which there were not many:

> The first we come to is an island at which pleasure-parties usually land, and which is often visited by the angler. It rejoiceth in the name of Monkey Island, a name which it has received from a pleasure-house built on it by the late Duke of Marlborough, the drawing room of which is painted over with monkeys in all sorts of positions. The house is hastening to decay, and is only kept from entire ruin by the occasional attention of the fisherman and his family who live in a cottage on the island, and who rent the water for the fishery, and two or three of the neighbouring aits for the purpose of growing basket-rods, and who supply boiling water and the like for visitors.

Later in the 19th century, there was a hotel on Monkey Island. In 1879, it was advertised as being 'one of the most comfortable Hotels on the Thames' with 'Every accommodation for Picnic Parties and Excursionists', while there were boats and fishing punts to let and a fisherman was always in attendance. The *Monkey Island Hotel* is still in existence.

Water Oakley Court, downstream of Monkey Island, was described by Henry Taunt as 'a fine mansion in the castellated style', while *Salter's Guide to the Thames* of 1913 stated that it was once the property of the late Lord Otho Fitzgerald, but now belonged to Sir W.E.T. Avery. Today, the mansion, set in spacious grounds by the river, is a hotel known as the *Oakley Court Hotel.*

Boveney Lock is the next lock downriver. Henry Taunt observed that from this lock 'we catch the first good peep of the Royal Castle of Windsor; and all the way on we get pleasant views every now and then; till, passing under the Great Western Railway bridge, it bursts upon us in all its splendour'. The author added:

> The view of Windsor from the Brocas is the grandest on the River Thames. It should be seen with the red light of sunset glinting upon it; then the warm lights, contrasting so finely with the cold grey shadows, make every part stand out with boldness and reality; and the noble Round Tower, raising its head far above the surrounding buildings, gives a breadth and airiness to the whole.

W.G. Fearnside, in *Tombleson's Thames,* commented on the name and situation of **Windsor**:

> The place designated *New* Windsor, in contradistinction to the village of *Old* Windsor, which is of higher antiquity, is a borough and a market town ... The name is derived from the serpentine directions of the river, which in Saxon is *Windleshora*, or *Winding shore or banks*. It is about twenty-two miles from London by land, and forty-six by water. The delightful situation of the place has made it the favorite resort of most of our monarchs, even from the time of William the Conqueror.

Windsor Castle was founded by William the Conqueror. Succeeding monarchs have constructed and improved it over the centuries. This royal residence is said to be the

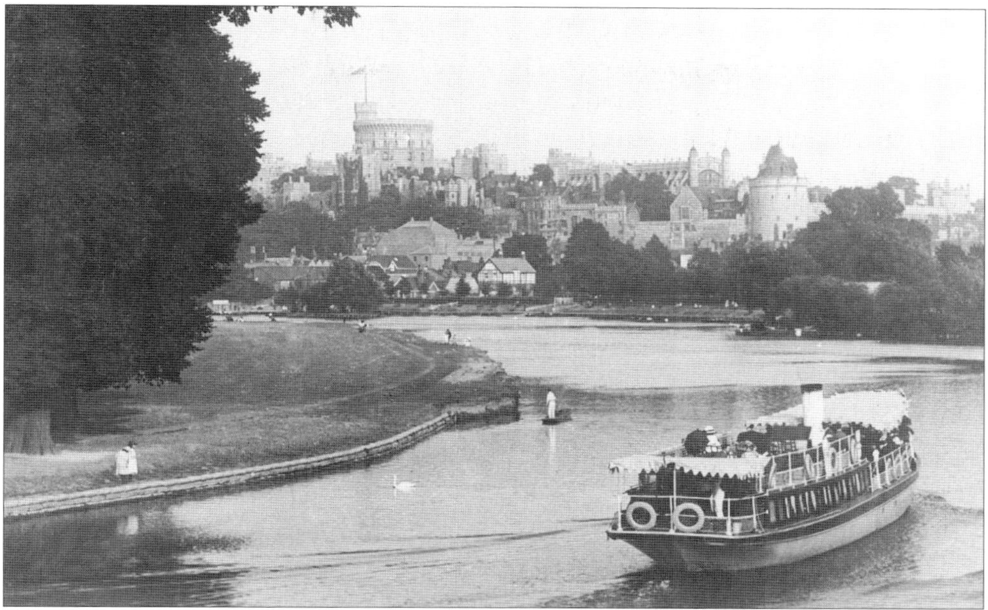

6 This postcard of Windsor Castle from the River Thames was postally used on 2 October 1916.

largest inhabited castle in the world. In the Lower Ward of the castle is the renowned St George's Chapel, while in the Middle Ward is the Round Tower. The private apartments and the State Apartments are in the Upper Ward. James Thorne, in *Rambles by Rivers: The Thames*, commented, 'Whatever of interest attaches to Windsor is centred on the Castle. The town is of goodly extent, has a large and busy population, yet it is quite lost sight of in the deep shadow of the mighty pile beneath which it lies.'

There are, of course, other aspects of Windsor which are worthy of note. The Town Hall, in High Street, was designed to accommodate a corn market beneath the meeting chamber. It was completed by Sir Christopher Wren in 1689. The four Portland stone pillars in the centre of this open area were added to allay fears that the floor of the room above might collapse without any support. However, the architect, who was certain of the original design, made sure that the pillars did not touch the beams, proving that the unsupported floor was secure.

Windsor Castle stands above two great parks, the Home Park, bordering the Thames, and the Great Park. In 1847, James Thorne referred to the Home Park, on the south and east, as the Little Park:

> The Little Park is united to the Great Park by a magnificent avenue of elms, called the Long Walk. This 'walk,' which consists of a perfectly straight road, three miles long, having on each side a double row of elms, was laid out in the reign of Queen Anne, and the trees are now in their maturity. At the termination of it in the Great Park, is a colossal statue of George III., by Westmacott. Both parks originally formed part of Windsor Forest. About them are vast numbers of noble old trees; and in the Great Park there are plenty of deer. The Little Park is entirely private; but the Great Park is open.

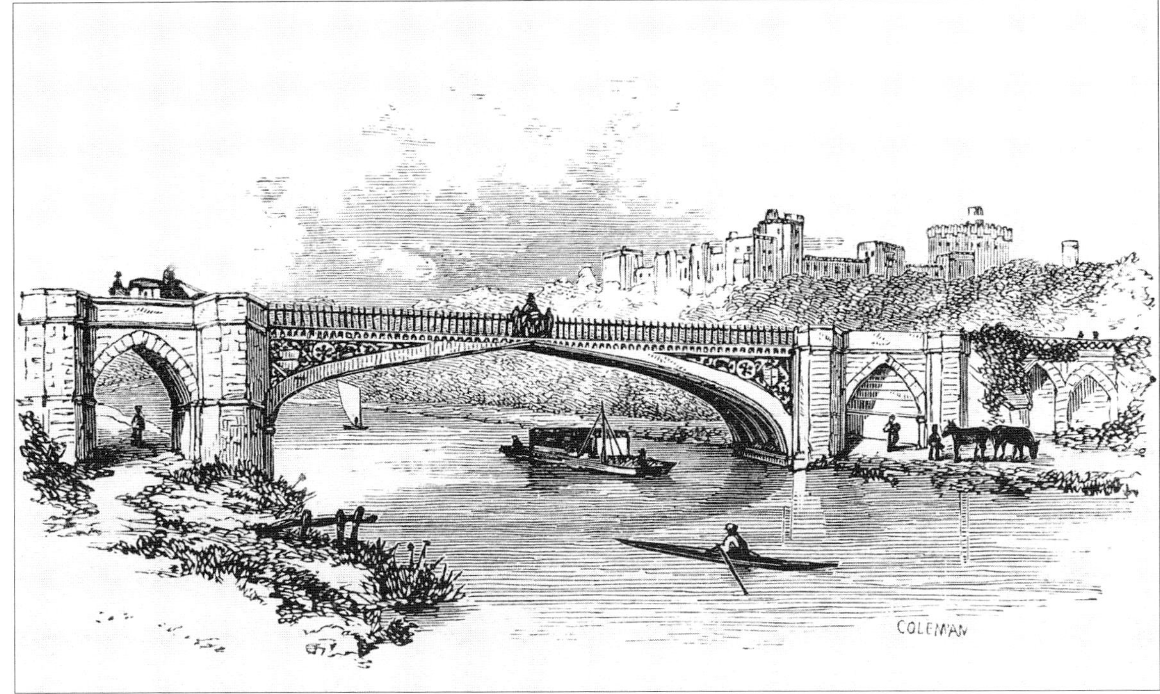

7 Victoria Bridge, 1859. Replacing the old Datchet Bridge, Victoria Bridge and Albert Bridge were opened in 1851. Both bridges have since been rebuilt. Victoria Bridge was opened in 1967 and Albert Bridge in 1928.

Mr and Mrs S.C. Hall noted, 'Eton is in Buckinghamshire, Windsor is in Berkshire. The river divides the counties — a very pretty bridge joining the towns.' However, although they wrote about Eton College, they had nothing further to say about the town of **Eton**. James Thorne stated, 'There is nothing in Eton that requires notice besides its famous college.' *Salter's Guide to the Thames* of 1913 mentioned that the town consisted mainly of one extensive street and gave the opinion that, to the visitor as to the world, Eton meant Eton College.

In *Tombleson's Thames*, W.G. Fearnside gave this description of the river downstream of Windsor Bridge. 'Soon after passing through Windsor bridge the stream divides; the main body of the water flowing over a weir to the left, and washing the meadows of Eton college, while a canal has been formed to the right, through a lock, for the accommodation of the navigator.' *Dickens's Dictionary of the Thames* mentioned the island created by the lock cut and the Cobbler, the long point of the island on its upstream side. The Pennells warned about keeping to the right because many boats had been dashed against the Cobbler when the river was high and the current strong.

Downstream of **Romney Lock**, the next bridge across the river is Black Potts Railway Bridge, which was opened on 1 December 1849. Originally the bridge had ornamental cast-iron work, but this was later replaced by wrought-iron girders. Mr and Mrs S.C. Hall wrote:

> Under the railway bridge of the Great Western we then row, between another ait — 'Blackpott's' — and 'the Home Park,' until we arrive at VICTORIA BRIDGE, a new and exceedingly graceful structure, which connects Windsor with the pretty and picturesque village of Datchet. The bridge, which has its companion a mile or so lower down the stream — the Albert Bridge — was built in 1851, from the design of Thomas Page, Esq., civil engineer, the acting engineer of the Thames Tunnel, and the engineer for Westminster Bridge.

Between Victoria Bridge and Albert Bridge, **Datchet**, on the left bank, is in Buckinghamshire. Henry Taunt observed, 'There are on the green, a few old English houses, but nothing else worthy of note, the Church having been newly restored in a style too modern to suit an English village landscape.' Datchet Mead is the renowned spot where Sir John Falstaff was ducked for his behaviour in William Shakespeare's *Merry Wives of Windsor*.

The Pennells remarked that the weir at **Old Windsor** seemed to them to be the most dangerous they had come to, while **Old Windsor Lock** was by far the most dilapidated that they had encountered. The lock was rebuilt in 1889 so they must have been referring to the period prior to its reconstruction. Downstream of Old Windsor Lock, a ferry once crossed to **Wraysbury**, on the left bank. A short distance downriver, at the *Bells of Ouseley*, on the right bank, there was 'fishing in abundance', according to Henry Taunt. George D. Leslie described the *Bells of Ouseley* as being at 'a very pretty turn of the river, and from here to Magna Charta Island the beauty is quite up to the mark'.

The next feature of interest is **Magna Carta Island** of which Henry Taunt wrote:

> MAGNA CHARTA ISLAND is well known to all readers of English history as being the place where, on the 19th of June, 1215, the Barons forced King John to sign the document known as the Great Charter of England, and which has borne fruit in the liberty that forms the birthright of every Englishman. The Charter is said to have been signed upon a stone, which is now made into a table in the cottage.

Today, **Runnymede**, on the right bank of the Thames, is held to be the place where Magna Carta was signed though the actual spot is not known. Runnymede is one of three different 'medes', or meadows, owned by the National Trust here. Downstream of these meadows and below **Bell Weir Lock** is Runnymede Bridge, which carries the M25 Motorway over the Thames.

At Bell Weir Lock, the Pennells found that the gates were closed. They commented, 'Too many barges had crowded in from the lower side, and the last had to back out, an operation which took much time and more talk.' However, it was worse coming out as, in trying to get clear of the waiting barge, they ran aground and became stuck, while all the other craft which had been behind them in the lock went past.

Mr and Mrs S.C. Hall wrote, 'We are now approaching the ancient town of Staines; — its bridge and its church steeple are in sight; but before we reach them there is an object standing on one of the aits that claims our especial attention. We must step ashore to examine it, for it is the BOUNDARY STONE of the City of London.' Henry Taunt referred to this marker as the 'London Stone', which was on 'the boundary of the counties of Middlesex and Buckinghamshire, and also the mark of the ancient jurisdiction of the city of London up the Thames'.

Charles G. Harper, in *Thames Valley Villages Vol. II,* asserted that **Staines** was an important place in the coaching age as it was situated on the greatly travelled Exeter road. Henry Taunt noted that, with its bridge 'of white granite built by Rennie', it was a 'clean town but has nothing to call for notice, excepting an old house near the Church, called Duncroft'. James Thorne stated that Staines had 'a long street of ordinary looking houses, a market-place of the usual kind, and a patch-work sort of church'. However, George D. Leslie commented, 'Staines has indeed gone all to the bad with gas-works, railway bridge, dirty houses and vulgar villas', while the Pennells remarked disparagingly, 'The town is thought to be the rival of Reading in ugliness.'

Salter's Guide to the Thames of 1913 mentioned the small bungalows with pleasing little gardens and the several camping grounds which were downstream of Staines. A popular place for camping was on the banks of the horseshoe loop of the river at **Penton Hook**. This stretch of the river was also a favourite location for fishing as chub, roach and perch were to be found, while there were trout and barbel at the weir. **Penton Hook Lock** and its lock cut bypass this channel. A lock was first opened here in 1815, but it was reconstructed in 1909.

According to Henry Taunt, **Laleham**, a short distance downriver, was another splendid place for fishing. He commented that both Penton Hook and Laleham were 'much frequented by anglers from London', adding, 'It is, without exception, the best neighbourhood for fly-fishing on the Thames, and the takes are generally heavy.' Some anglers camped out, while others stayed at the *Horseshoes* in Laleham where there were 'Good beds and accommodation for boating and fishing parties'. Henry Taunt noted, too, that 'Gentlemen who stop here often go into Chertsey to sleep, where are inns.'

Between Laleham and **Chertsey Lock**, the M3 Motorway bridge crosses the Thames. Chertsey Lock was first opened in 1813 and reconstructed by the Thames Conservancy a century later. Below the lock, the seven-arched Chertsey Bridge, connecting Surrey and Middlesex, was completed in 1785. The town with the same name as lock and bridge is on the Surrey side of the river. *Dickens's Dictionary of the Thames,* while noting that **Chertsey** had 'a number of good houses and a few shops of some importance', added that it could be described as 'quiet and dull'.

Henry Taunt had this to say about the town:

> Chertsey is an ancient town, but there is little of antiquity in its appearance. It contains a Church not remarkable for its beauty, though scarcely so ugly as that of Laleham on the other side of the Thames. The ancient importance of the town was mainly owing to the noble Abbey, originally founded in 666 for the Benedictines.

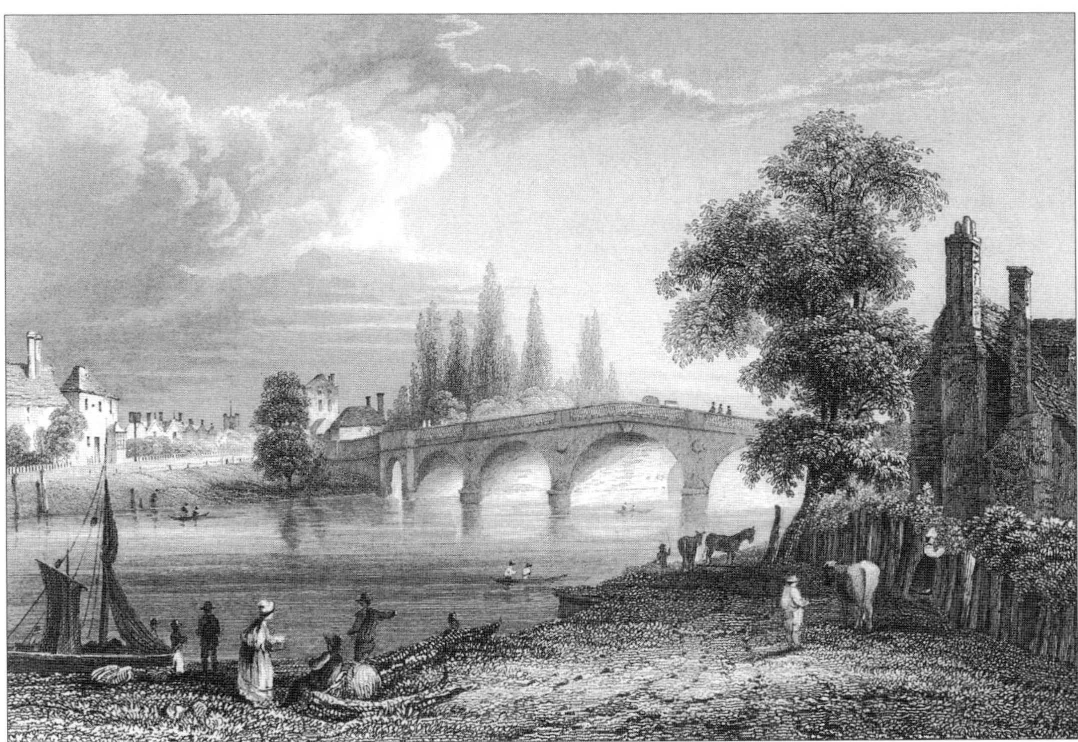

8 An engraving of Chertsey Bridge from *Tombleson's Thames*, *c.*1834. W.G. Fearnside commented, 'The river becoming very shallow, runs with considerable strength, until it reaches Chertsey weir and lock, on escaping from which it passes through Chertsey-bridge, which is built of stone, and consists of five principal and two collateral arches.'

Mr and Mrs S.C. Hall, in *The Book of the Thames*, mentioned that Chertsey Mead was said to produce 'the best hay in England; and where, during a large part of the year, there is a right of commonage, of which the neighbouring farmers avail themselves to fatten cows that supply London with pure milk'. Downstream of Chertsey Mead, the River Wey joins the Thames. The Halls noted, 'The Wey enters the Thames at a mill in the curve of the stream, but the ordinary course for boats is to the lock at Shepperton.'

Henry Taunt described the location of **Shepperton Lock** and the confluence of the River Wey with the Thames:

> SHEPPERTON LOCK is situated on a short cut, the main river making a détour through the Weir. Weybridge lies a little away from the river, up the back-water leading to the Weir. It is a long straggling place, boasting a monument on its green, and a very elegant new Church. The Wey joins here by two streams, the upper one being the navigable one, by which the oarsman can proceed to Guildford or Basingstoke. The old route, by the Wey and Arun Canal, is now impracticable, in consequence of the abandonment of navigation on it.

In the late 19th century, **Shepperton** was a place favoured by anglers. Henry Taunt's 1879 edition of his Thames book carried an advertisement for the *Anchor* family hotel at Shepperton, which offered 'Excellent accommodation for Fishing, Boating, and Picnic Parties'. Another advertisement was for 'G. Purdue, Boat and Punt Builder, fisherman, etc.' Purdue was a local surname. Fred S. Thacker, in *The Thames Highway Volume II: Locks and Weirs*, remarked that a Purdue had the ferry at Shepperton in the 15th century.

Opened in 1935, the Desborough Cut bypasses Shepperton and **Lower Halliford** though the original channel of the river is still navigable. Thames guidebooks often mention Cowey Stakes, just upstream of the bridge at Walton. Henry Taunt noted that it was supposed to be the ford by which Caesar crossed the Thames, as stakes had been found there not many years back. He described Walton Bridge as 'an ugly iron structure'.

From the 15th century, a ferry crossed the river at **Walton-on-Thames** until the first bridge was erected in 1750. This was a wooden lattice structure which only lasted until 1783. A second bridge, built of brick and stone, was completed in 1788, but in 1859 the two central arches collapsed and it was replaced by an iron lattice-girder bridge. The latter was damaged in an air raid in 1940 and was superseded by a fourth 'Callender Hamilton' bridge, which was erected in 1953, though the third bridge remained alongside until its removal in 1985. The fourth bridge is now used by cyclists and pedestrians, while a fifth bridge, erected in 1999 on the site of the third bridge, carries traffic. Recently, a new replacement Walton Bridge has been proposed.

In *Rambles by Rivers: The Thames*, James Thorne described Walton as 'a good-sized busy country-village, without anything remarkable in its appearance. The church is a strangely patched affair — extremely old and extremely ugly'. Mr and Mrs S.C. Hall mentioned 'the scold's bridle', which was kept in Walton Church, having been presented to the parish by a man who had lost an estate 'through the instrumentality of a gossiping, lying woman'. Henry Taunt referred to it as 'one of those curious instruments of punishment, a scold's bit, the use of which was to make the offender hold her tongue'. The iron band fitted over the head and a flat piece of iron entered the mouth, keeping down the tongue.

James Thorne wrote, 'Below Walton the river presents no features of especial prominence or beauty.' However, he did add that 'numerous genteel residences, with their smooth lawns and cheerful gardens, enrich the shores, and the aits in the river generally afford a pleasing variation to the ordinary character of the scenery'. He observed that **Sunbury,** on the Middlesex side of the river, 'exhibits a great many good houses, and the grounds show some noble cedars'. Henry Taunt was rather dismissive about the village, stating, 'There is nothing of importance at Sunbury, the Church being anything but pretty or antique.'

In late Edwardian times, Charles G. Harper was of the opinion that, on leaving Walton-on-Thames, long stretches of the once beautiful scenery of the river had been spoiled by 'the waterworks engineer and the speculative builder'. The latter author wrote of the embankments of the great reservoirs on the Surrey side of the river and of the 'unlovely line of engine houses and pumping stations' of the waterworks on the Middlesex bank.

Mr and Mrs S.C. Hall described the scene downstream of Sunbury:

> Flat and uninteresting are the meadows that stretch away from the Surrey bank of the Thames as we voyage below Sunbury. Tall osiers for the most part, shut out all distant views from the water. The villages of West and East Moulsey succeed in their turn. Between the former village and the river lies the low open tract, or common, known as Moulsey Hurst, and memorable chiefly in the annals of pugilistic encounters and horse-racing. East Moulsey has very rapidly increased during the last few years. Fine trees have disappeared, and rows of genuine suburban residences have sprung up in their place.

The authors of *The Book of the Thames* wrote about the features on the opposite bank of the river:

> Situated on the Middlesex side of the Thames, the village of Hampton rises from the river's edge, and its long series of villas, with their orderly looking trees and well-kept gardens, with here and there a fishing cottage peering from beneath thick masses of overhanging foliage, skirt the stream. At the entrance into Hampton from Sunbury there are several good houses, that stand back at some little distance from the Thames; and in front of them the water-towers and other buildings of the London and Hampton works, for the supply of the metropolis with water, have been recently erected. An attempt has been made to impart an architectural character to these edifices, but they present a very questionable appearance after all. The passage across the water from Moulsey Hurst is effected by means of a truly primitive ferry-boat. Immediately adjoining the landing-place stands Hampton Church, occupying a commanding position on rising ground.

Henry Taunt wrote that **Hampton** was only noted for its races, which took place on the other side of the river. He looked more favourably on an island downriver, known as **Tagg's Island** and the location of a hotel, stating that it had been made into a 'first-class place for landing, picnic parties, and fishermen'. He added, 'the fishing all round the island, being strictly preserved, is good. Campers out will here find a good resting-place at a nominal charge, and at the Hotel will be found every convenience'.

A short distance downriver of Tagg's Island and its neighbour, Ash Island, is **Molesey Lock**. The Pennells noted how busy the lock was on a Saturday afternoon and on a Sunday and how the water in the lock 'never rose or fell without carrying with it as many boats as could find a place on its surface'. They mentioned the slide where there were two rollers for the boats going up and two for those coming down and how 'there were always parties embarking and disembarking'. On the road at this bustling place, the Pennells noticed ragged men and boys with ropes and horses offering to tow boats up to Sunbury, Shepperton, Weybridge and Windsor.

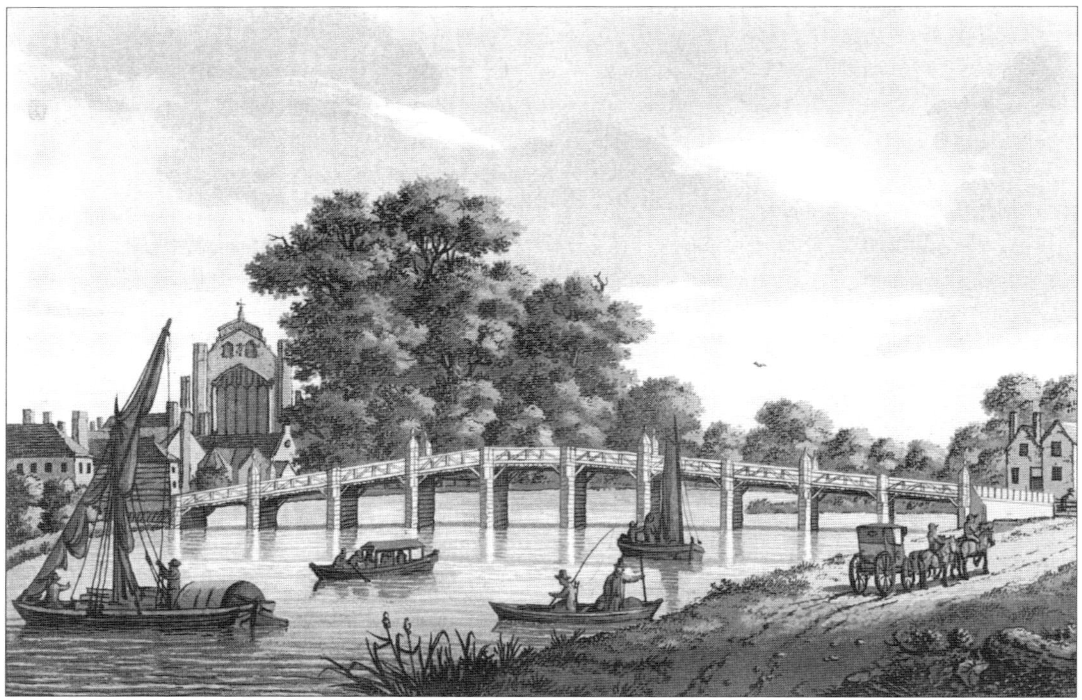

9 Samuel Ireland included this aquatint of Hampton Court Bridge in his *Picturesque Views on the River Thames*. He remarked, 'HAMPTON COURT bridge, which is of wood, has a light and pleasing effect, and was finished about twenty-five years since, under the direction of Mr. White of Weybridge; the former bridge was so ill constructed as only to remain fit for use about thirteen or fourteen years.'

Mr and Mrs S.C. Hall travelled along the river when the old Hampton Bridge was still in existence. They remarked, 'Hampton has the questionable fame of possessing the ugliest and the most inconvenient bridge on the Thames, although a toll is still demanded from passengers.' Henry Taunt, describing its replacement, wrote, 'HAMPTON COURT BRIDGE, just below the Lock, is rather a picturesque iron structure, which stands in the place of an old wooden bridge, and connects the village of Moulsey with that of Hampton Court.' In 1933, this iron bridge was superseded by the present ferro-concrete bridge, which is faced with red brick and Portland stone in imitation of the style of the nearby palace.

Thomas Wolsey, Archbishop of York, who later became Cardinal Wolsey, began building **Hampton Court Palace** in 1514. Its magnificence, however, annoyed Henry VIII and Wolsey tried to regain favour by offering the splendid property to the king. Henry VIII made additions to the palace including the Great Hall. After William III became king, some of the buildings were demolished and Sir Christopher Wren was commissioned to enlarge the palace. Besides its historical buildings, Hampton Court Palace had other features of interest for late 19th-century visitors. Henry Taunt commented, 'The gardens with the celebrated vine, are also objects of attraction; and the fun of being lost in the Maze has helped to brighten many a holiday at Hampton Court.'

Thames Ditton is situated opposite Hampton Court Park. W.G. Fearnside, in *Tombleson's Thames*, noted that 'the *Swan Inn*, pleasantly situated on the margin of the river, and divided from the main part of the Thames by two small islets, is much frequented by anglers, who are attracted by the barbel and ground fishing obtained in the vicinity'. Just over half a century later, *Dickens's Dictionary of the Thames* observed that, although still popular with punt-anglers and excursionists from London, the increased railway facilities had taken visitors farther away so that Thames Ditton was not such a favoured place as it once had been. Almost five decades on, it was noted, in Ward, Lock & Co.'s *The Thames*, that 'the ubiquitous bungalow-builder' had covered the large island here and that the river idler had lost 'a favourite lounging place'.

Mr and Mrs S.C. Hall thought that there was little to attract the voyager between Thames Ditton and Kingston. They remarked, 'The banks of the river are on both sides low, generally bordered with rushes, with occasional aits, on which grow the "sallys" which supply so many of the basket-makers of London.' Three decades later, *Dickens's Dictionary of the Thames* mentioned that **Surbiton**, a suburb of Kingston, had grown immensely in recent years. A reason for this increase in size may have been Surbiton's good access from London as it was on the main line of the London and South Western Railway. Henry Taunt, noting Surbiton's 'favourite promenade along the bank of the river, and rows of pretty villa residences behind', concluded, 'but there is nothing else to attract our attention'. However, in *The Thames from Mouth to Source* (1951), L.T.C. Rolt, having seen Surbiton from the water, wrote, 'I would say it has been maligned.'

10 This Edwardian postcard of Teddington Lock and rollers was postally used on 4 September 1909. The boat rollers allowed skiffs and small craft to be pulled out of the water and taken from one level of the river to the other.

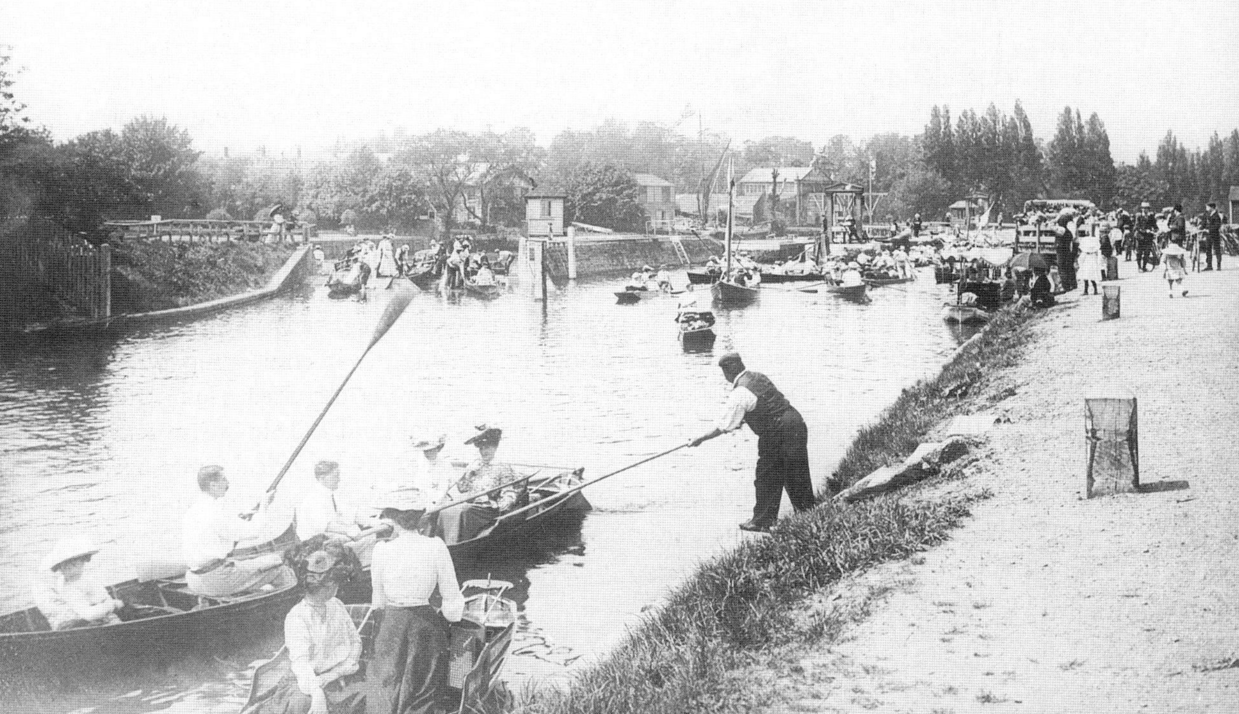

Henry Taunt was a little dismissive of **Kingston upon Thames**. Having noted that it was a royal town in Saxon times and that it still retained the celebrated kings' or coronation stone upon which the Saxon kings sat at their coronation, he remarked, 'The Church, which was built in the reign of Richard II., the market-place, town-hall, and the bridge, are the only objects of interest, besides the stone already mentioned.' He added that Kingston was also the headquarters of several rowing clubs, some of which took a leading part in the various regattas held here, and at other places on the river. Kingston Rowing Club used to be on **Raven's Ait**, an island between Surbiton and Kingston. The island was also once the home of a training centre for sailing, canoeing and boating. Now Raven's Ait is a venue for weddings and conferences.

In 1879, boats were housed and let at Kingston by J. Messenger, R.J. Turk, F. Eastland and C. and A. Burgoyne. The latter were advertised as 'Centre-board Yacht & Boat Builders', while R.J. Turk was 'Boat Builder and Waterman to her Majesty'. An advertisement in *Salter's Guide to the Thames* of 1913 noted, 'By appointment to H.M. the King. R.J. Turk & Sons, Boat, Punt, and Canoe Builders, Thames Side and Albany Park, Kingston-on-Thames'. The Turk boat building business was established in Kingston in 1710 and the firm, which now operates a fleet of passenger boats, is still run by a member of the Turk family.

In *The Book of the Thames*, Mr and Mrs S.C. Hall wrote:

> And so we leave Kingston, looking back on the pleasant and prosperous town, pursuing our course downward between low banks, with here and there a mansion of note, but meeting nothing of comment until we approach Teddington; its 'lock' being the last — or, more properly the *first* — lock on the Thames.

Henry Taunt observed that Teddington Lock was 'divided into two; the small lock on the left hand being for pleasure-boats'. He added, 'There is also a boat-launch at the lock.' The Pennells, noting that the large lock was for barges and steam tugs, described how the 'familiar smoky smell that always lingers over the Thames at Westminster or London Bridge' greeted them at Teddington. A new barge lock, measuring 650ft by 24ft 9in, was opened on 11 June 1904. The old lock measures 177ft 11in, while the skiff lock is 49ft 6in long and 5ft 10in wide. The locks at Teddington mark the end of the non-tidal navigable Thames, which flows for 125 miles from its head of navigation at Inglesham. They also mark the end of this historical journey from Sonning, along the Middle and Lower Thames, which has covered a distance of just over 52 miles. Below Teddington Lock, the tidal Thames continues the river's journey to the sea.

Sonning to Marsh Mills

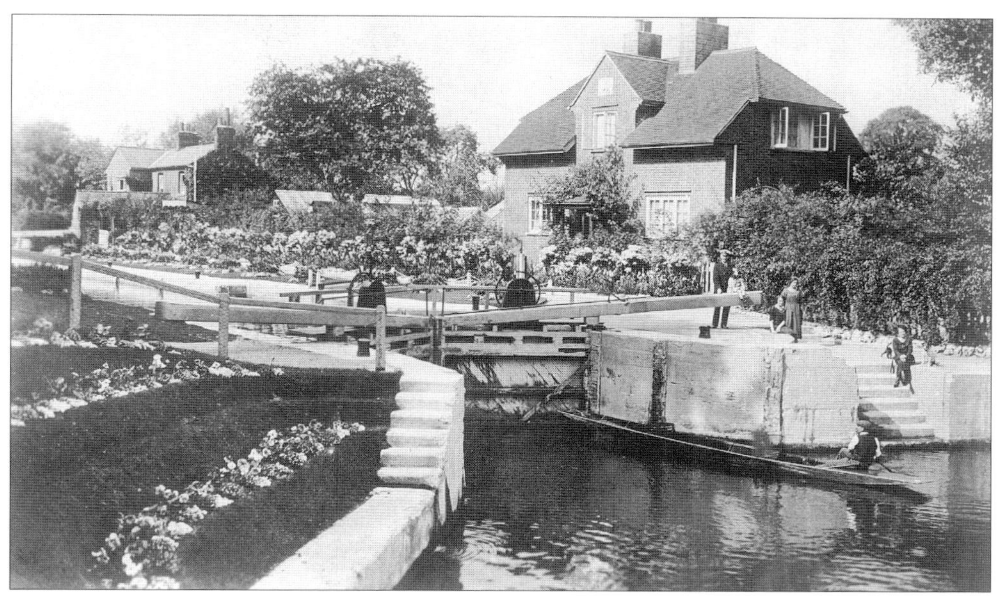

11 Sonning Lock was opened in 1773. It was rebuilt by the Thames Conservancy in 1868 and once more in 1905. A new lock house was built in 1916.

12 The tower of St Andrew's Church, Sonning, peeps over the trees in this early 20th-century view of a West Country barge moored by the riverbank. According to Peter H. Chaplin, in *The Thames from source to Tideway*, going up the Thames used to be termed 'travelling West Country' and hence upriver barges were known as West Country barges.

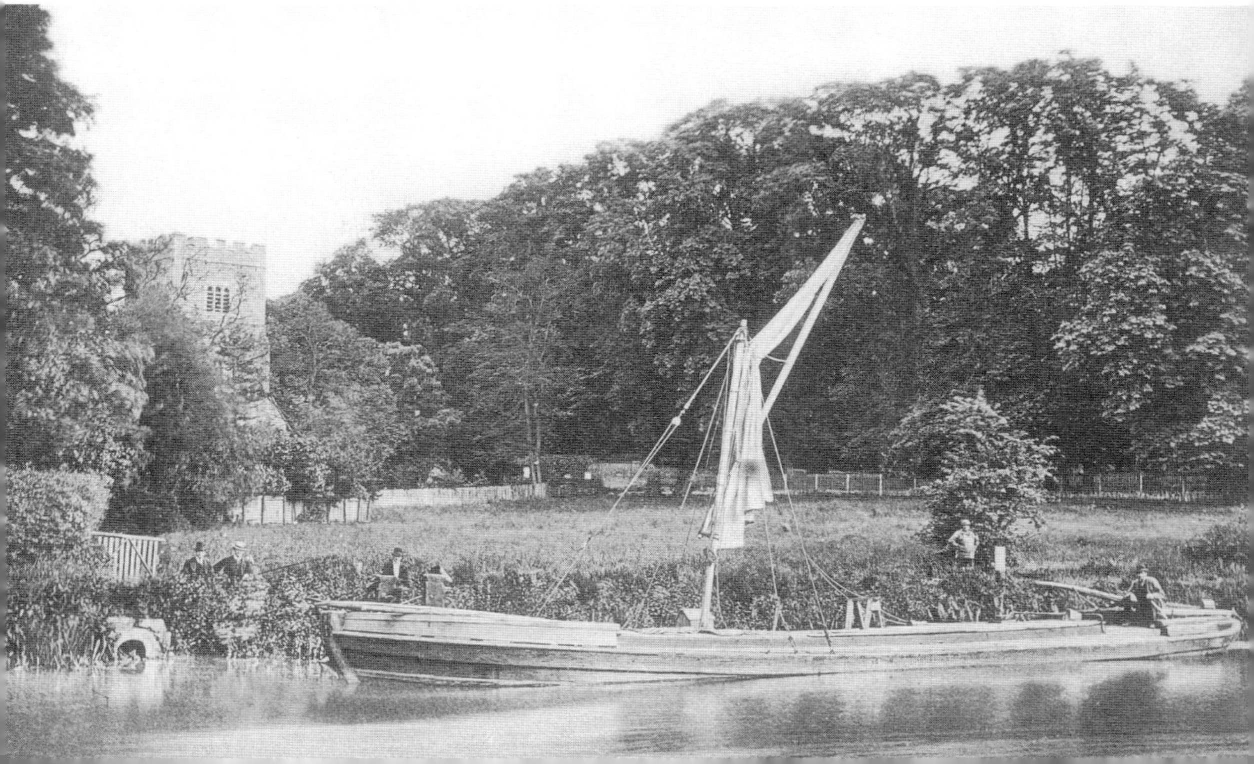

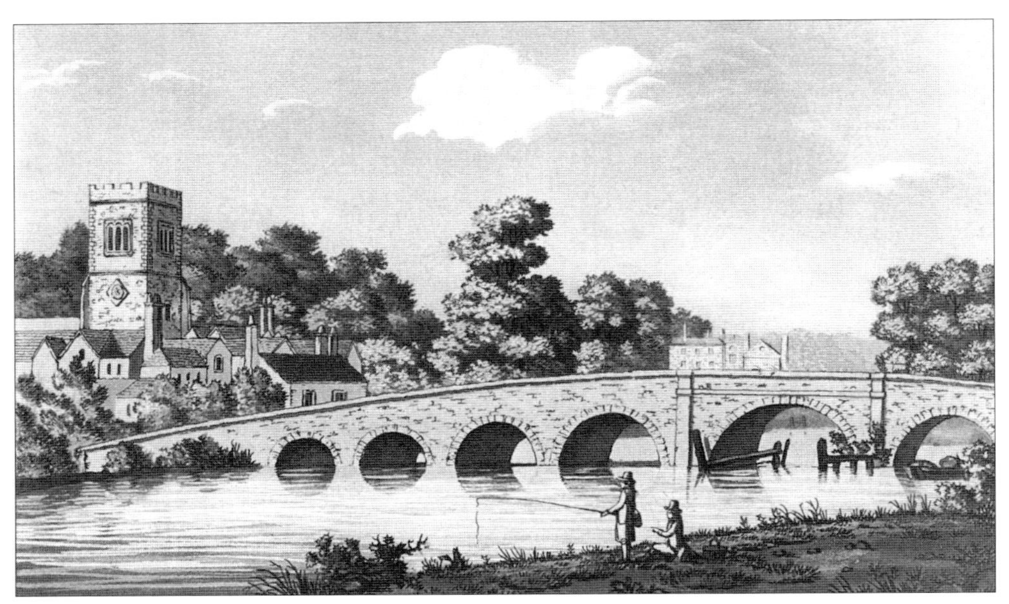

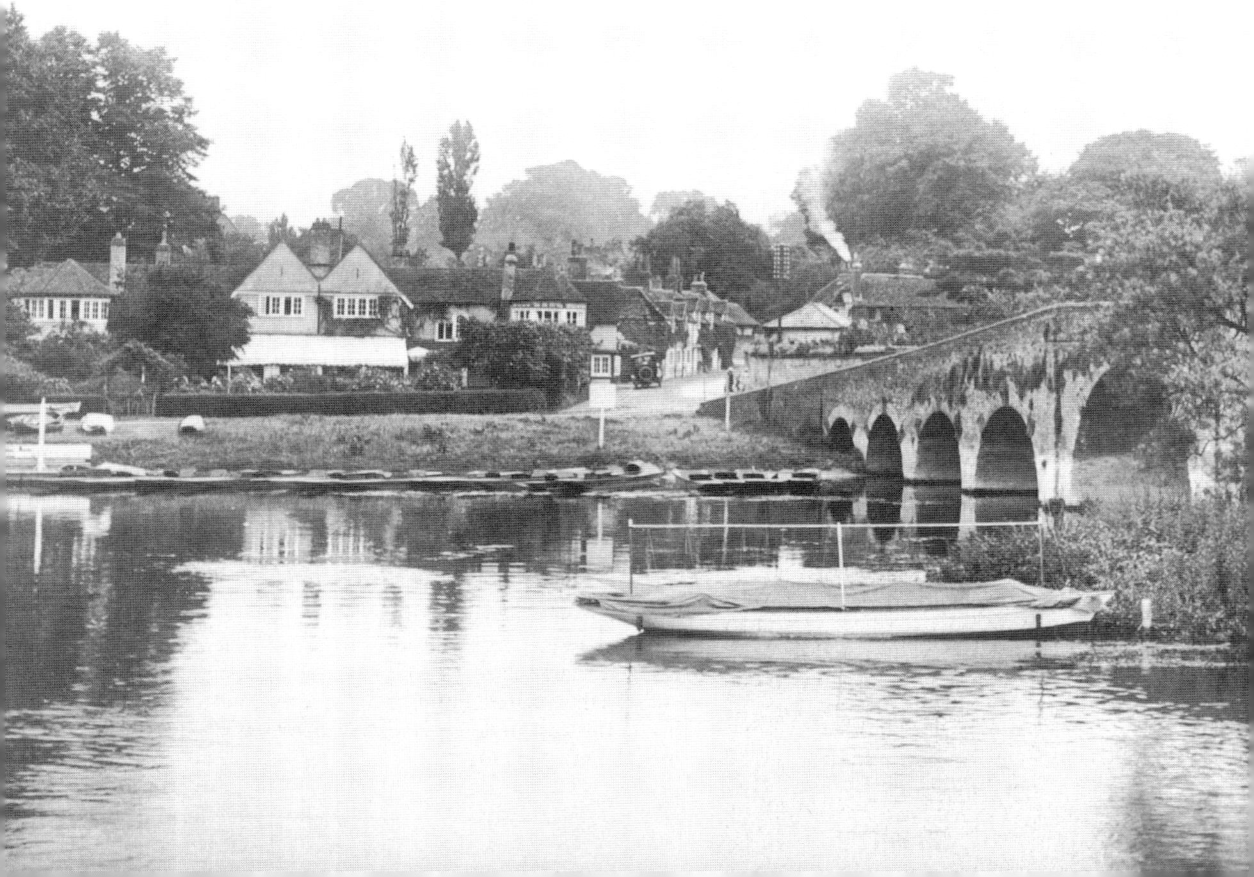

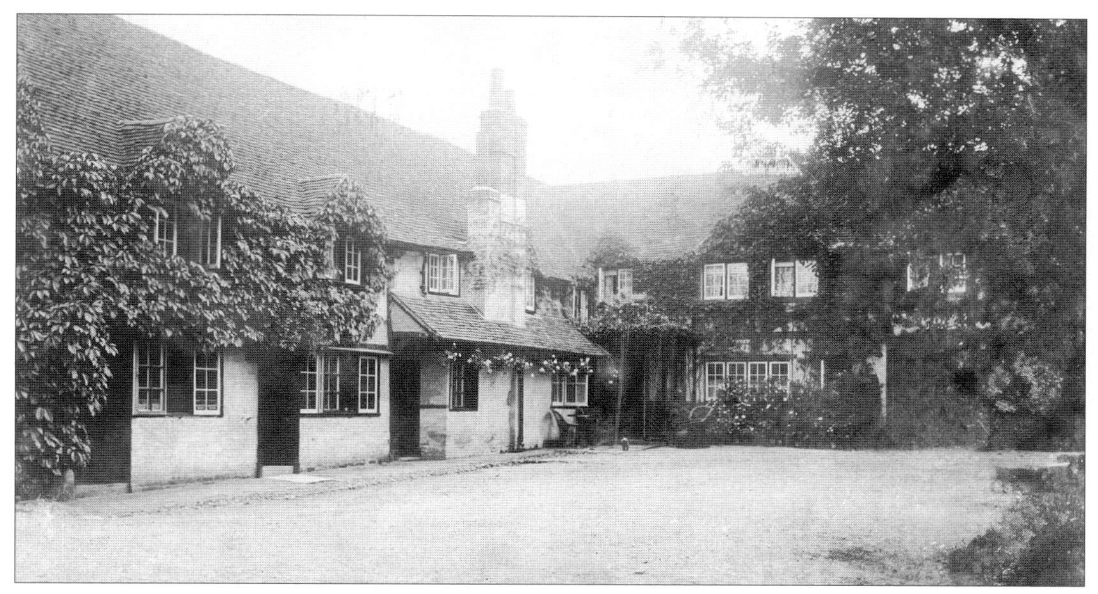

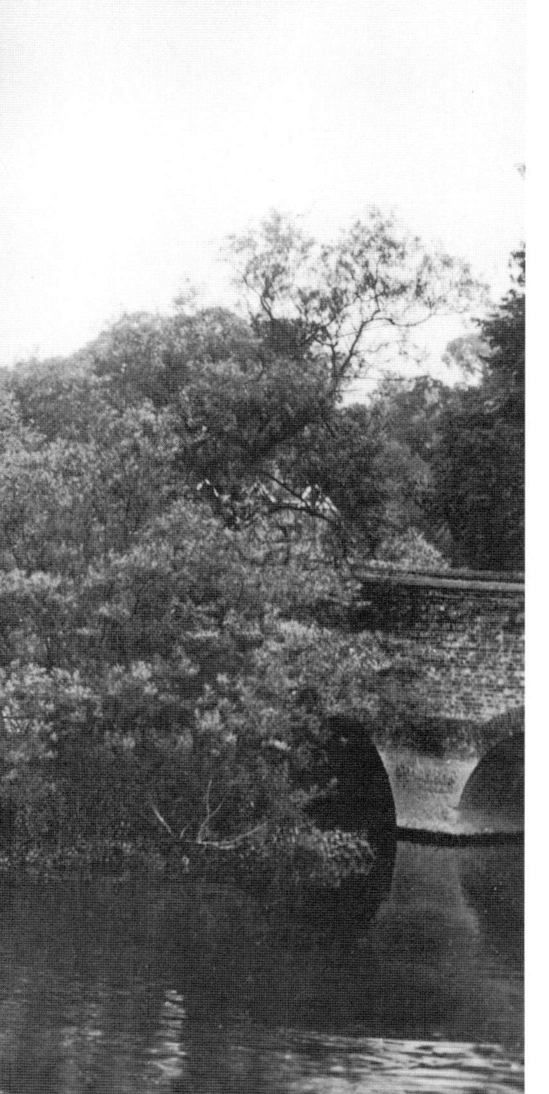

(Top left) 13 Samuel Ireland, in *Picturesque Views on the River Thames*, gave the title of 'Sunning-bridge' to this aquatint and described the scene:

> Sunning Bridge is a plain modern structure of brick, well adapted for convenience and durability. The annexed view was taken from below the bridge, as the objects there combined most happily to afford a picturesque landscape. The house, which appears over the bridge, is the residence of Lady Rich, whose family has long occupied this spot.

(Left) 14 On the left of this view of Sonning Bridge is the *White Hart*. In the late 19th century, it was a public house kept by Edward Stanley Lockley in 1887 and John Stephens in 1899. Known as the *White Hart Hotel* in 1913, when Mrs Bertie Hull was proprietress, its gardens sloped to the river where there were launches, skiffs, punts and canoes to let.

(Top right) 15 In *The Stream of Pleasure*, Joseph and Elizabeth Robins Pennell described the *Bull* at Sonning as being 'low and gabled, running round two sides of a square, with the third shut in by the churchyard wall and a row of limes'. This view of the *Bull Hotel*, Sonning was postally used on 29 September 1908.

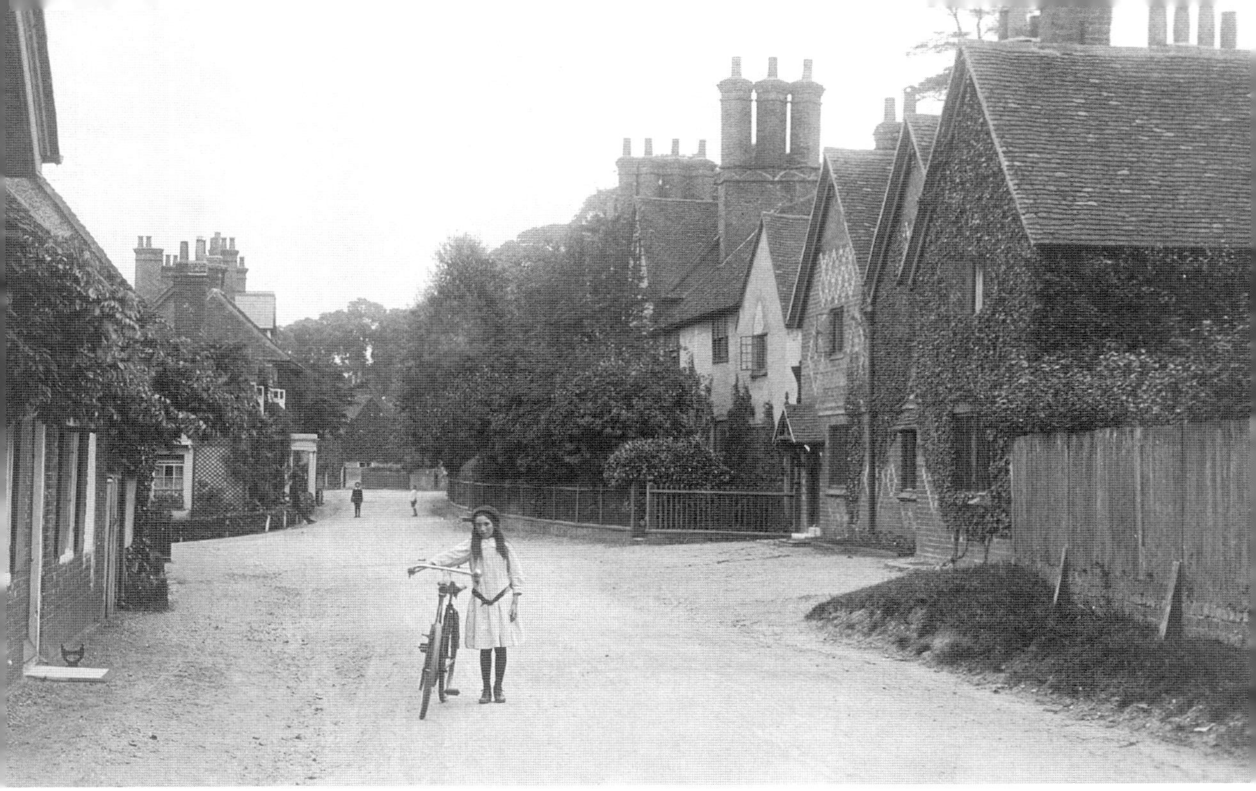

16 Writing in the early 20th century, Horace Bamford, in *The Old-World Village of Sonning-on-Thames*, noted that every cottage or house, large or small, had 'a profusion of flowers growing in all directions' and that many a flower border was open to the main road.

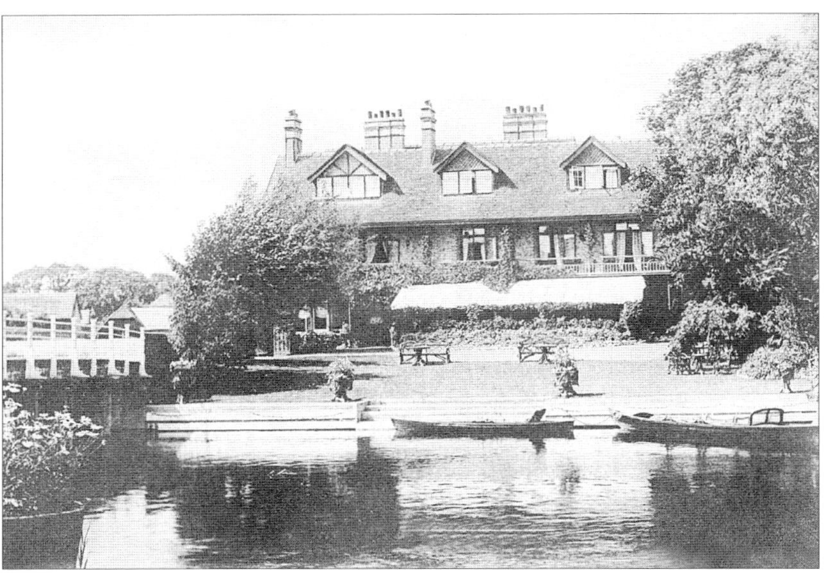

17 The *French Horn Hotel* was described in the late 19th century as being 'pleasantly situated on the Banks of the Thames, on the Oxfordshire side, within one minute's walk of the Village of Sonning'. At that time, the establishment made up 12 beds and offered good accommodation for fishing, boating and private parties.

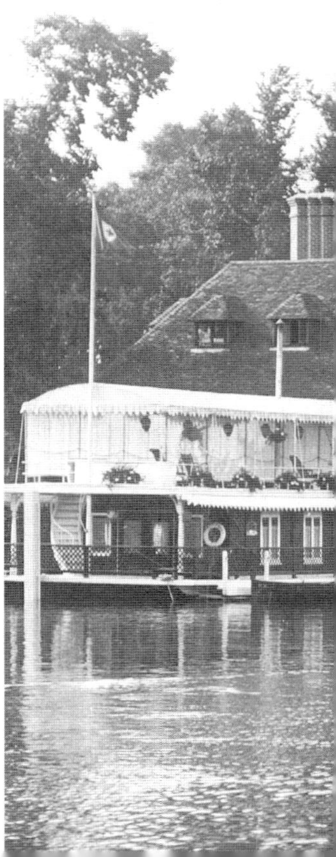

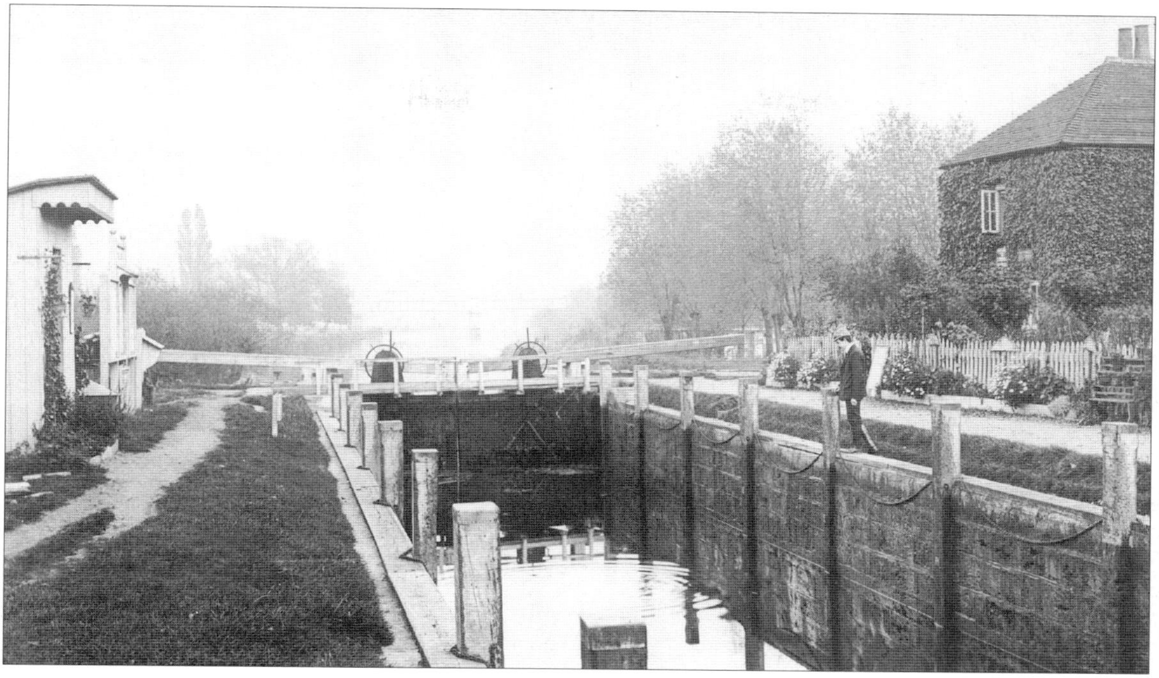

18 An early 20th-century postcard of Shiplake Lock. According to Fred S. Thacker, in *The Thames Highway Volume II: Locks and Weirs*, there was a weir here called 'Cotterell's Lock' in 1746. The pound lock was opened in 1773, but was rebuilt in 1787 and entirely reconstructed in 1874. For many years the lock island has been used as a camping site, the tents erected there being a familiar feature.

19 Postally used on 29 September 1910, this postcard view shows houseboats at Shiplake.

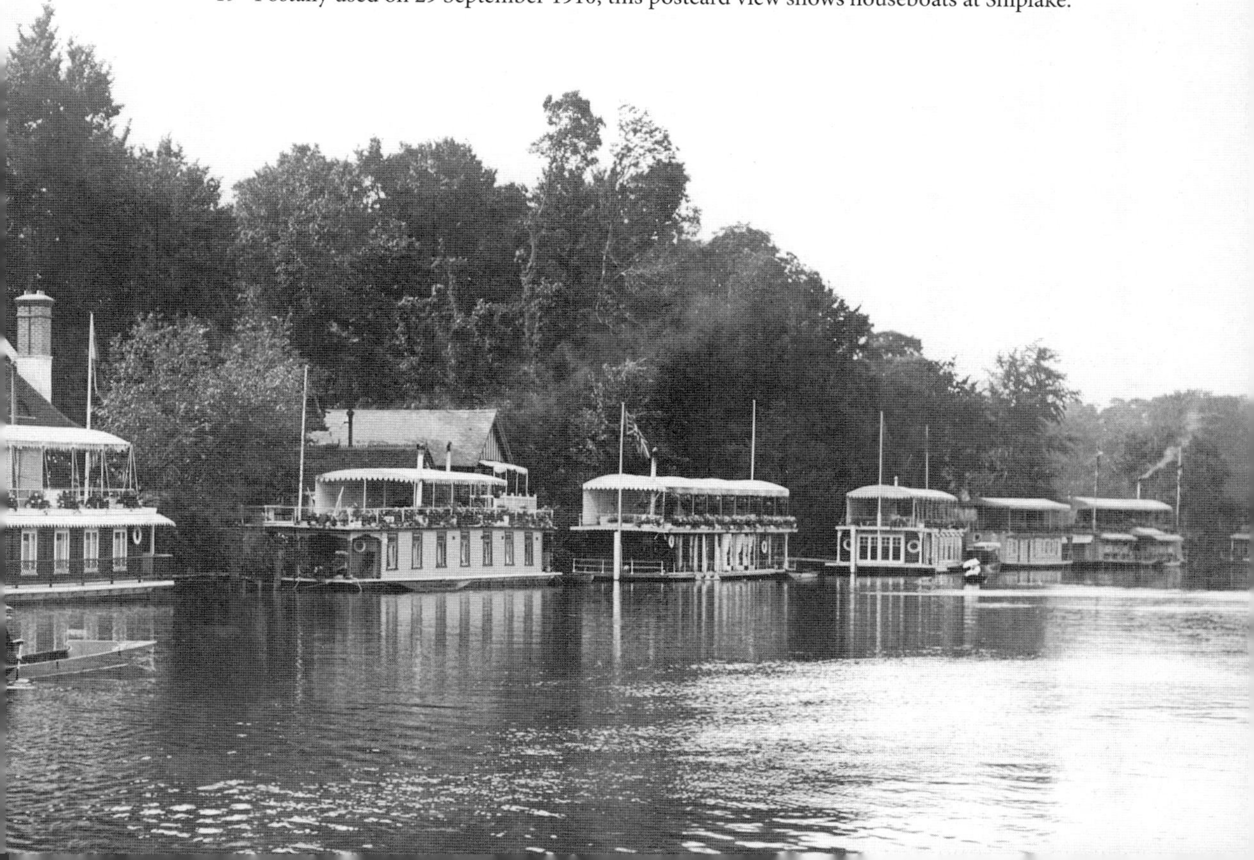

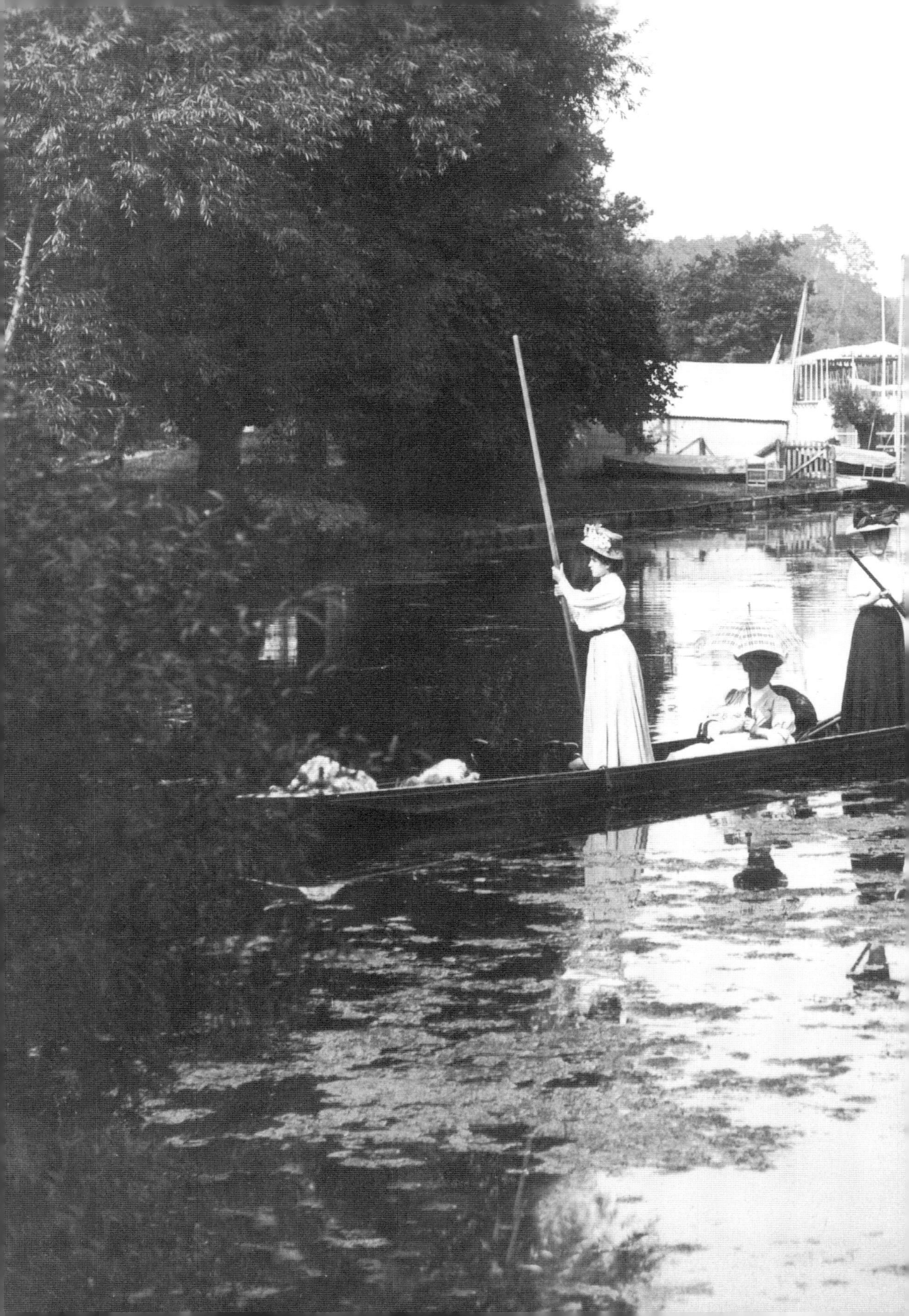

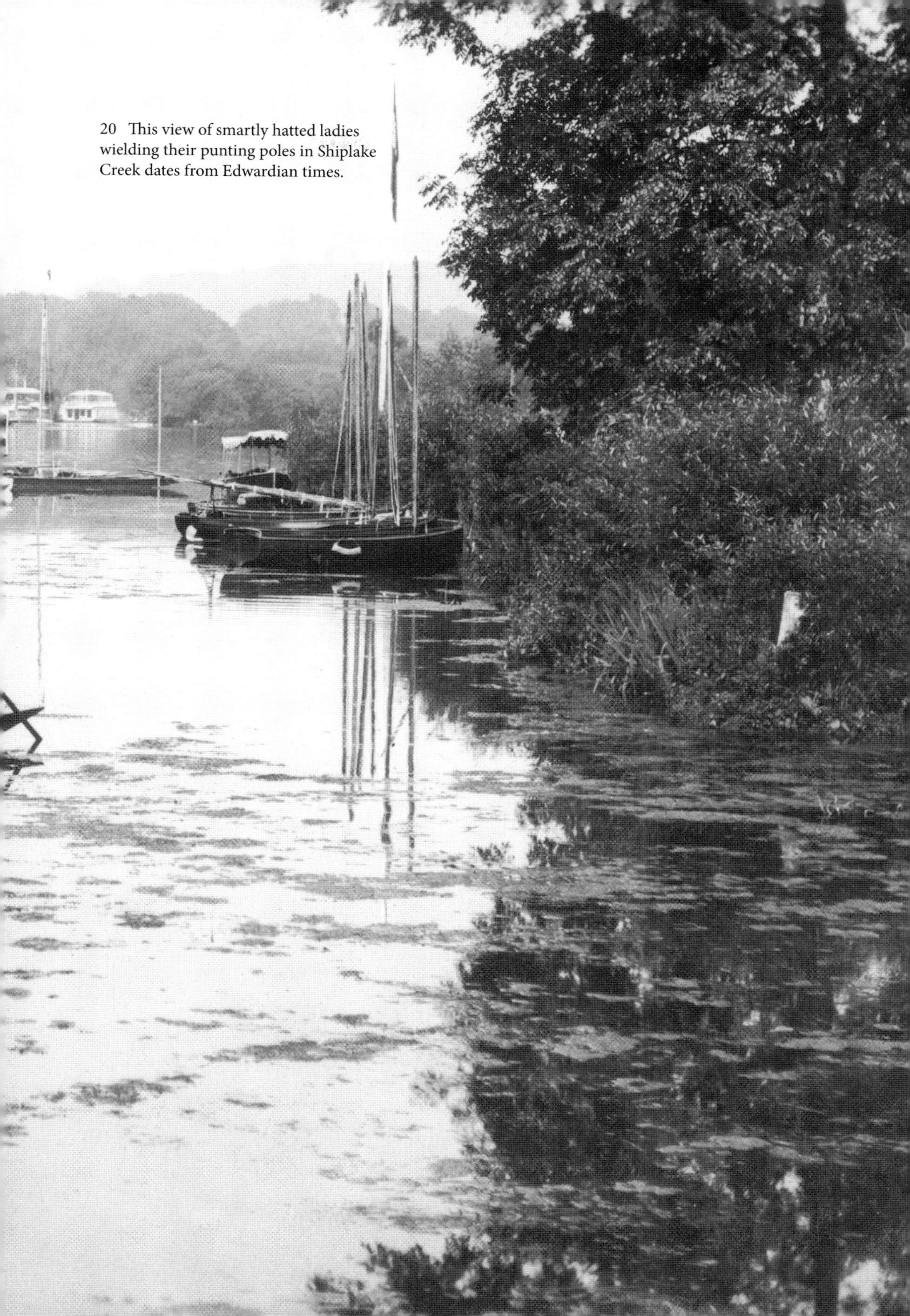

20 This view of smartly hatted ladies wielding their punting poles in Shiplake Creek dates from Edwardian times.

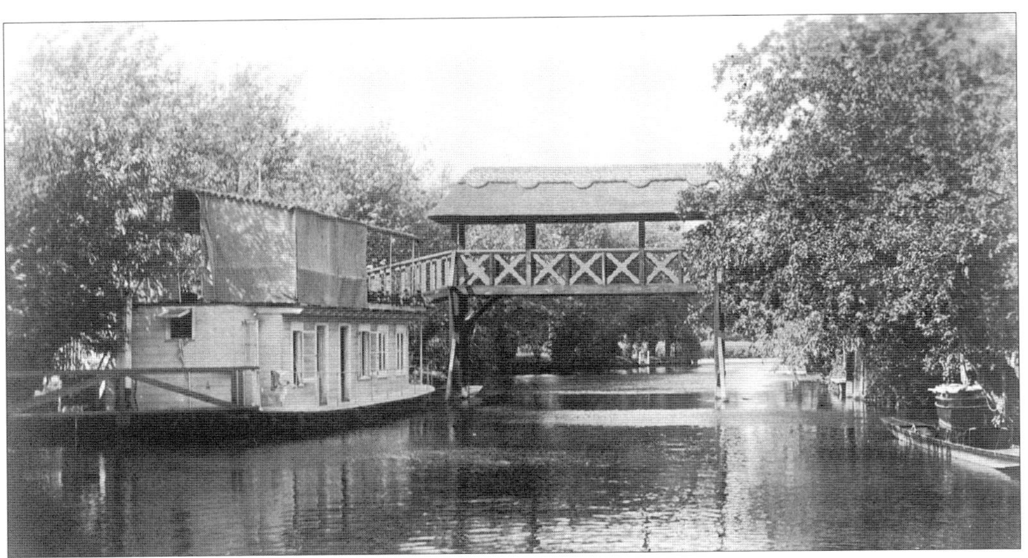

21 A postcard view of Loddon Mouth, Wargrave, where the River Loddon flows into the Thames. The message on the back of the postcard reads, 'Having a week around Henley in our boat ... Do you need a cook? Am becoming quite proficient.'

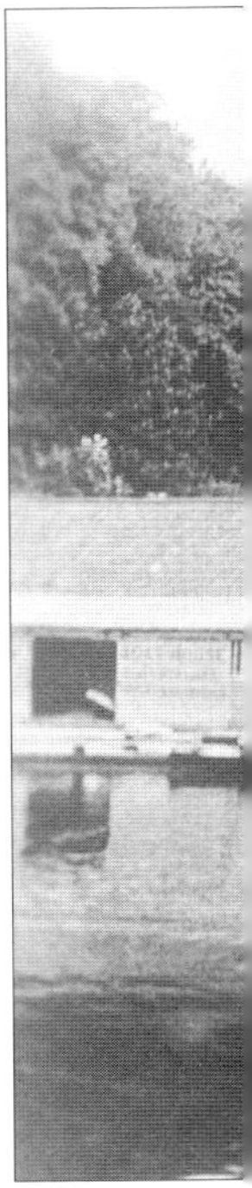

22 *St George & Dragon*, Wargrave. Past proprietors were Francis Wyatt in 1899 and Mrs Kate Wyatt in 1915.

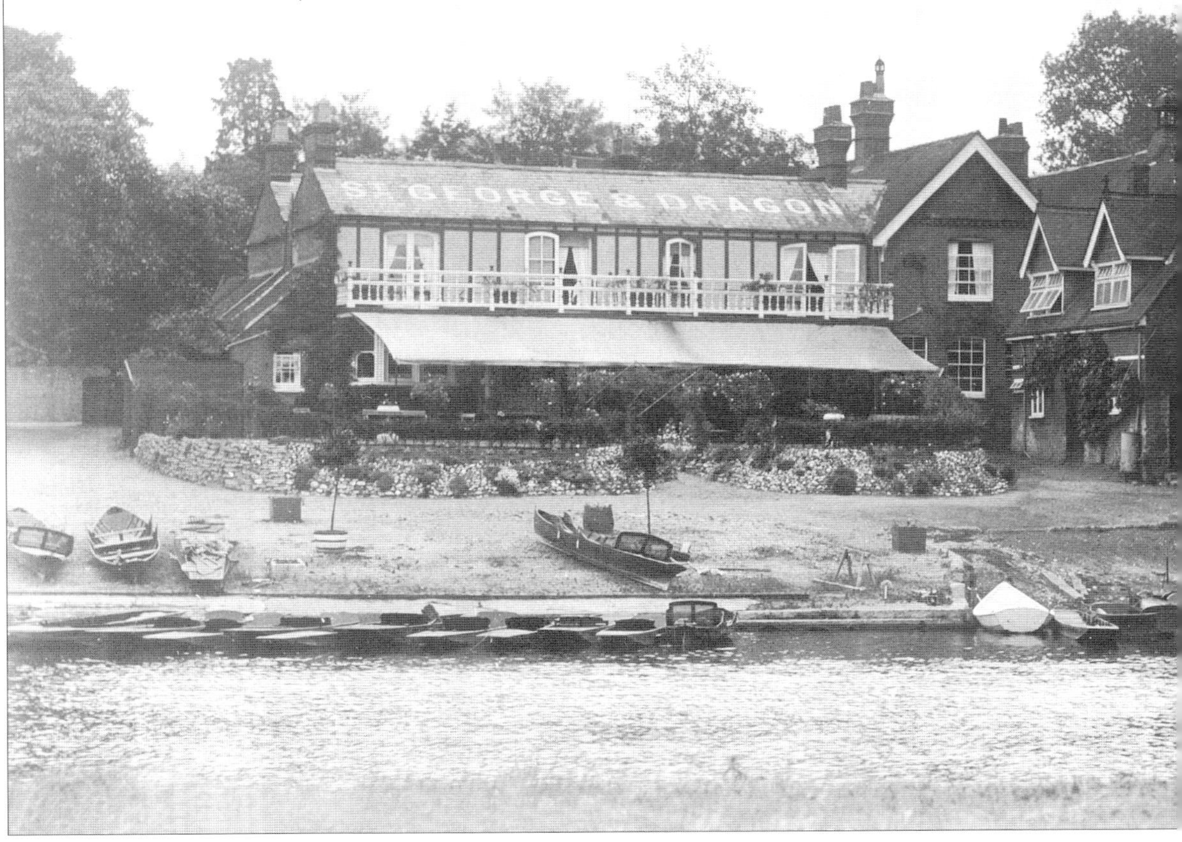

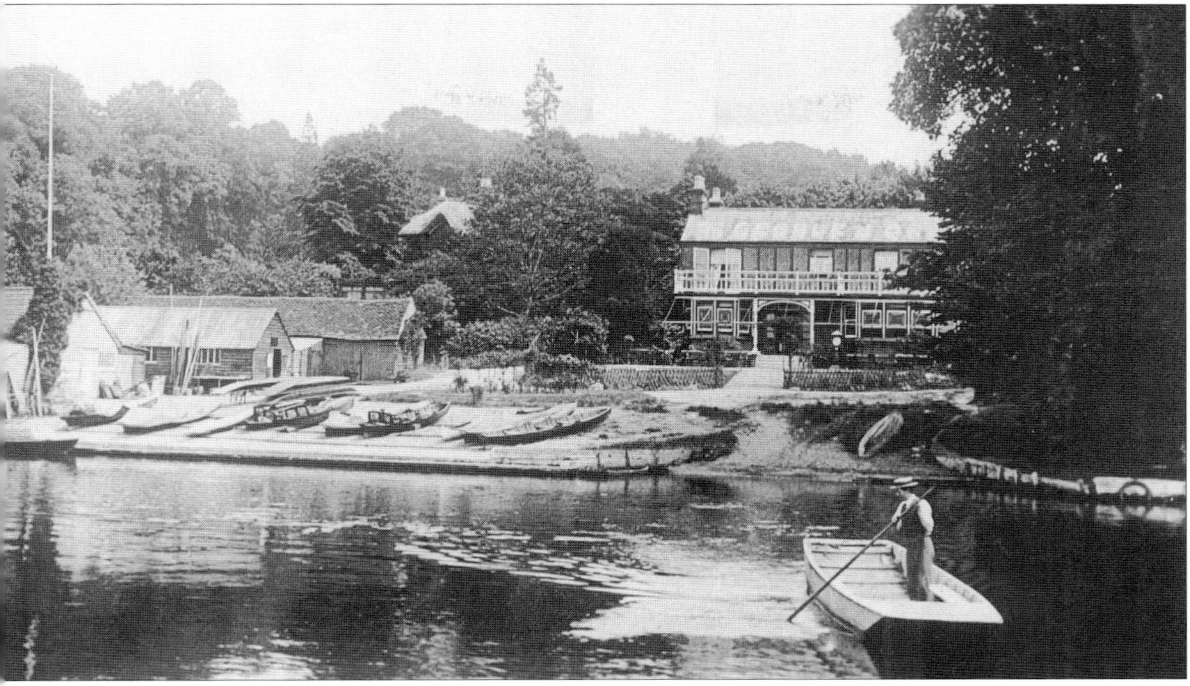

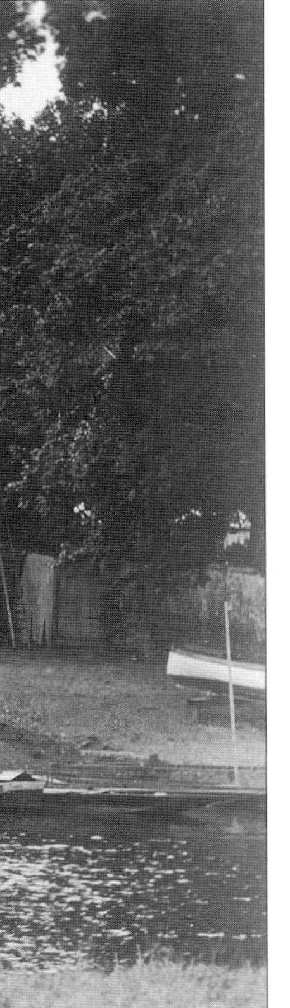

23 The ferry at the *St George & Dragon*, Wargrave. Before Wargrave railway station was opened in 1900, passengers wishing to travel on the railway could cross the Thames here to reach Shiplake railway station on the other side of the river. There was another ferry a short distance downriver.

24 The shops in High Street, Wargrave, had their awnings out on the day when this view, dating from *c*.1915, was taken. Tradespeople and businesses in Wargrave at this time included baker, grocer, butcher, greengrocer, confectioner, draper, fishmonger, boot repairer, chemist, stationer, hairdresser and tobacconist. Besides the *St George & Dragon Hotel*, there was a Temperance Hotel and three public houses.

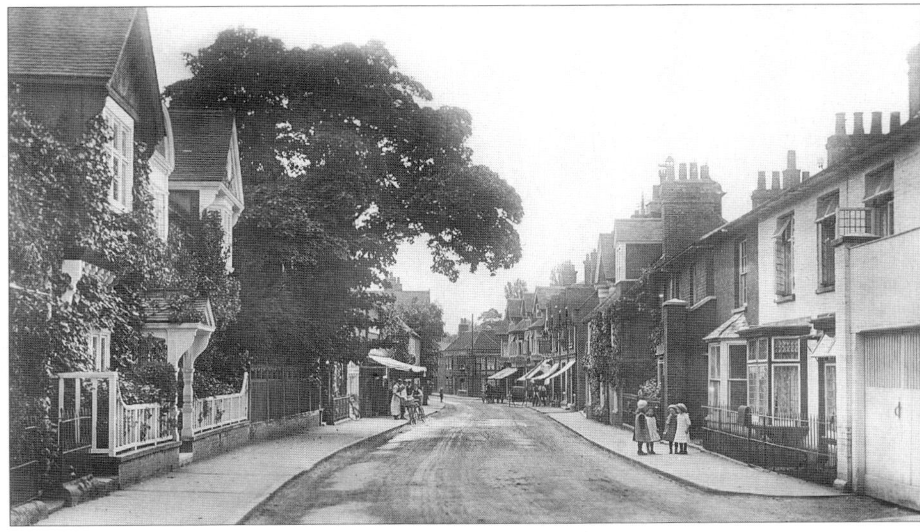

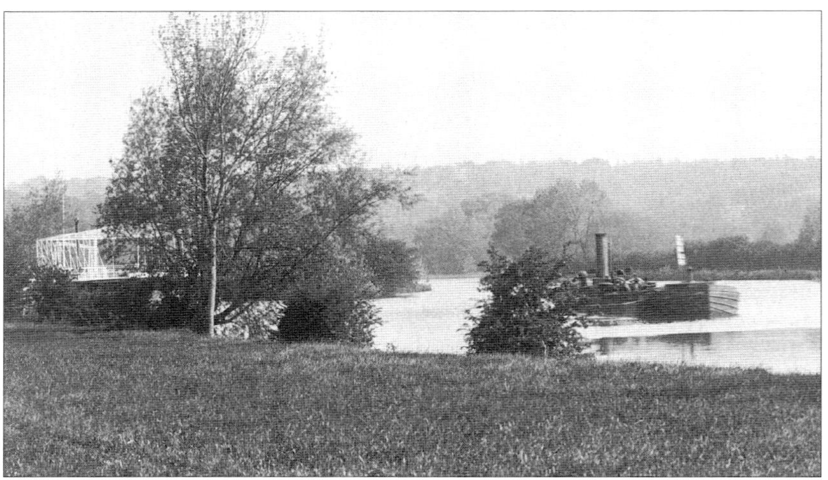

25 A steam tug pulling a barge on the Thames at Bolney, near Henley-on-Thames.

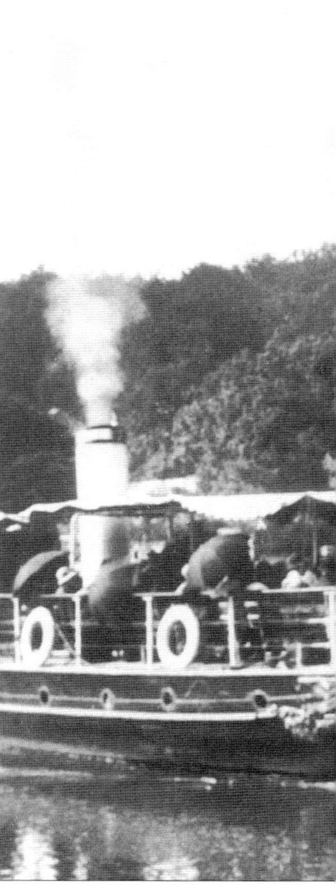

26 An engraving of Park Place, dating from *c.*1834 and included in *Tombleson's Thames*. W.G. Fearnside gave this recommendation:

> A visit to Park-place, now the property of the Maitland family, and once the residence of George IV, when prince of Wales, will be found uncommonly gratifying, not only for its extensive woods, lawns and superb views, but for the taste displayed in the mansion and pleasure grounds, wherein are seen some interesting ruins of a druidical temple, found in the island of Jersey, and transported hither at great expense.

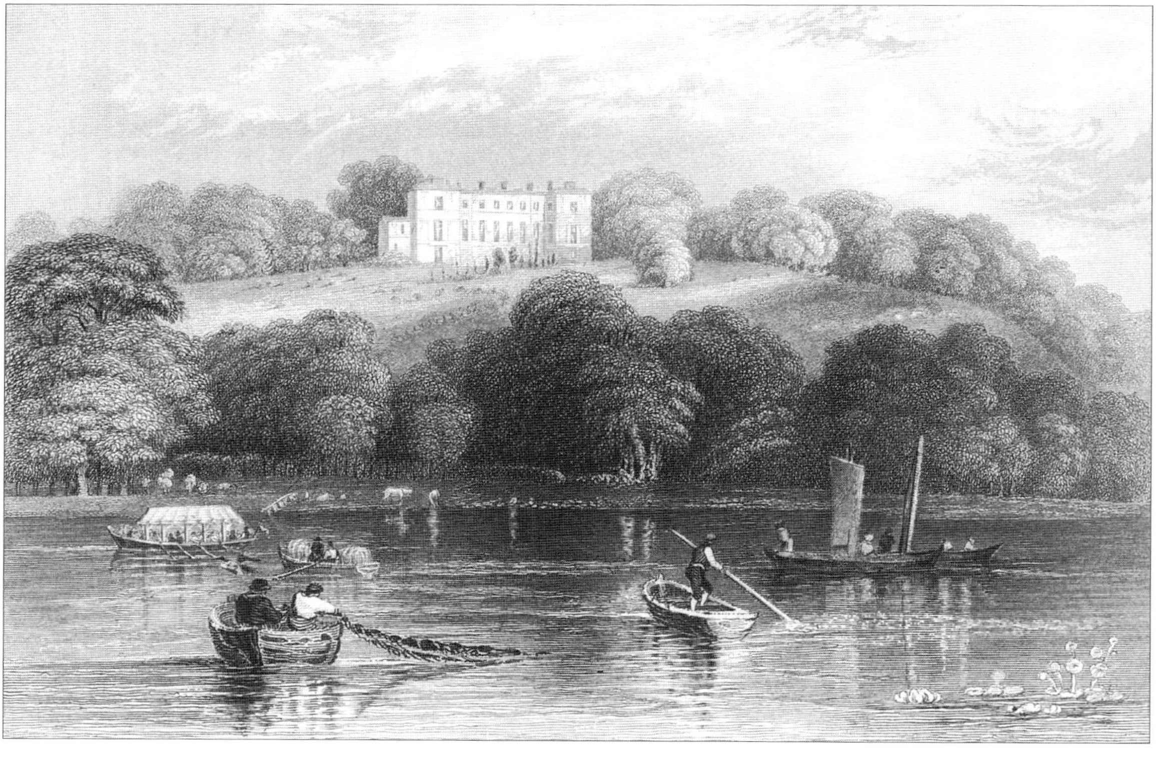

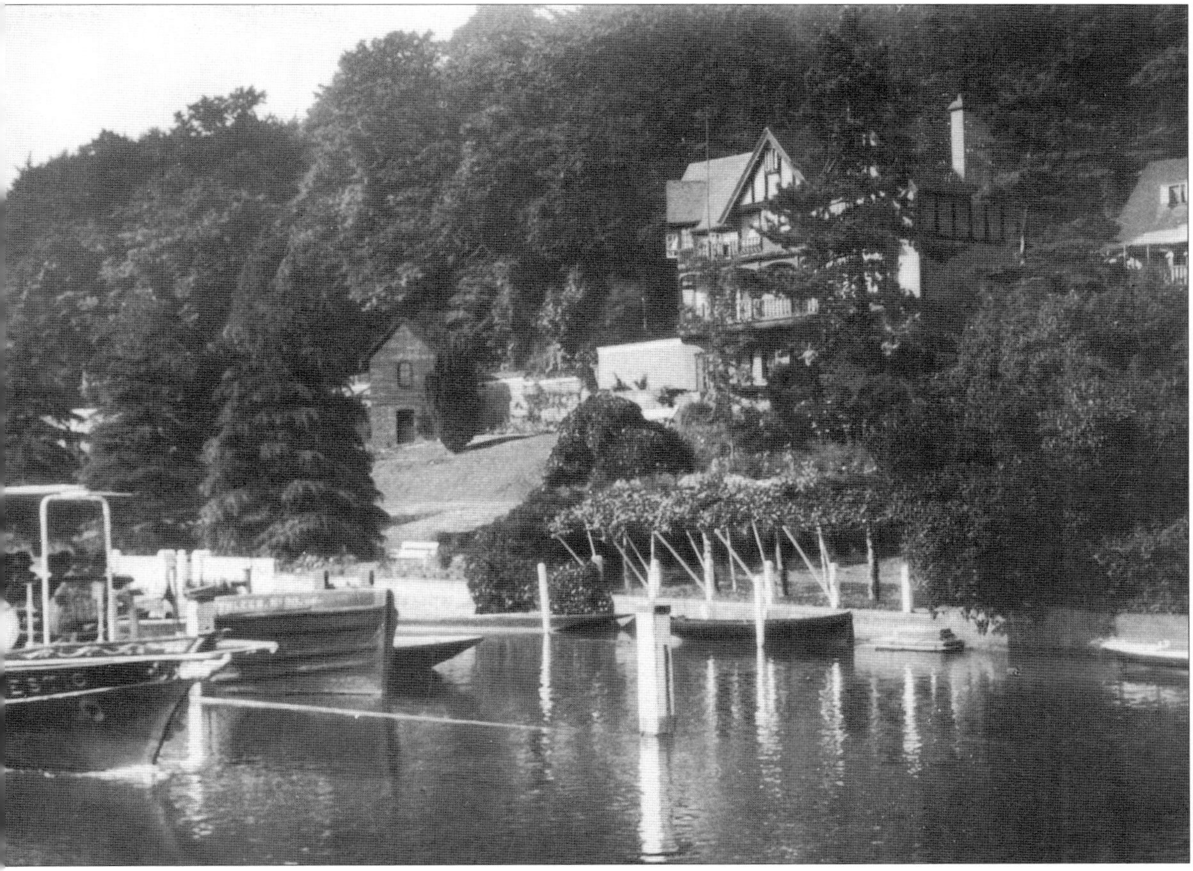

27 The *Majestic*, a steamer built by E. Cawston of Reading in 1908, near Marsh Lock, Henley-on-Thames. This 88ft-long vessel was acquired by Salter Brothers in 1945.

28 Marsh Lock, near Henley-on-Thames, *c.*1910-14. Fred S. Thacker noted that the pound lock here was opened in 1773, its first lock keeper being John Ward who was paid 5s. per week. The lock was rebuilt in 1787, 1886 and 1914.

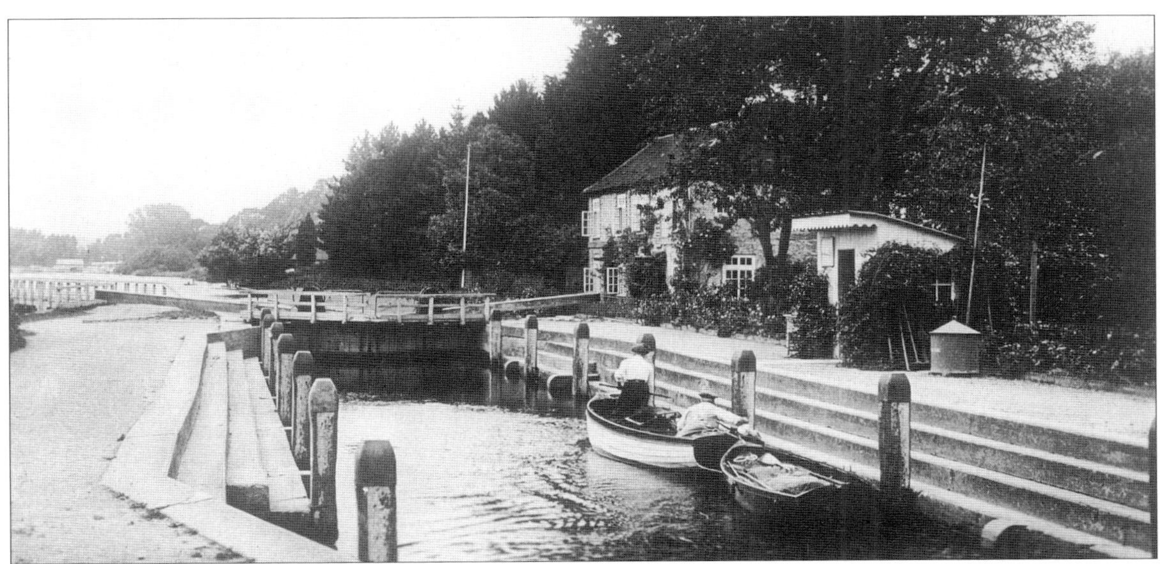

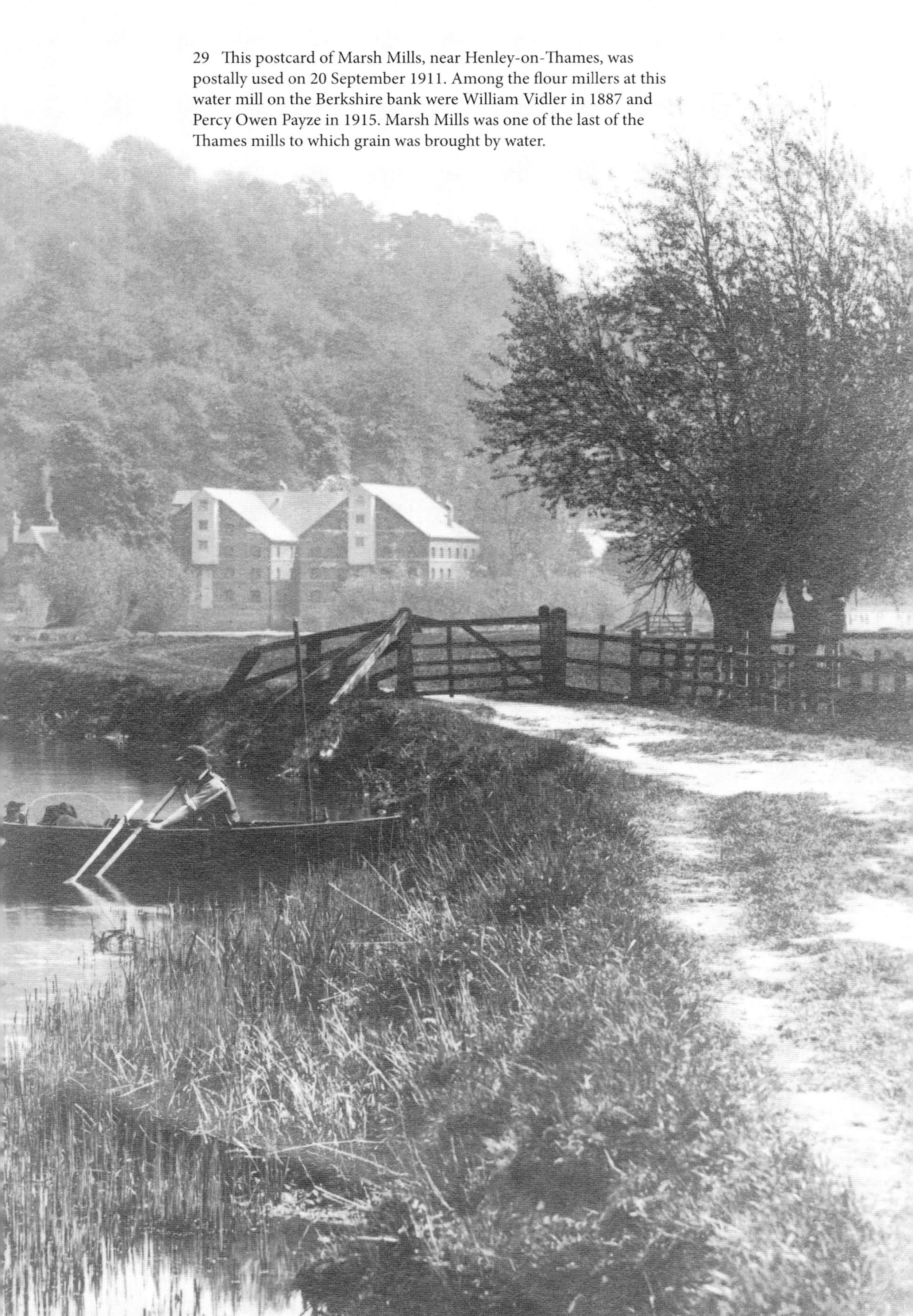

29 This postcard of Marsh Mills, near Henley-on-Thames, was postally used on 20 September 1911. Among the flour millers at this water mill on the Berkshire bank were William Vidler in 1887 and Percy Owen Payze in 1915. Marsh Mills was one of the last of the Thames mills to which grain was brought by water.

Henley-on-Thames to Medmenham Abbey

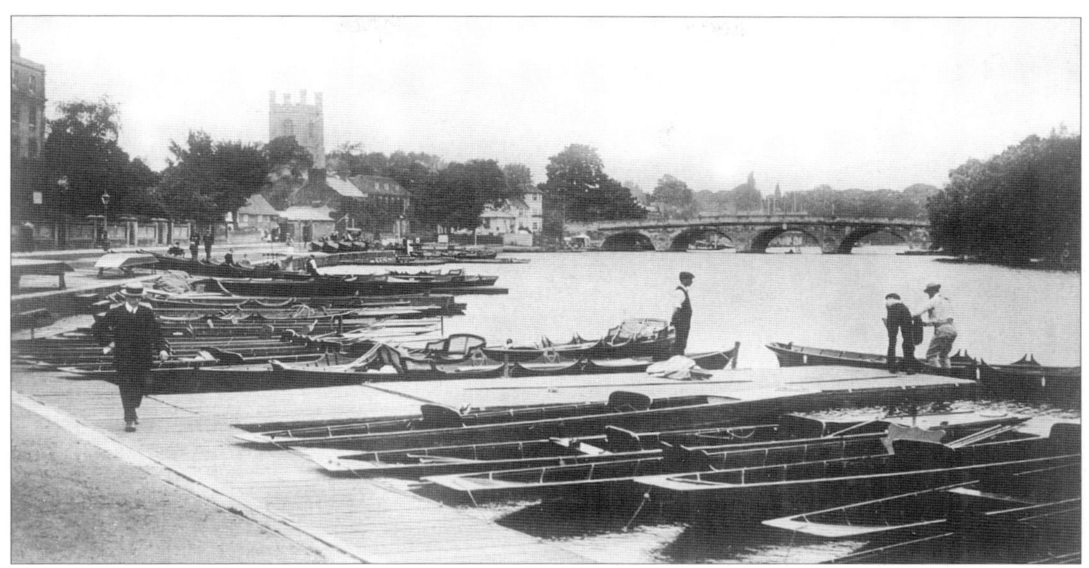

30 This scene above the bridge at Henley-on-Thames, dating from *c.*1910-14, shows that there were plenty of small rowing boats and punts for people to indulge in the favourite pastime of 'messing about on the river'. In 1913, Hobbs & Sons Ltd, launch and boat builders, had two boathouses at Henley, one within a minute of the railway station and the other near the winning post and overlooking the Regatta course.

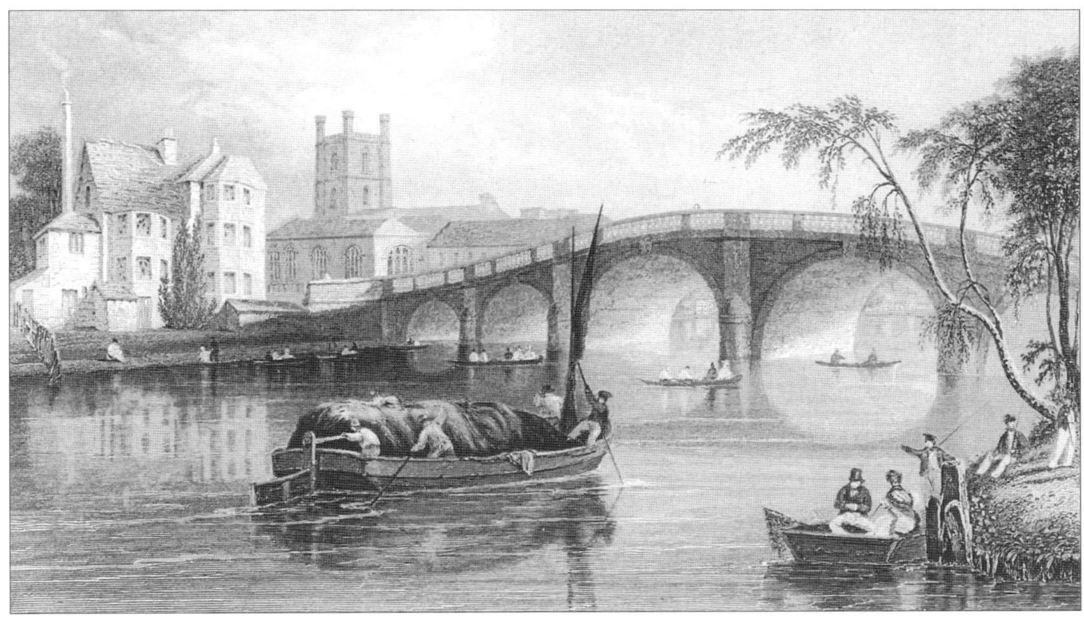

31 Henley Bridge, *c.*1834. In the late 18th century, William Combes described the bridge as built of white stone and added, 'The pavement which runs along either side, is guarded by a low balustrade; and both fronts are enlivened by pilasters supported on semicircular projections of the piers, the whole forming an uncommon design of simplicity and elegance.'

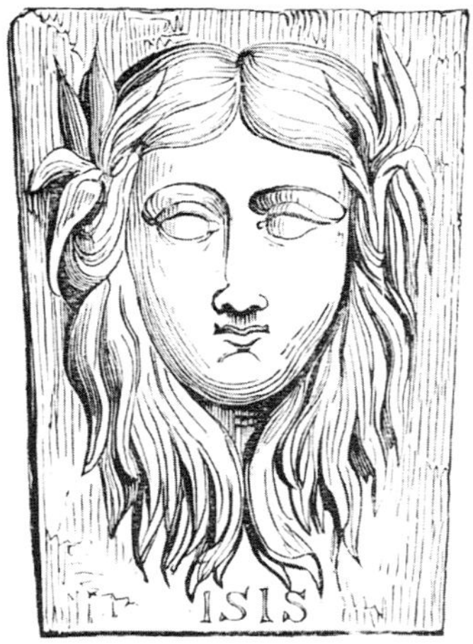

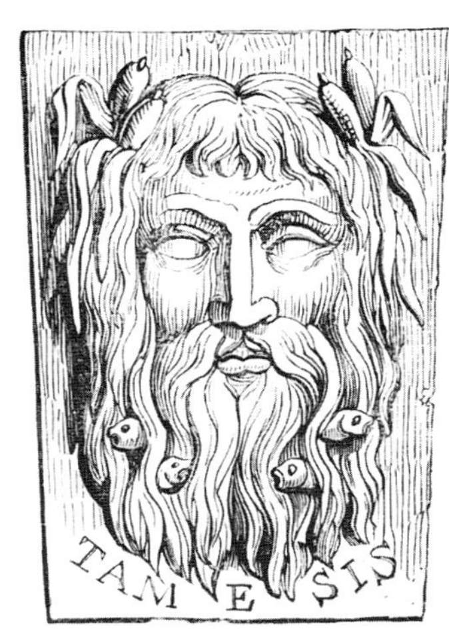

32 Isis and Tamesis on Henley Bridge from *The Book of the Thames* by Mr and Mrs S.C. Hall, who commented that Henley Bridge 'will be interesting to Art-lovers as containing two sculptured works — MASKS OF THE THAMES AND ISIS — from the chisel of the Hon. Mrs. Damer, they decorate the consoles of the central arch'.

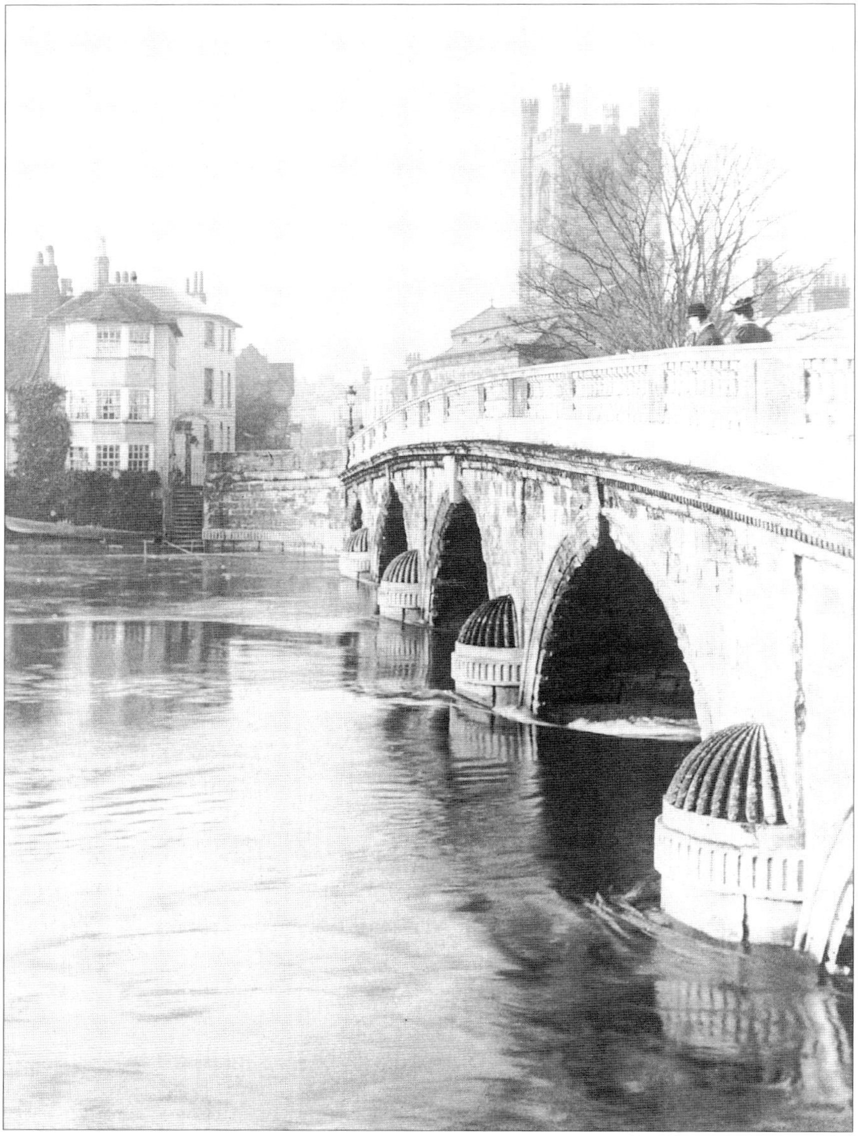

33 Floodwater was lapping at the piers of Henley Bridge when this photograph was taken. In the background can be seen the 17th-century *Angel Hotel*.

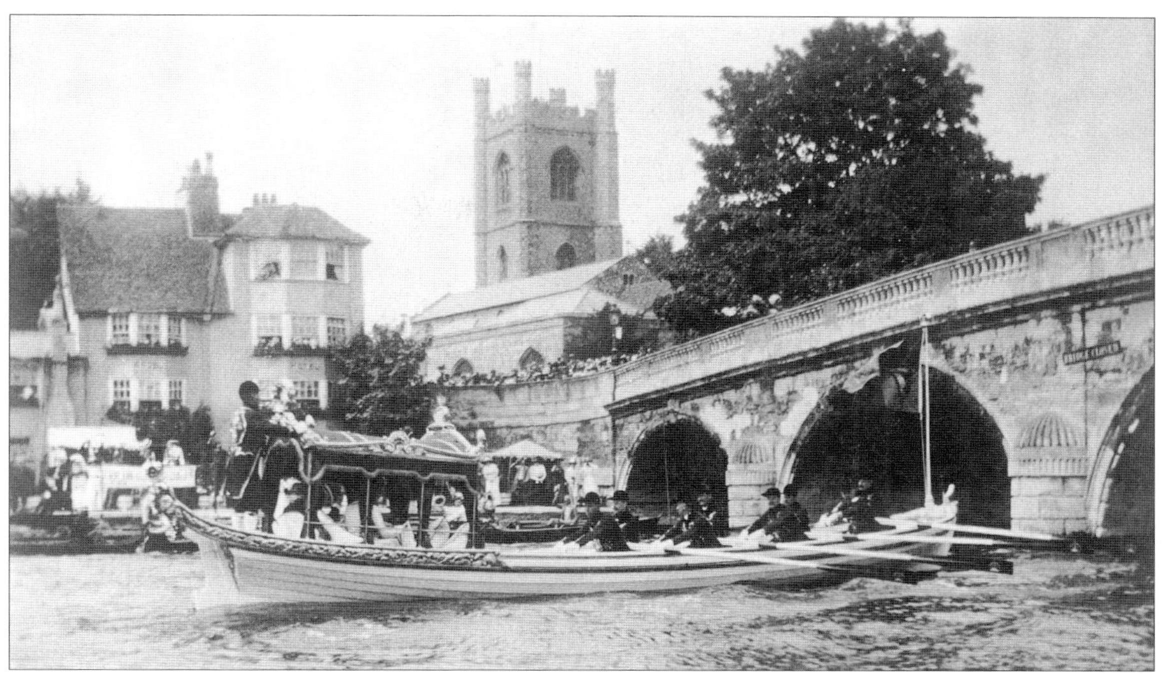

34 In 1912, King George V and Queen Mary visited Henley for the Regatta. This postcard view of the royal barge at Henley Bridge was postally used the same year with the message, 'This is King and Queen on here at the Regatta'.

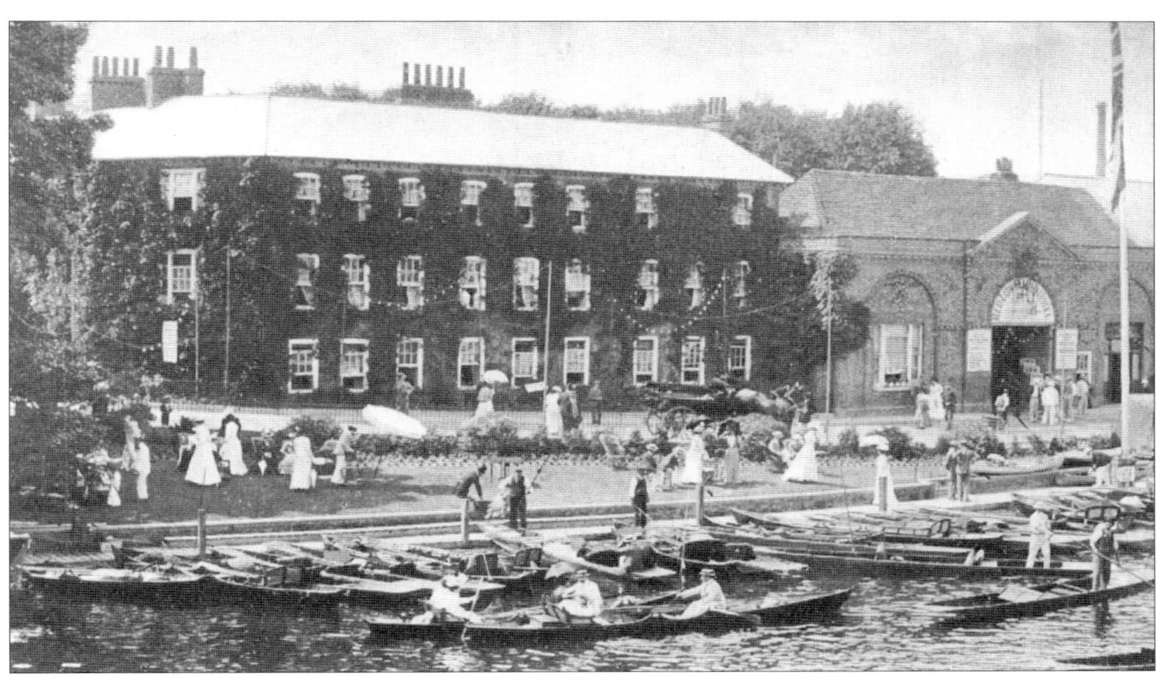

35 Situated next to Henley Bridge, the *Red Lion Hotel* was once one of the main coaching inns of the town. Among Royalty who are said to have used the inn are Charles I, George III and George IV. Popular during the Regatta, the hotel was depicted on this trade card dating from *c.*1906. *Kelly's Directory of Oxfordshire* listed Charles H. Burkard as manager of the *Red Lion Family Hotel*, Thames side in 1907.

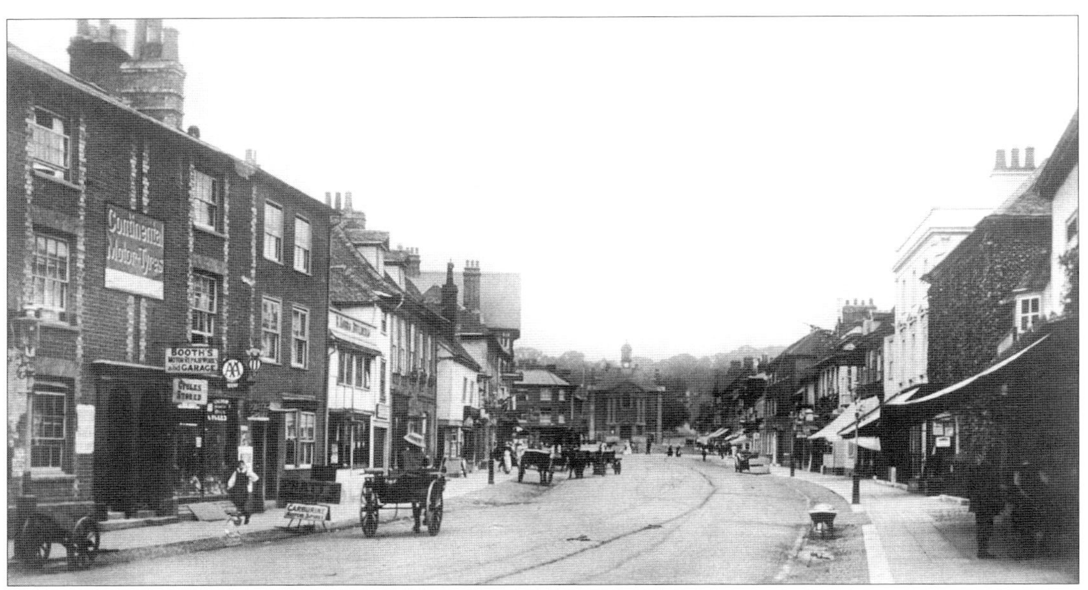

36 Hart Street, Henley-on-Thames, *c.*1910-14. Prominent on the left of this view is a sign for Booth's Motor Repair Works and Garage. James Booth, motor agent, was listed at 34 and 36 Hart Street in *Kelly's Directory of Oxfordshire* of 1911. In the distance can be seen Henley's Town Hall, situated in the Market Place. This large red-brick building with stone dressings was erected between 1899 and 1900 in commemoration of the Diamond Jubilee of Queen Victoria, which had taken place in 1897.

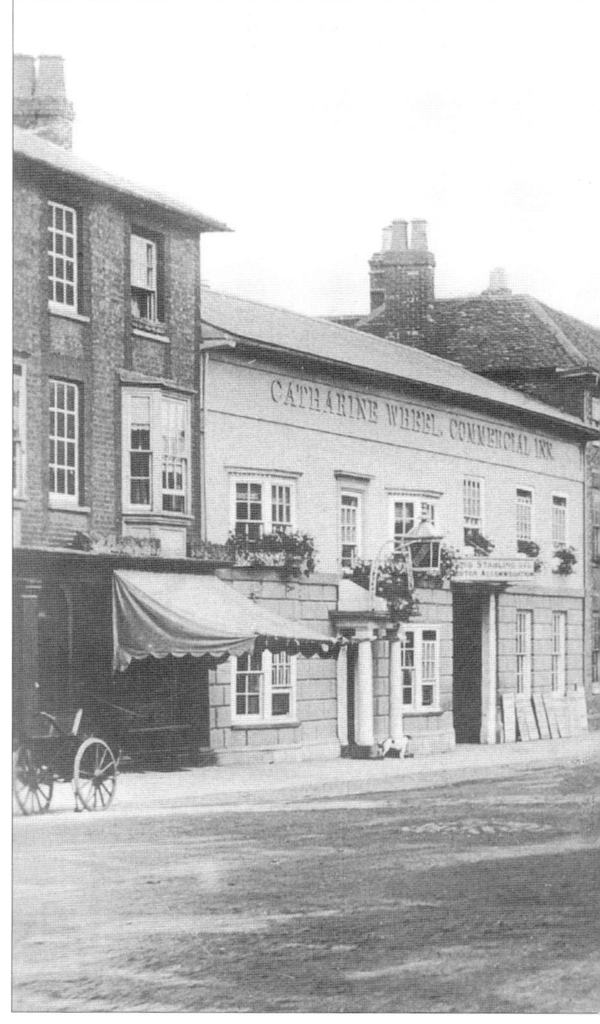

37 This postcard of Hart Street, Henley-on-Thames was postally used on 23 August 1916, but the view may have been taken in the first decade of the 20th century. On the left is the *Catharine Wheel Commercial Inn*. By 1907, *Kelly's Directory of Oxfordshire* listed the premises as the *Catherine Wheel Hotel*. Mrs Buchanan was manageress at this time, while in 1911 Ernest Barton ran the hotel at 7 and 9 Hart Street. In 1913, the hotel provided accommodation for passengers on the Salter's Oxford and Kingston steamers at the special inclusive tariff of 8s. 6d. for dinner, bed, breakfast and attendance. A porter met the steamers and conveyed luggage to and from the hotel free of charge.

38 Pleasure craft moored alongside the *Little White Hart Hotel*, at Thames side, Henley-on-Thames. In the early years of the 20th century, this establishment had a private landing stage and motor garage plus the 'Largest Dining Hall in Henley for Parties'. In the background of this view, the Henley Brewery can be seen.

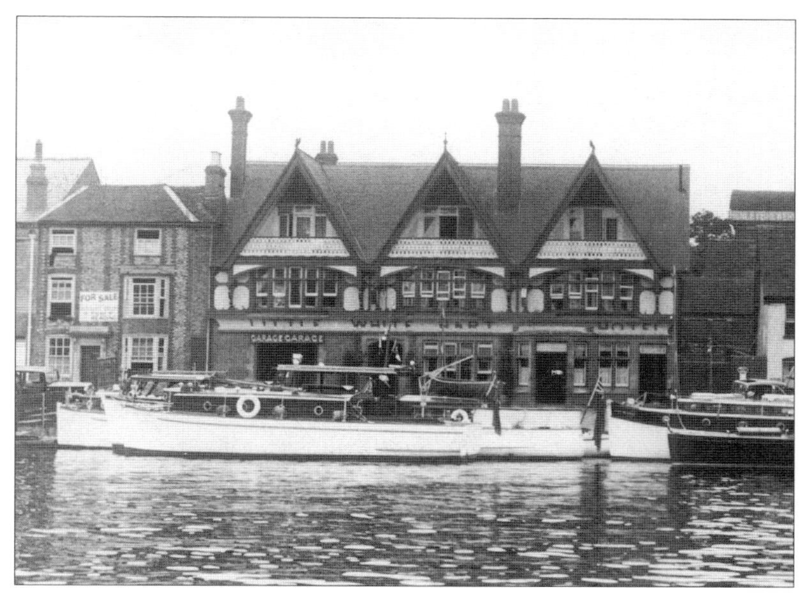

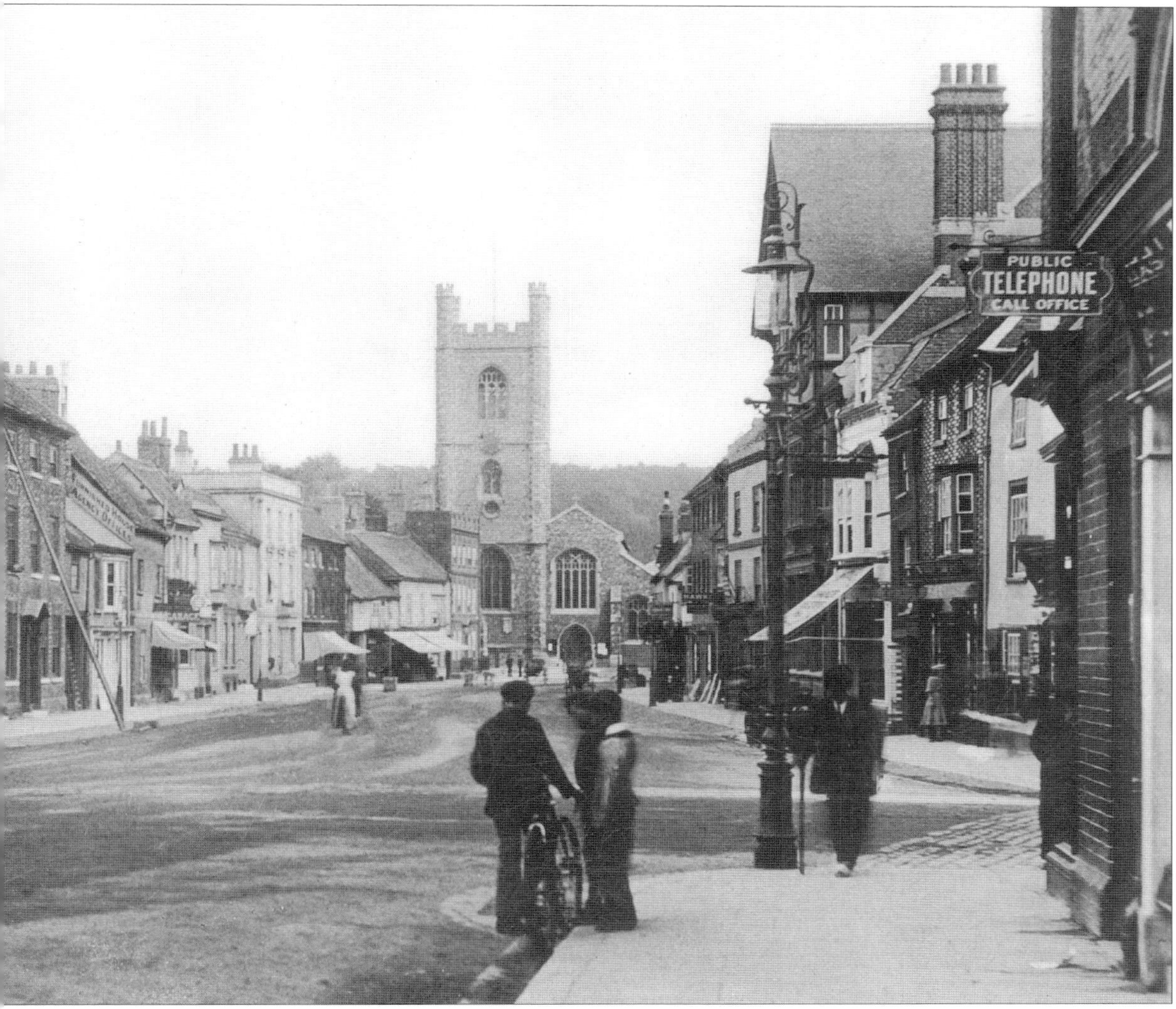

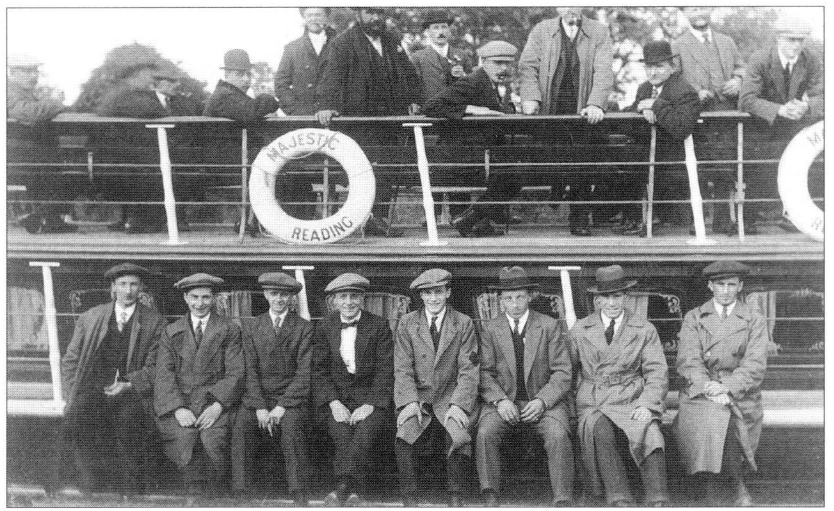

39 Passengers on the *Majestic* steamer, owned by Cawston's of Reading, posed for the photographer at Henley-on-Thames in 1919.

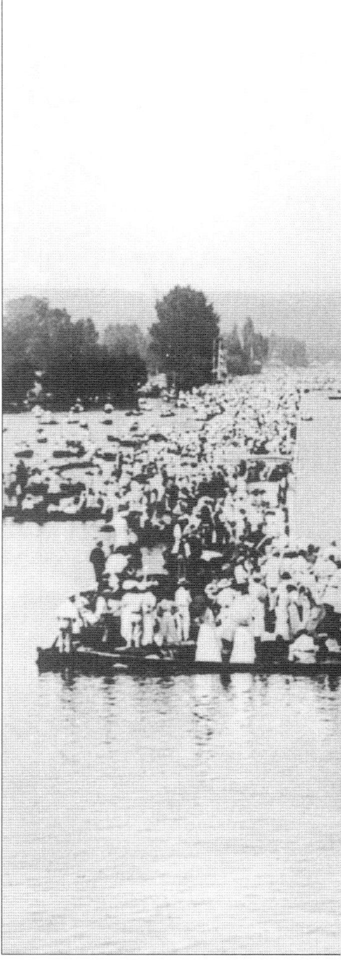

40 View on the river, Henley-on-Thames, *c.*1910-14. At this time, Hobbs & Sons Ltd advertised 'A large stock of punts, canoes & rowing boats to let' plus 'Steam, electric and motor launches of various sizes for hire'.

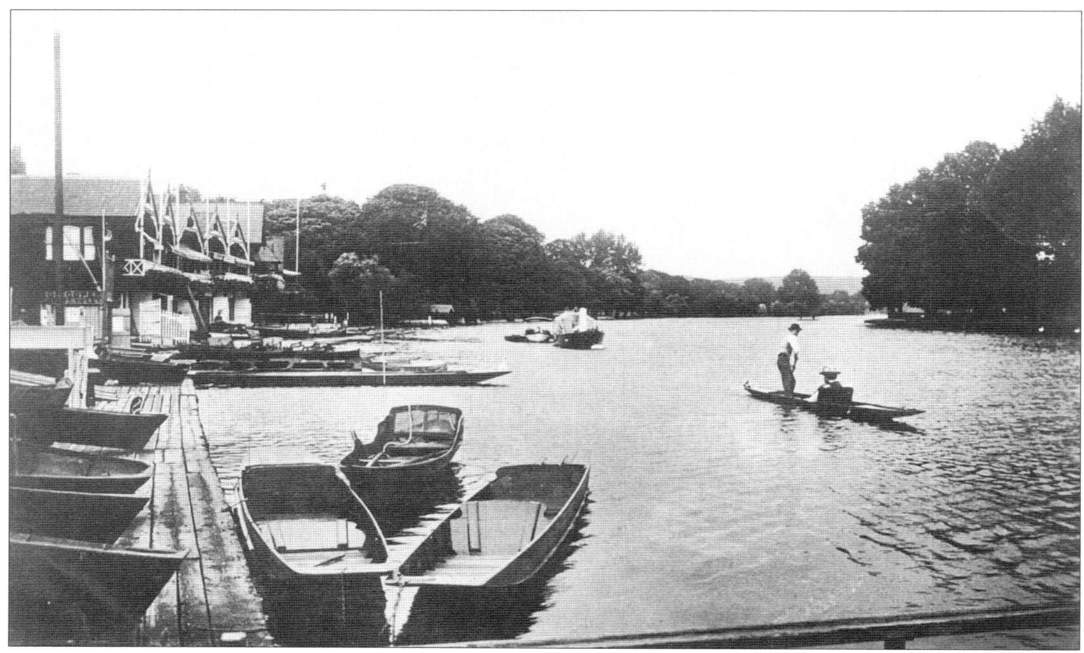

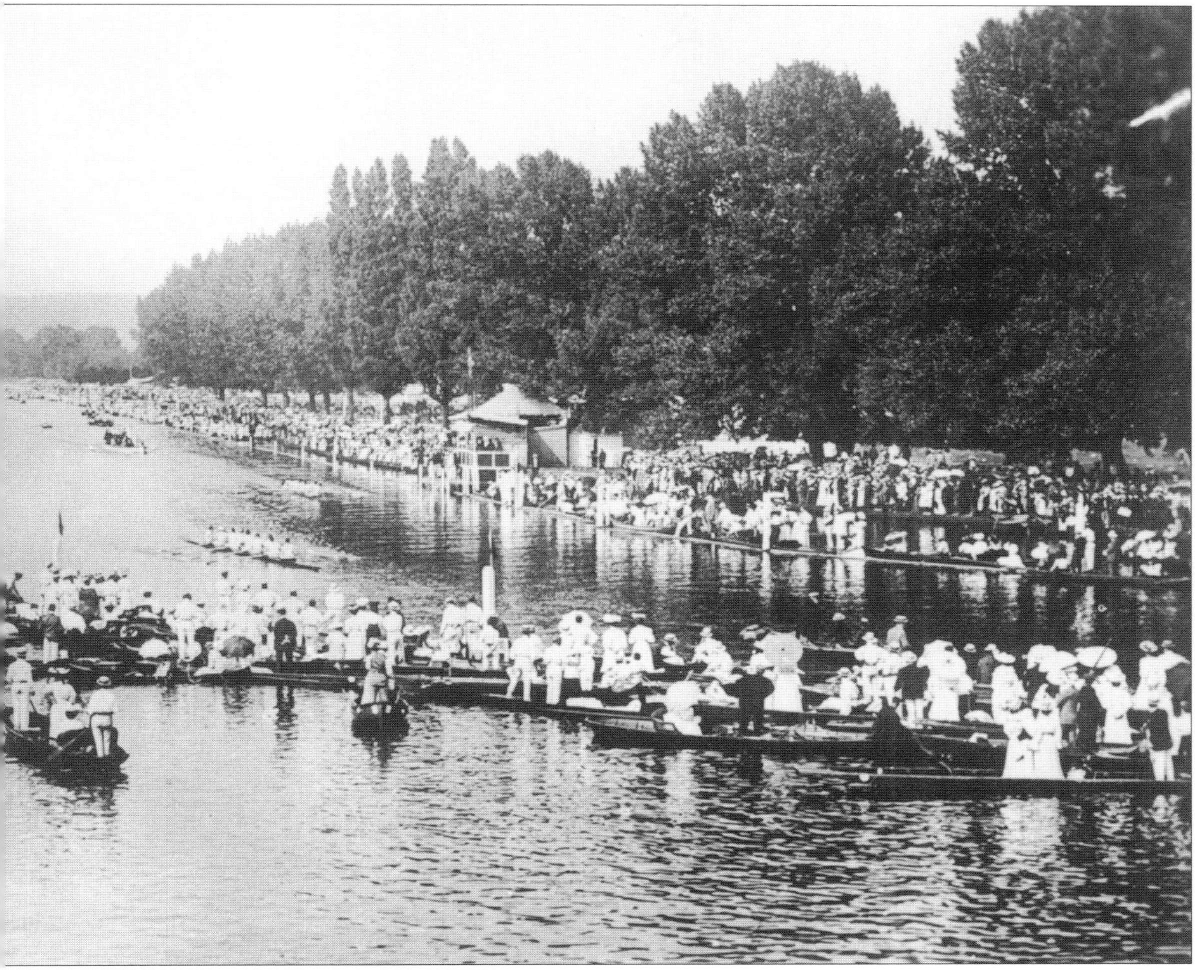

(Above) 41 The Regatta course, Henley-on-Thames, *c.*1907. The prizes included the Grand Challenge Cup and the Thames Challenge Cup for eight oars, the Stewards' Challenge Cup and the Wyfold Challenge Cup for fours, the Silver Goblets for pairs and the Diamond Challenge Sculls for scullers.

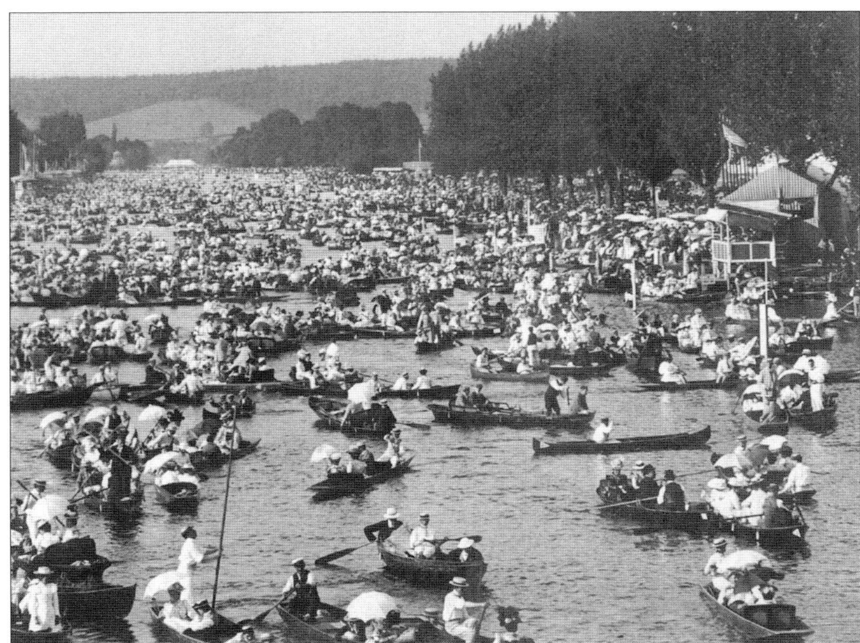

42 Small craft crowded the river at the time of the Henley Regatta, *c.*1907.

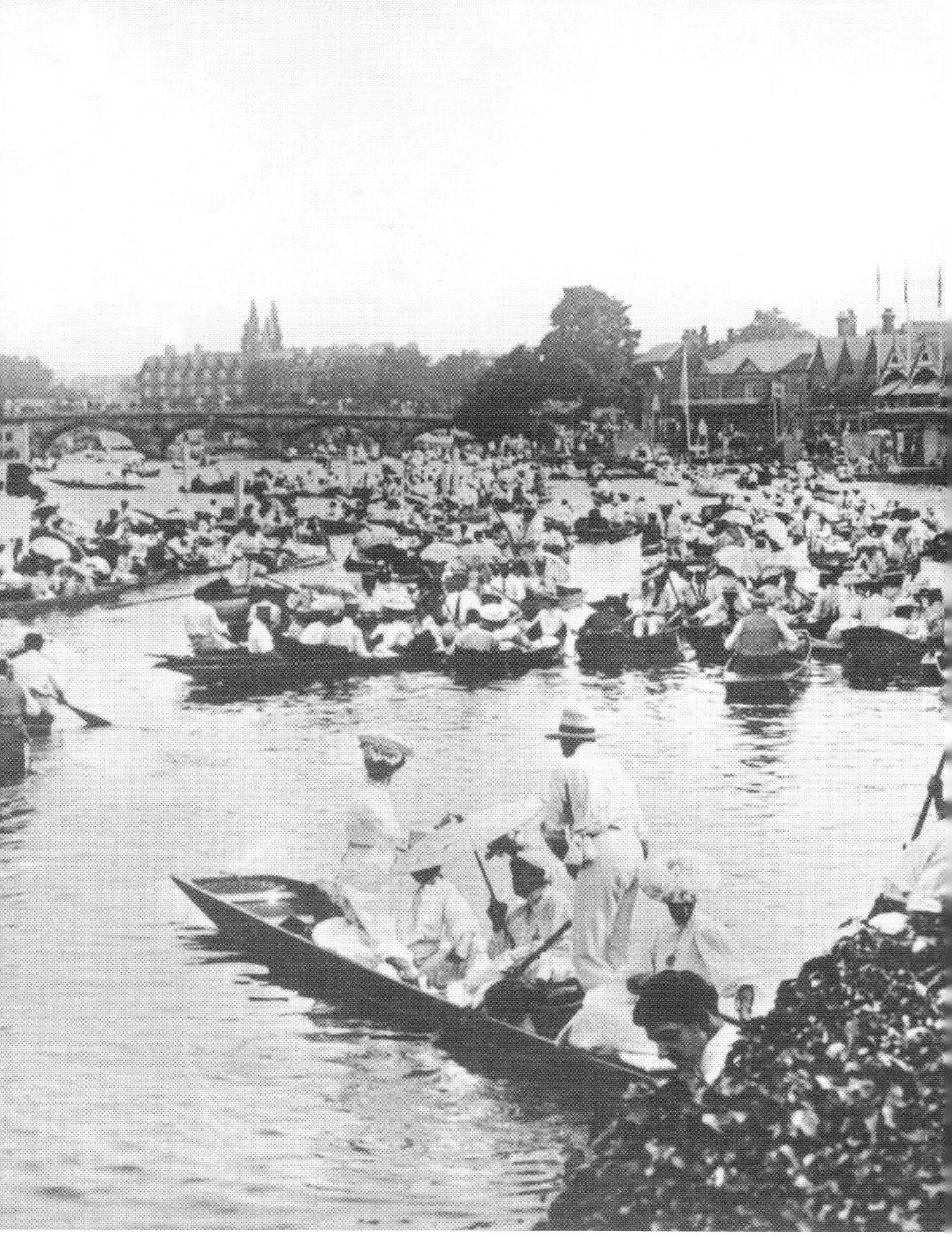

43 Henley-on-Thames from Phyllis Court, *c.*1907. The old manor of Phyllis Court once stood on the riverbank to the north of the town. Most of it was pulled down in the late 18th century and

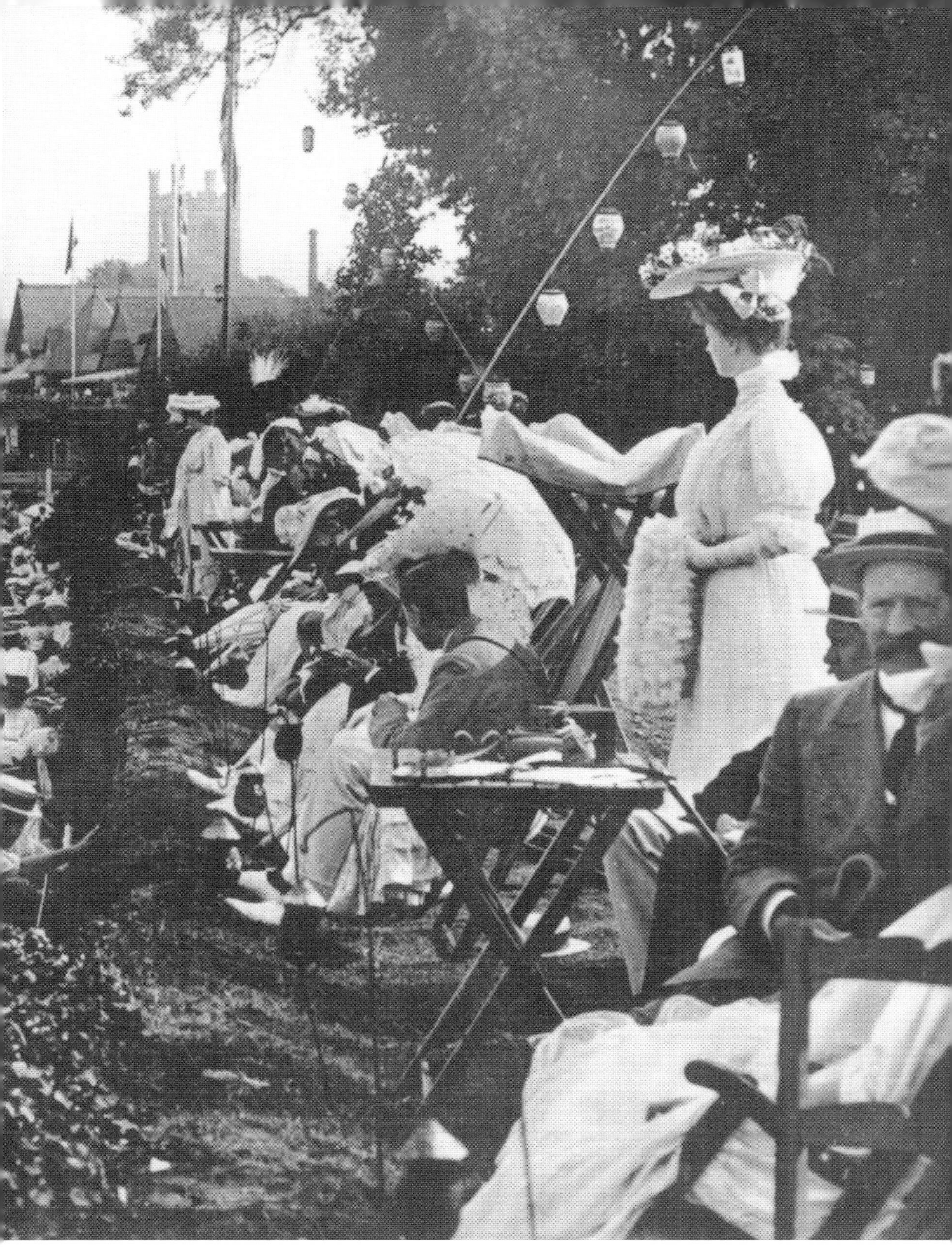

the remainder was later removed and replaced by the building, which was occupied by Phyllis Court Club. This Edwardian view shows the Thames during Regatta week.

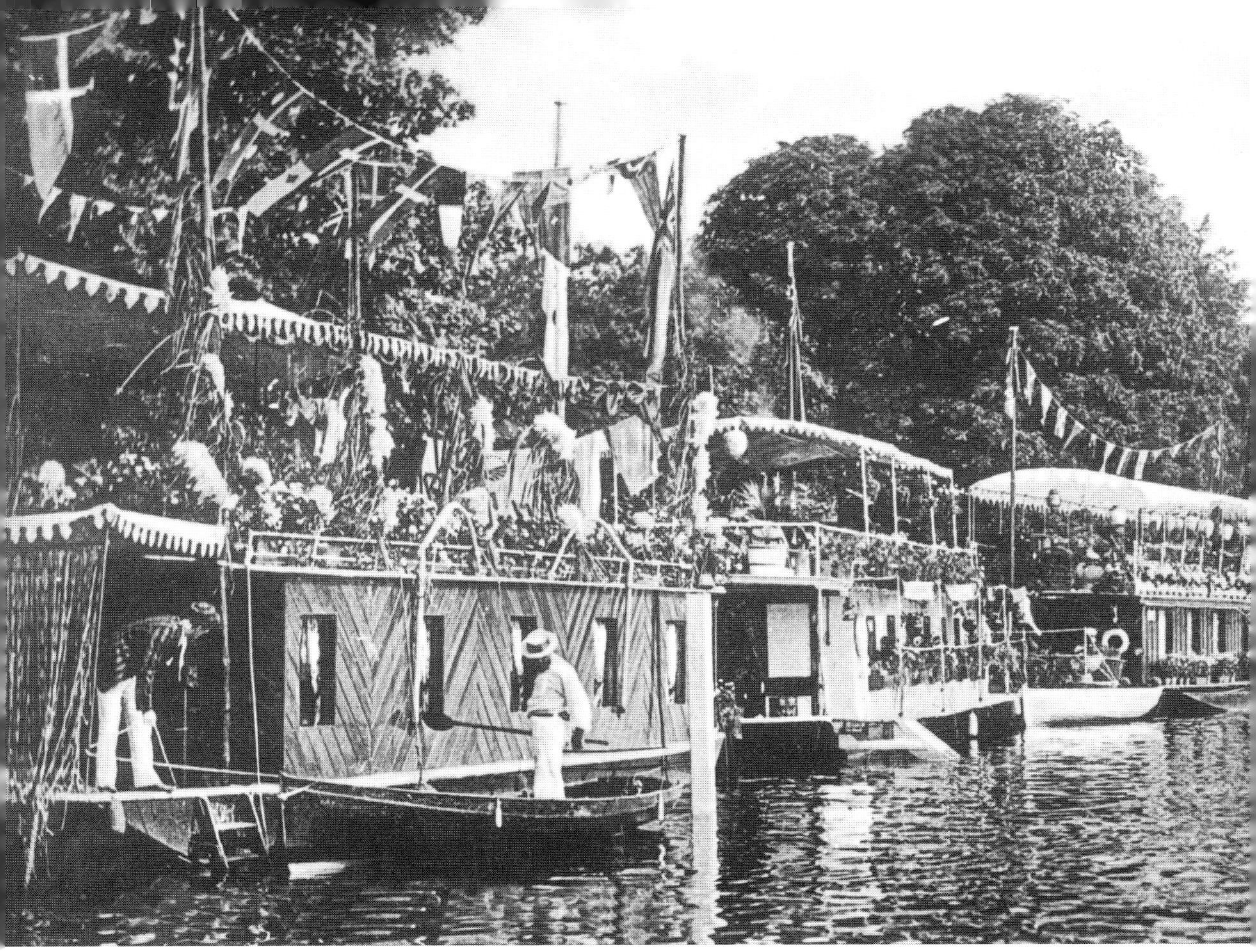

(Above) 44 Houseboats at Henley Regatta, decorated with flowers and bunting, made a good subject for a postcard of the annual event. This one was postally used on 31 January 1914.

(Right) 45 This illustration from *Tombleson's Thames* shows Fawley Court, downstream of Henley-on-Thames. W.G. Fearnside commented, 'the seat of Mr. Freeman, with its lawns and thick woods, has a noble appearance: the mansion was erected from the designs of Sir Christopher Wren'.

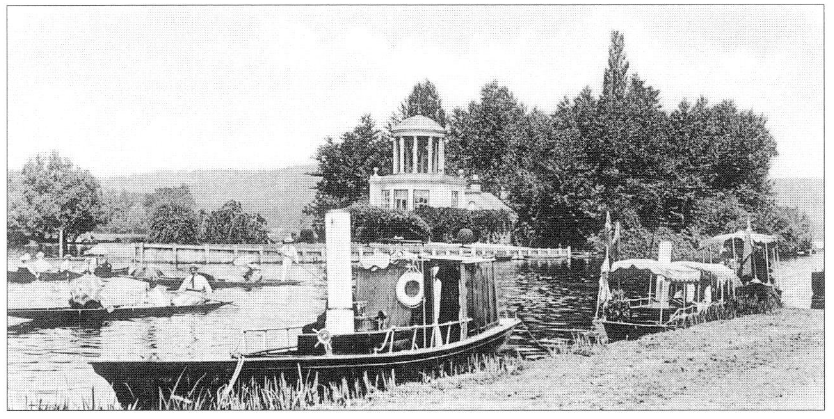

46 Temple Island, downriver from Henley-on-Thames, is the backdrop to this Edwardian boating scene.

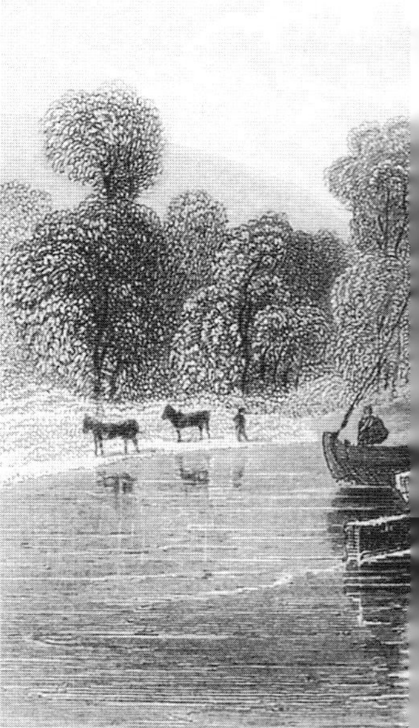

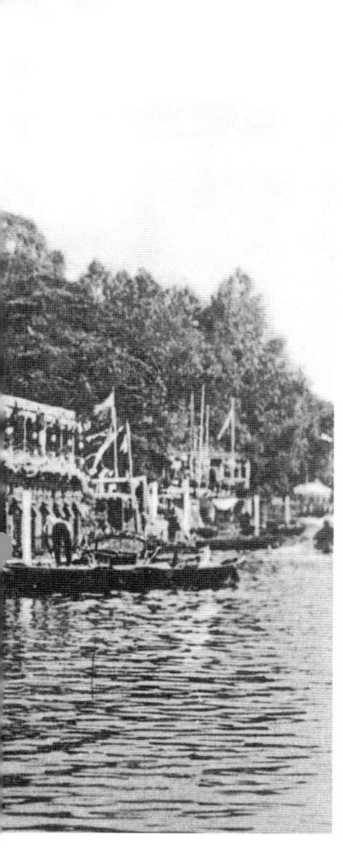

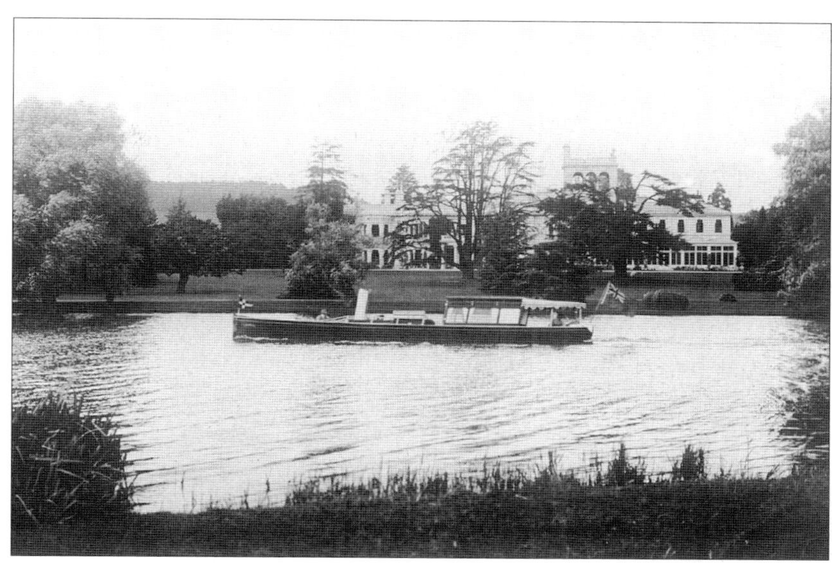

47 In 1915, Greenlands, near Henley-on-Thames, was the seat of William Frederick Danvers Smith, 2nd Viscount Hambleden, who belonged to the renowned firm of newspaper vendors, W.H. Smith & Son. At this time, besides flower gardens on a large scale, the grounds contained some fine cedars of Lebanon and a Wellingtonia.

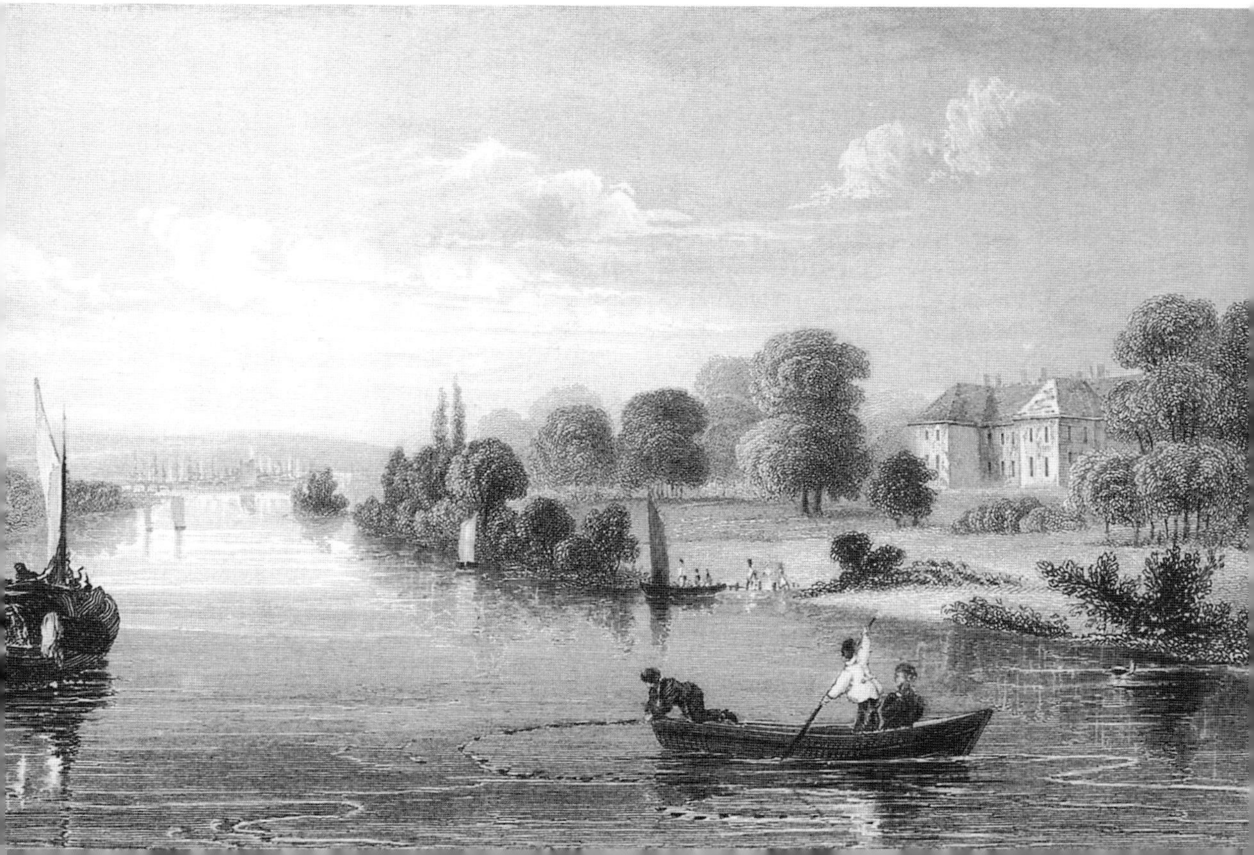

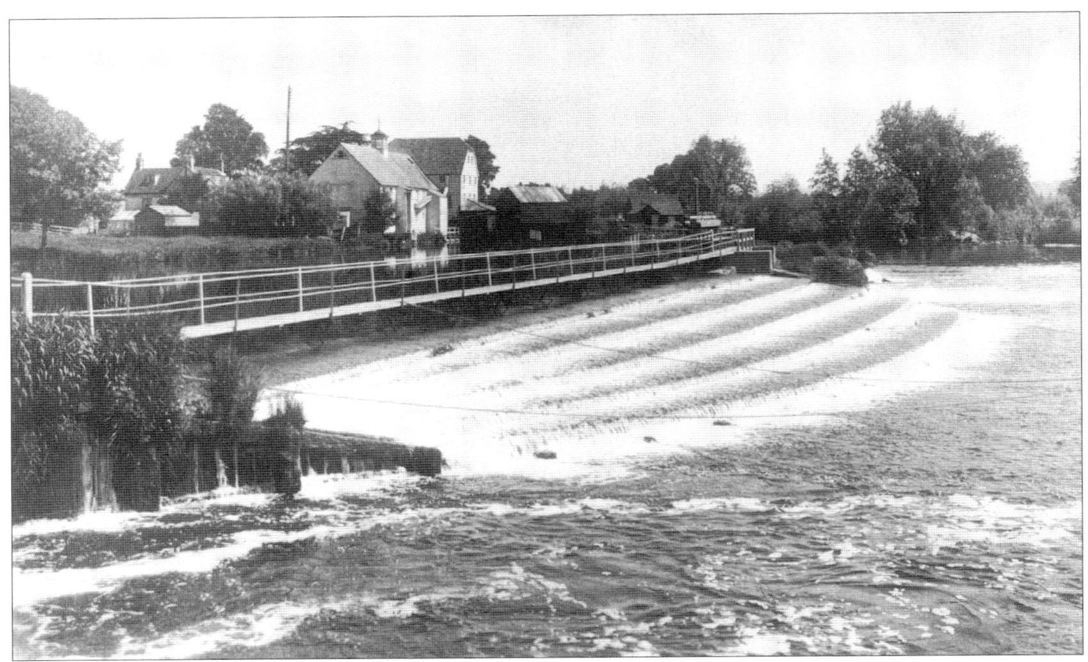

48 Hambleden Mill can be seen in the background of this view of Hambleden Weir. C. Barnett & Sons were millers at Hambleden Mill in the early years of the 20th century.

49 In the early 20th century, the area around Henley was used for army manoeuvres. This postcard view, which was postally used in 1904, shows motors crossing a pontoon bridge at Aston.

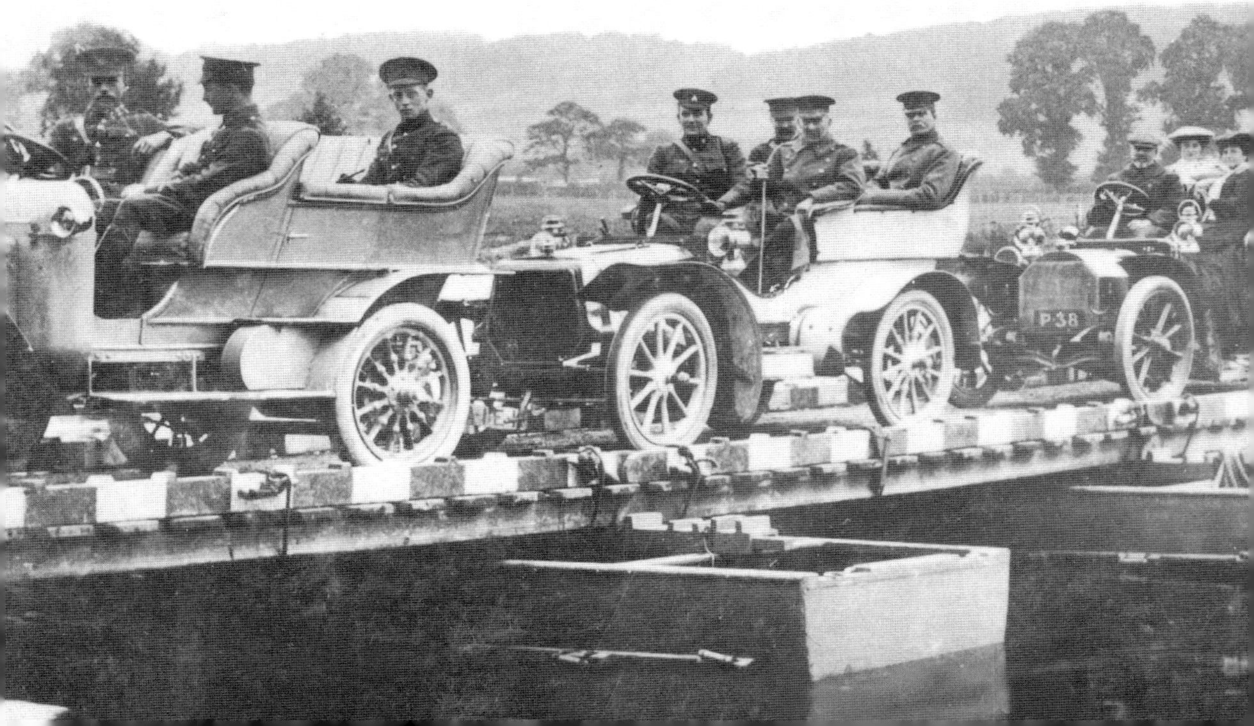

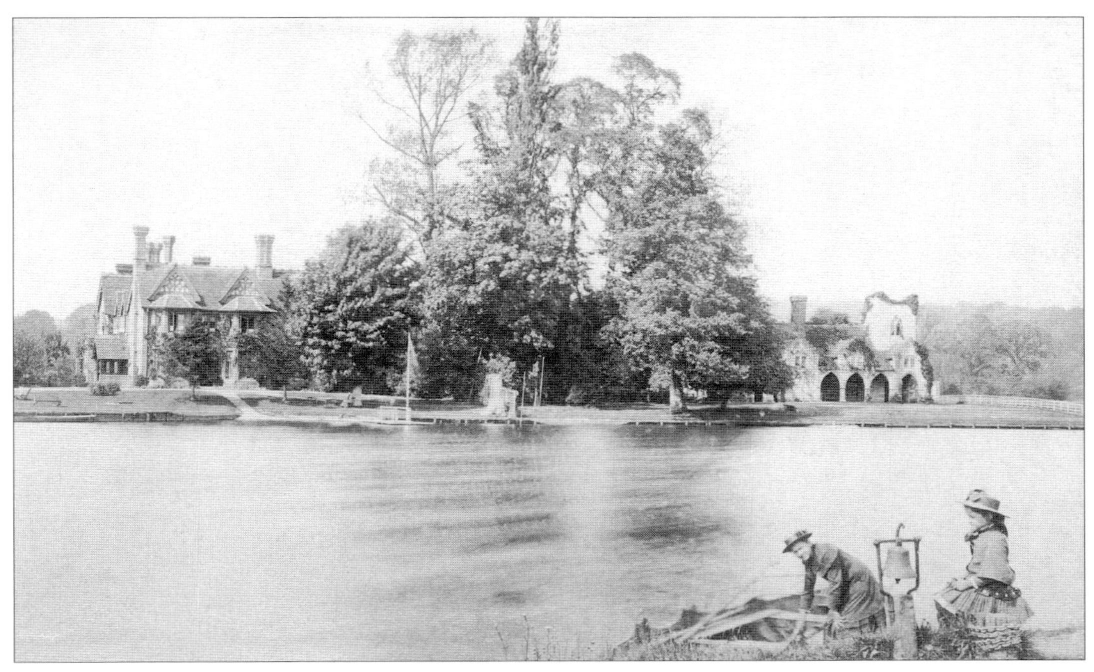

50 A ferry used to cross the river at Medmenham Abbey. The bell in the right-hand corner of this old photograph was presumably used to call the person who operated the ferry. The hotel here was called the *Ferry Hotel* in Henry Taunt's time.

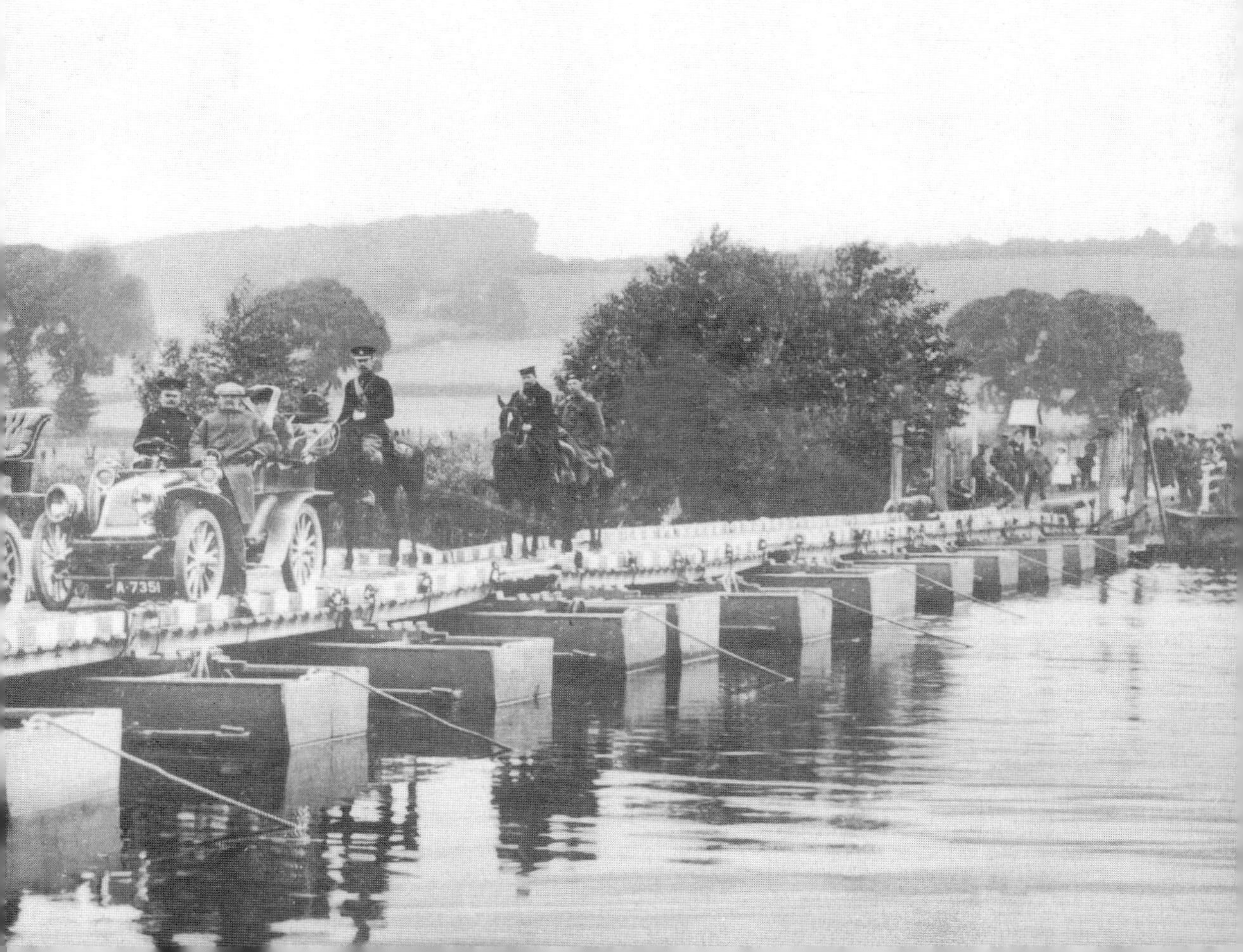

Hurley to Cookham Lock

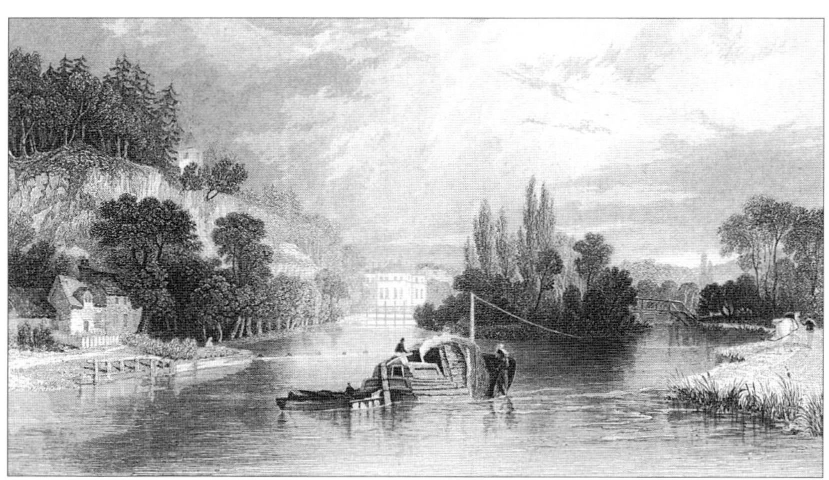

51 'View near Hurley' from *Tombleson's Thames*, *c*.1834. The large house illustrated was Harleyford House, now known as Harleyford Manor.

52 Hurley Lock was opened in 1773. Fred S. Thacker noted that in 1910 it was 'one of the oldest looking on the River', having timber sides like Day's Lock.

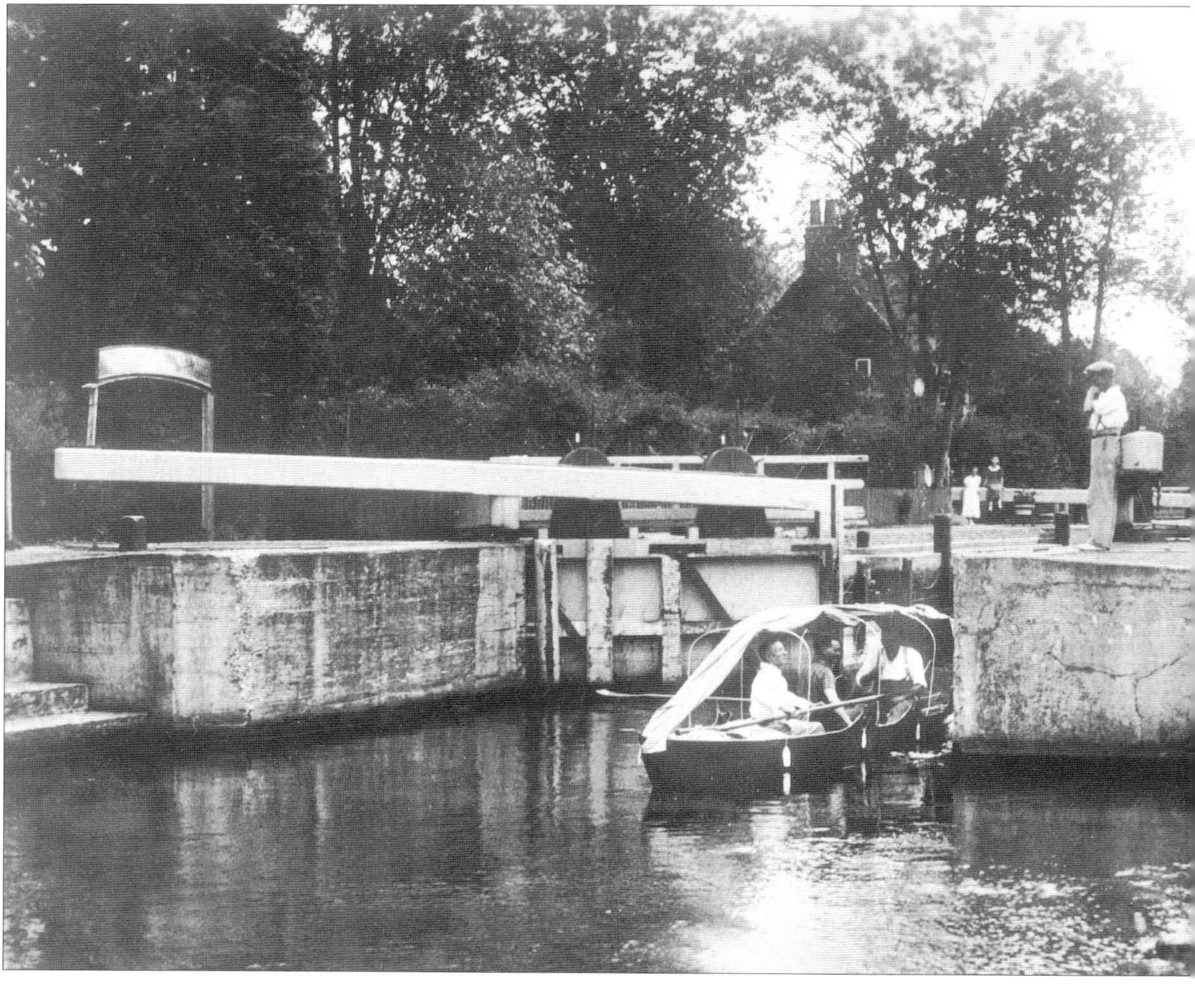

53 *Ye Olde Bell Inn*, Hurley, is said to have been built in 1135 as a guest house for the nearby Priory of St Mary. The original building was reconstructed in medieval times. The gabled and half-timbered hostelry, shown here, was kept by John F. Oliver in 1913.

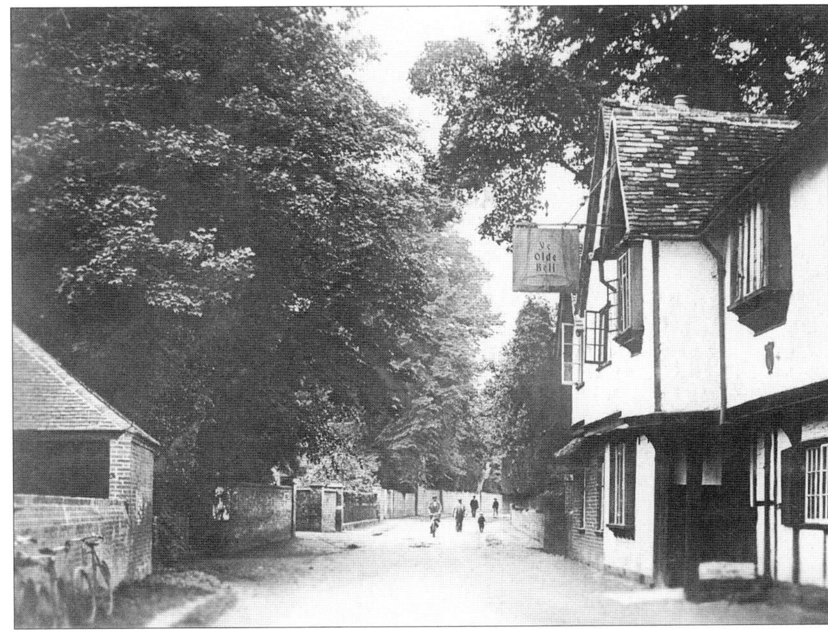

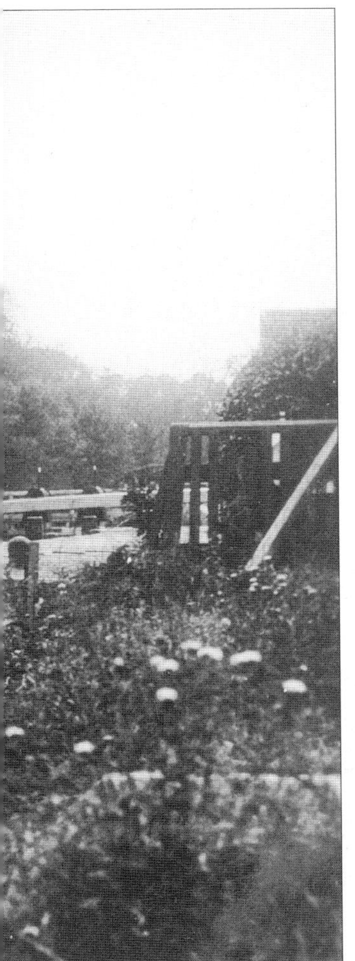

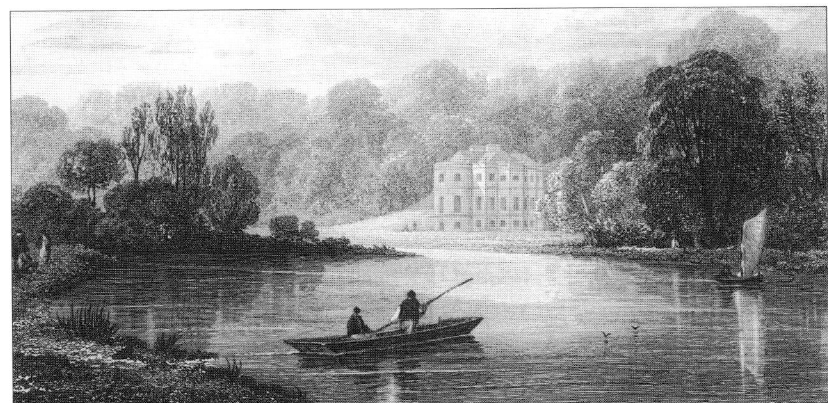

54 'HARLEYFORD HOUSE, Seat of Sir Wm. Clayton Bart.' from *Views on the Thames* by W.B. Cooke and George Cooke. Drawn by S. Owen and engraved by W.B. Cooke, this view was published on 1 January 1817.

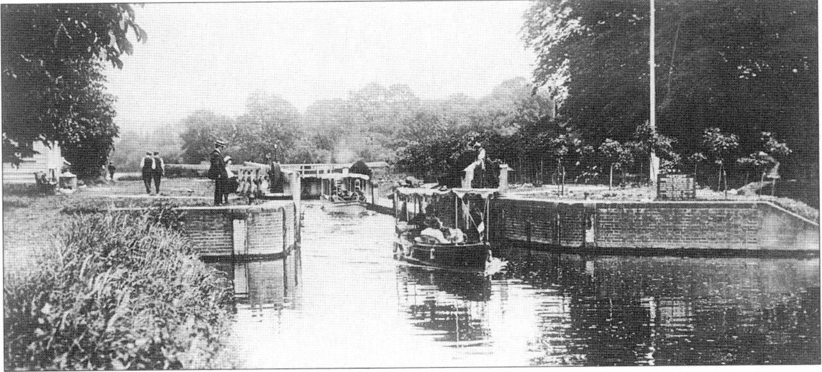

55 Temple Lock, *c*.1906-10. Opened in 1773, the lock here was rebuilt in 1782. A new lock was constructed alongside the old one in 1890.

56 Temple House, drawn by S. Owen and engraved by George Cooke, from *Views on the Thames*. In the 1830s, the property was described by W.G. Fearnside as 'Temple-Hall the seat of Mr. Williams, member of Parliament for the town of Marlow, to whom belong the copper-mills here erected, which are esteemed the most complete and powerful in England'.

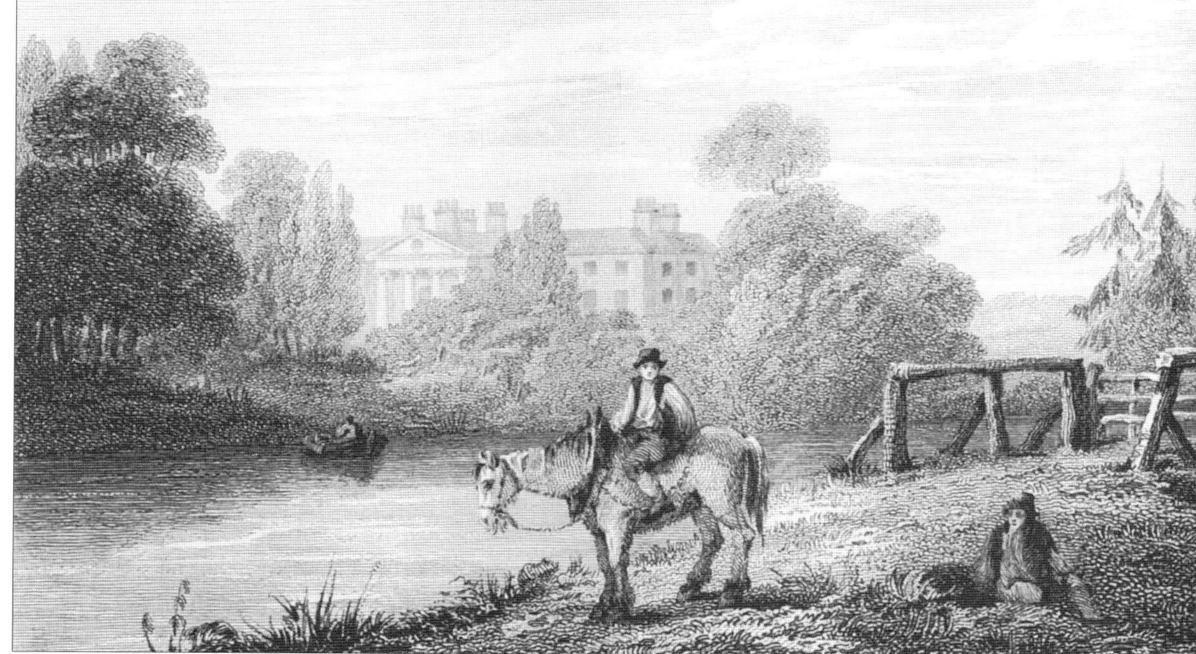

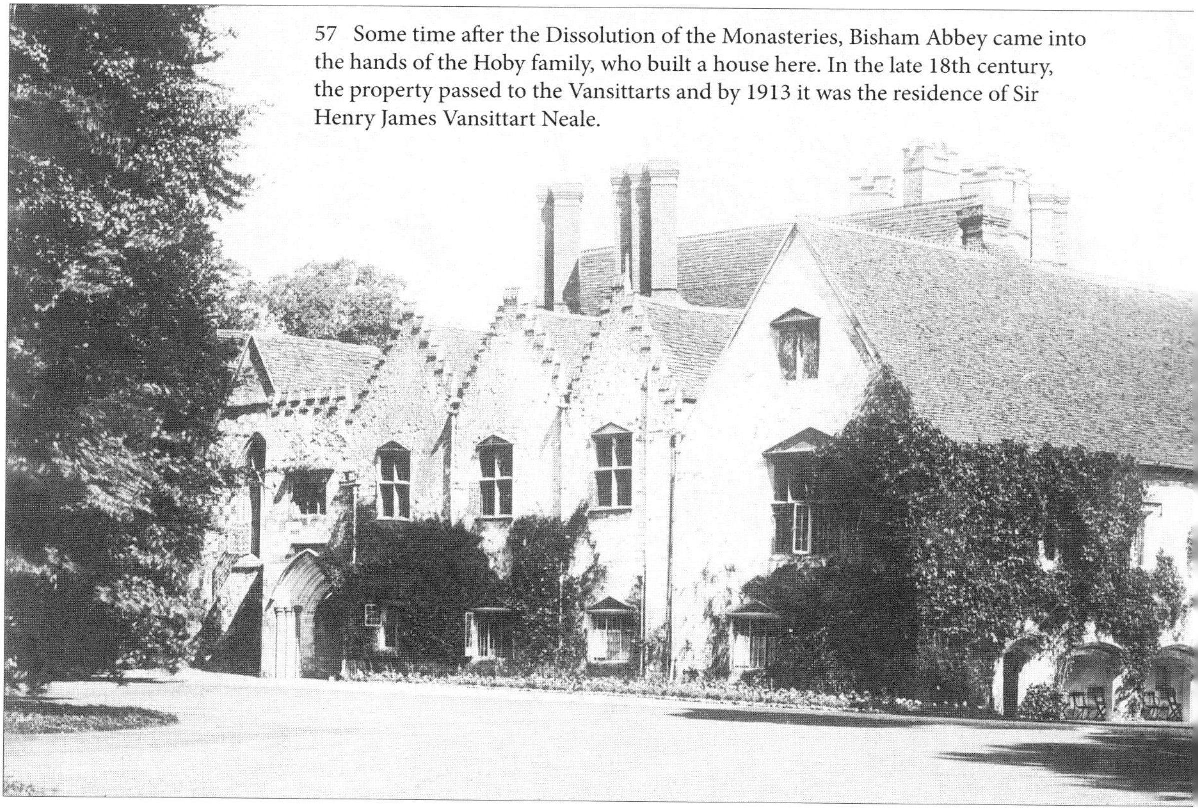

57 Some time after the Dissolution of the Monasteries, Bisham Abbey came into the hands of the Hoby family, who built a house here. In the late 18th century, the property passed to the Vansittarts and by 1913 it was the residence of Sir Henry James Vansittart Neale.

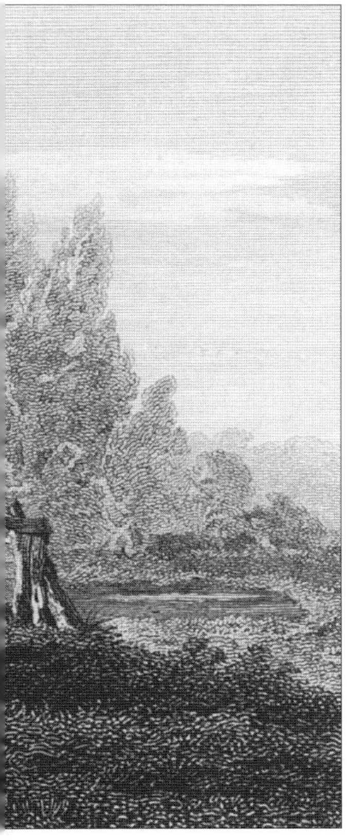

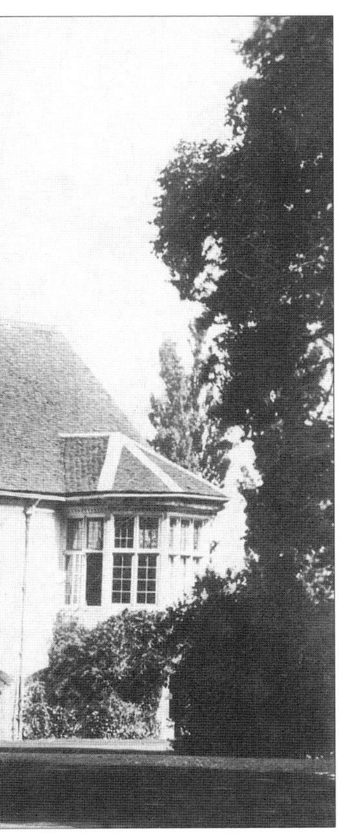

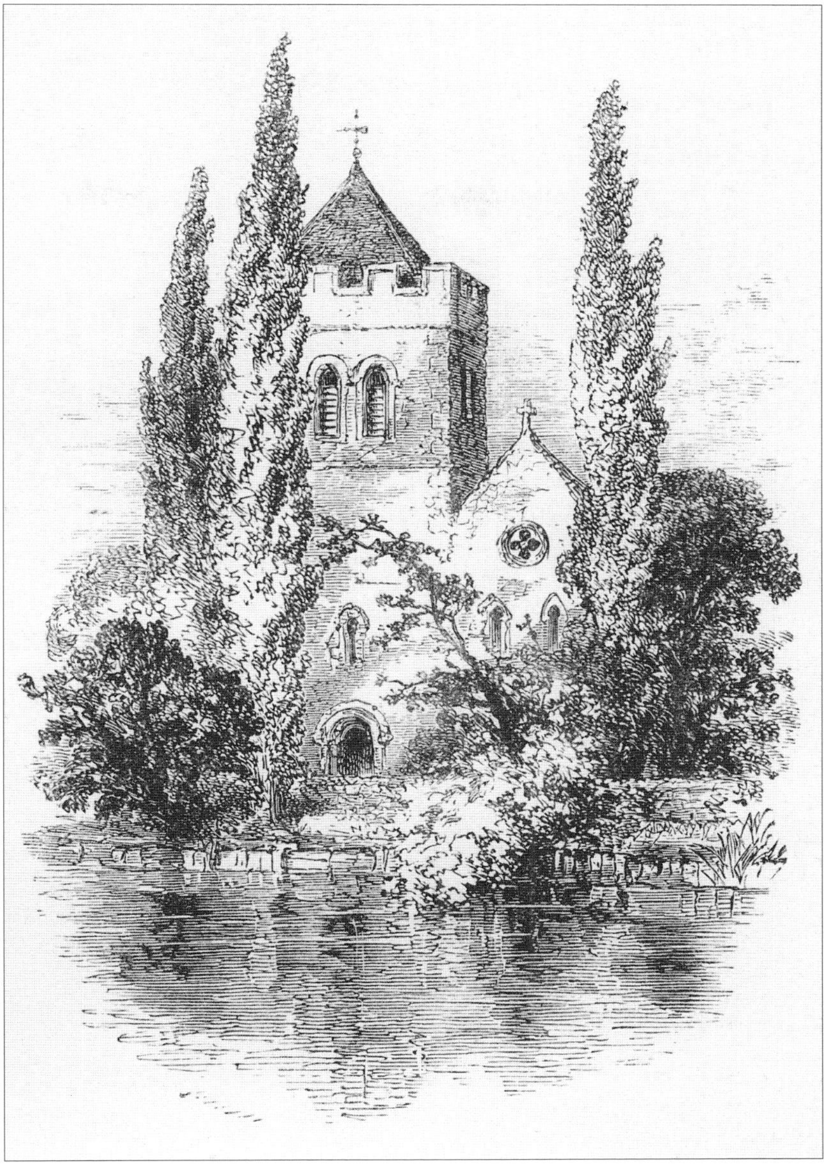

58 Bisham Church has a 12th-century tower with 15th-century additions. Over the centuries, the building was enlarged and great alterations took place in the 19th century. Constructed during Elizabethan times, the Hoby Chapel contains the tomb of two knights, Sir Thomas Hoby and his half-brother Sir Philip Hoby, and the striking tomb of Lady Hoby, wife of Sir Thomas, which also depicts the sons and daughters from her two marriages.

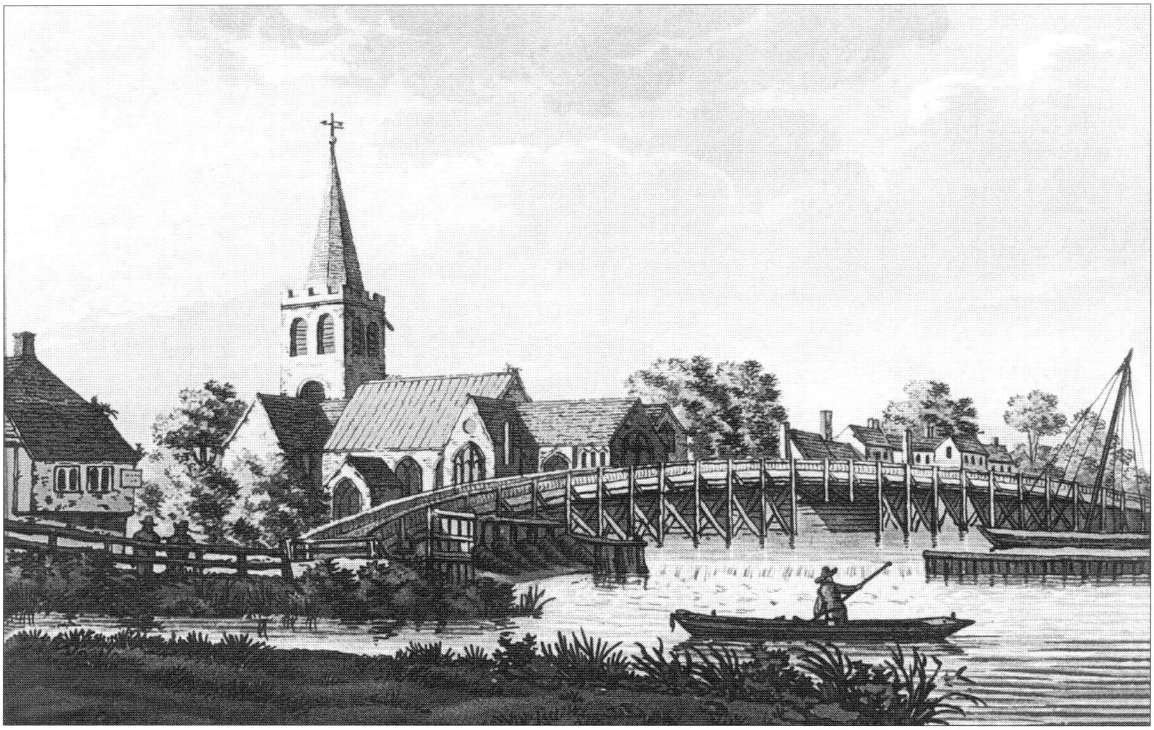

59 An aquatint entitled 'Marlow bridge &c.' from Samuel Ireland's *Picturesque Views on the River Thames.*

> From Bisham Abbey, the town of Marlow, considered as a picturesque object, receives much addition from the New Bridge, which is of wood, and has been recently finished at an expence of about eighteen hundred pounds. It has a remarkable ascent, and forms the best object as a wooden bridge, that I remember to have seen. The ballustrades are painted white, in imitation of stone-work; And the whole scenery contiguous is pleasingly variegated by the rich verdure of the adjacent woods.

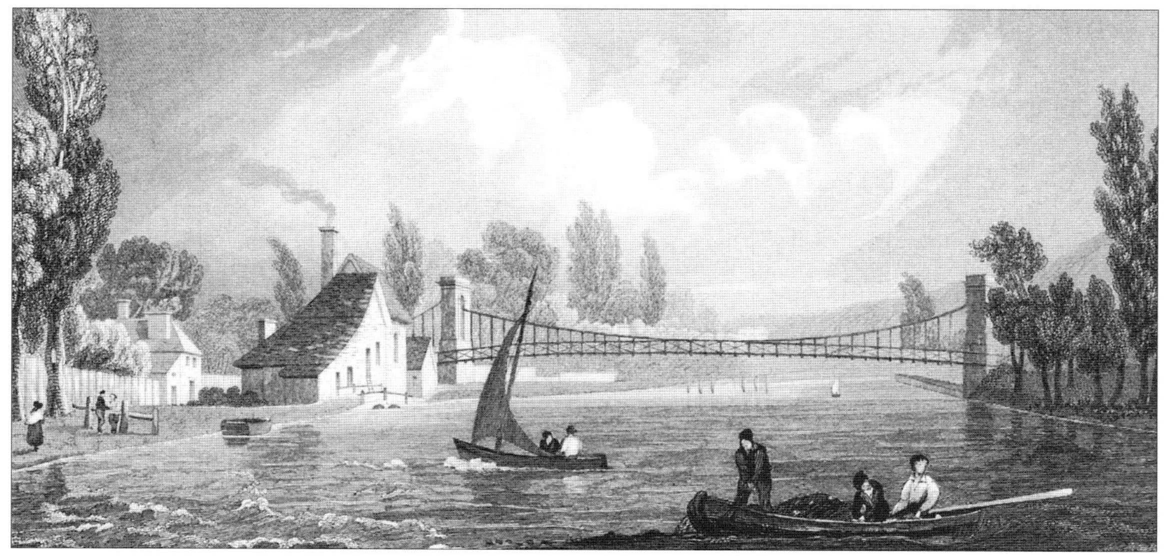

60 This engraving entitled 'Suspension Bridge, Great Marlow', dating from *c.*1834, was included in *Tombleson's Thames.*

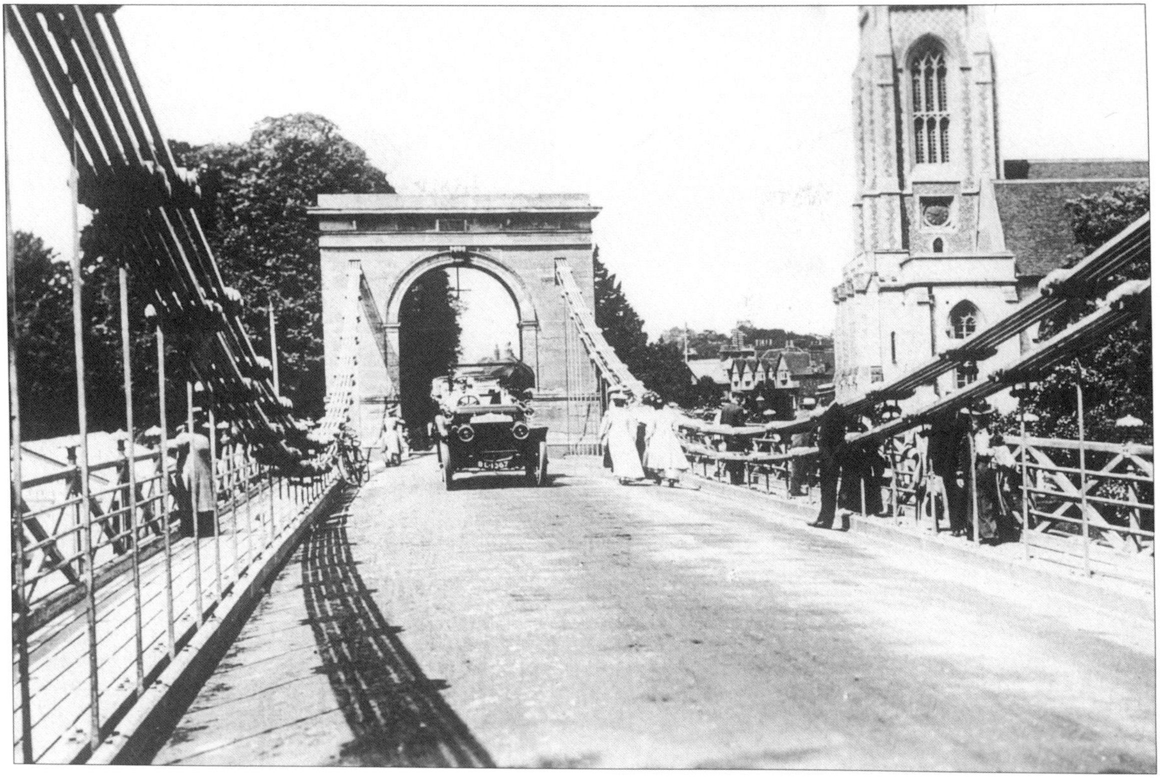

61 A plaque at Marlow's Suspension Bridge commemorates the designer of the bridge, William Tierney Clark, 1783-1852, and its opening in September 1832. The suspension bridge was restored in 1965. This view dates from *c.*1906-10.

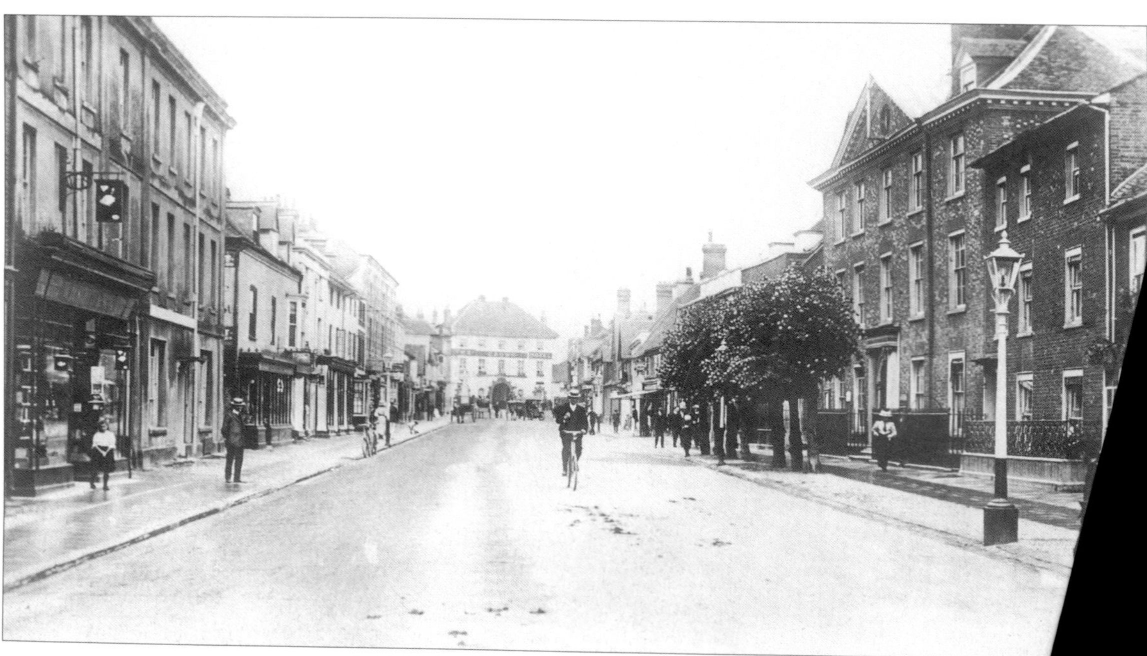

62 In this Edwardian view of High Street, Marlow, dating from *c.*1906-10, the *Crown Hotel* can be seen in
Market Square in the distance. In 1903, Miss M.J. Feltham was manageress of this family and commercial
while Thomas Halse Hull was proprietor in 1907.

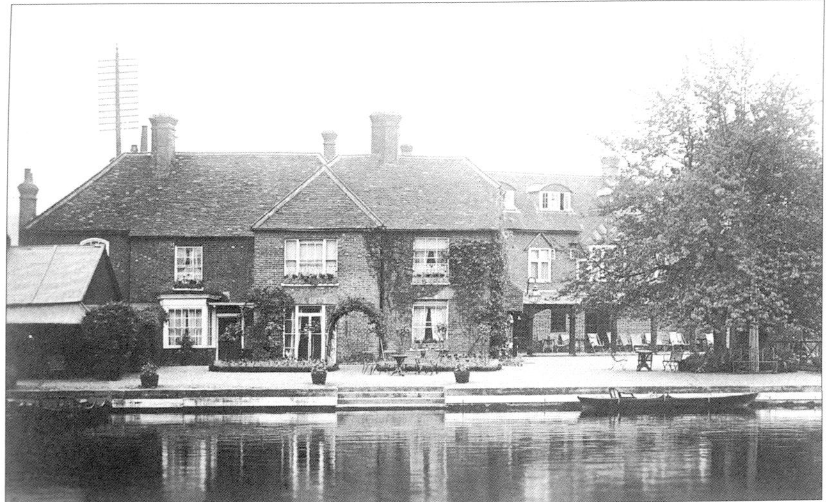

63 The *Compleat Angler Hotel* on the Berkshire bank of the river at Marlow was run by Robert B. Kilby in 1913, when it was advertised as an 'old-established, high-class Family Hotel, standing in its own grounds' and 'beautifully situated on the River Bank, adjoining the Weir'.

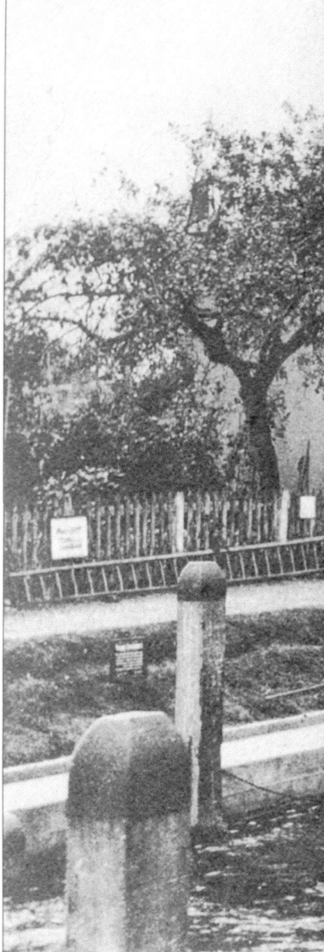

64 The tall spire of Marlow's All Saints' Church, which was added in 1898-9 and restored in 1990-3, is a landmark. This postcard view of the river and church at Marlow, taken from near the lock, was postally used on 6 June 1908.

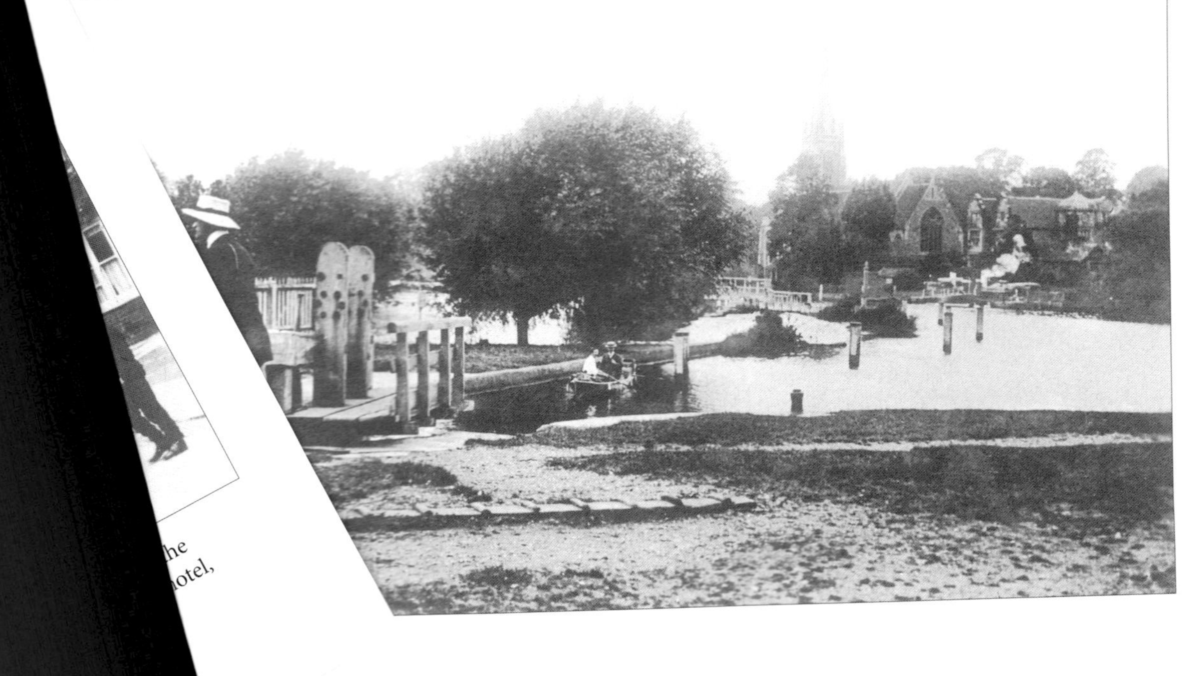

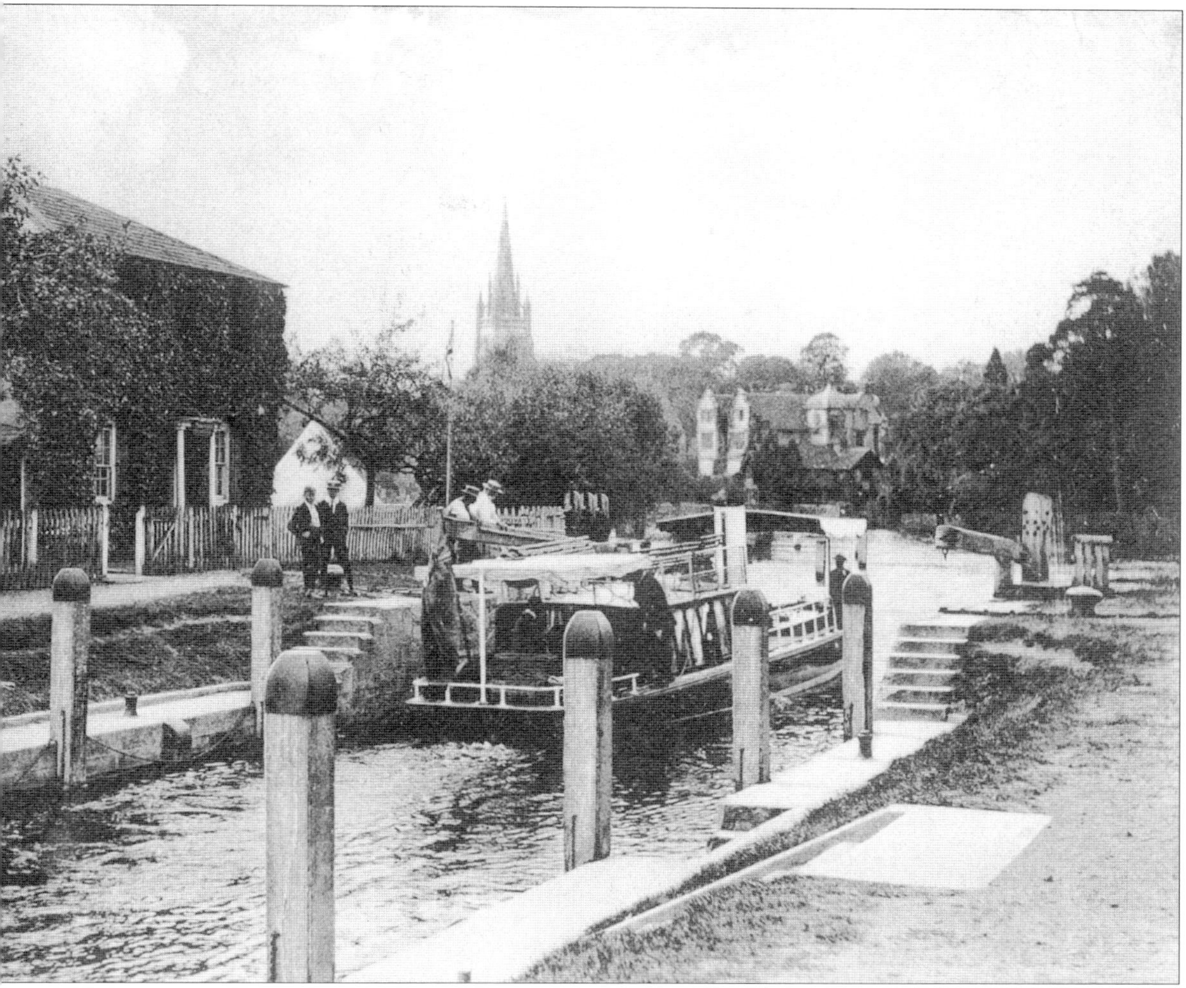

65 A steamer makes its way out of Marlow Lock in this postcard view, which was postally used on 12 September 1908. Fred S. Thacker stated that the first pound lock at Marlow was opened in 1773 on the Buckinghamshire side of the river opposite the lock shown here. A new pound lock was built on the modern site in 1826. In *The Thames from source to tideway*, Peter H. Chaplin noted that Marlow Lock was reconstructed by the Thames Conservancy in 1927.

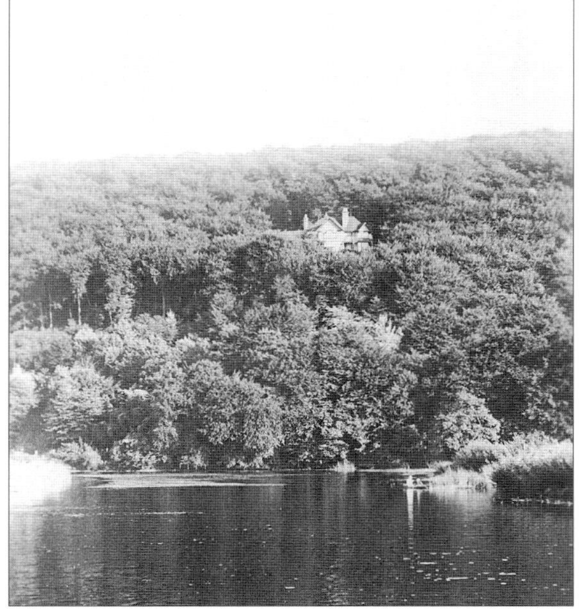

66 Quarry Woods, Marlow, *c.*1910-14. *Salter's Guide to the Thames* of 1913 commented that the Quarry Woods, rising boldly 'in uninterrupted beauty on the Berkshire shore', were now intersected with roads and paths, which were freely accessible to visitors, the woods half concealing a number of houses and bungalows. The guidebook stated that from Winter Hill, where the woods come to an end, there was a splendid view of almost the whole of the Thames Valley between Henley and Maidenhead. Nowadays, tall trees conceal much of this view.

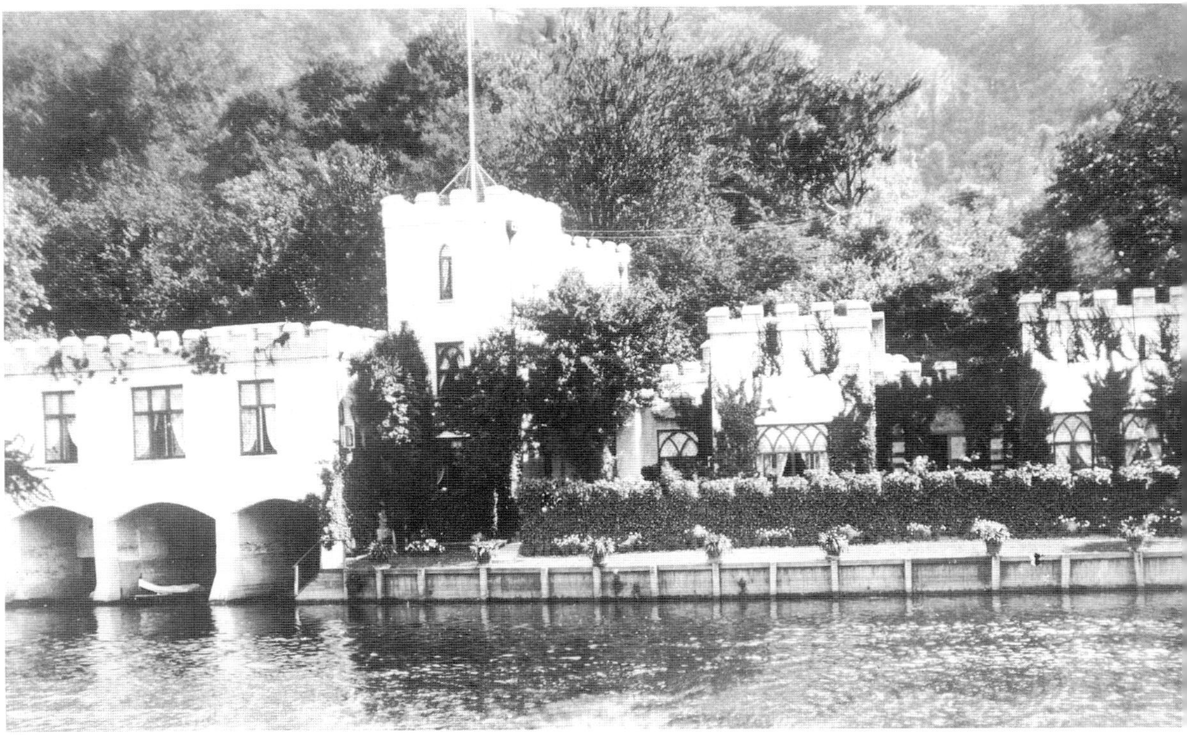

67 In *The Thames from Mouth to Source*, L.T.C. Rolt mentioned seeing 'an extraordinary castellated bungalow' beneath the slopes of Quarry Woods on the Berkshire side of the river. This postcard of the exotic-looking residence, Quarry Wood Hall, was postally used on 1 August 1914. A.J. (Jock) Cairns, in *The Book of Marlow* (1976), remarked that Quarry Wood Hall, 'a rendezvous for the celebrities of yesterday', was designed by Aubrey Beardsley and built in 1901.

68 An engraving of Cookham from *Tombleson's Thames*, dating from *c*.1834. Cookham's Holy Trinity Church dates mainly from the 13th century, while the tower was erected in the 16th century.

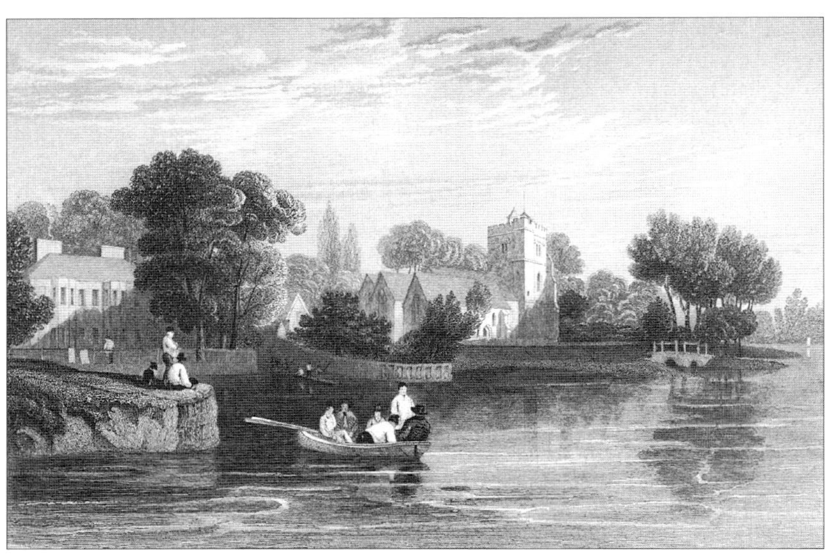

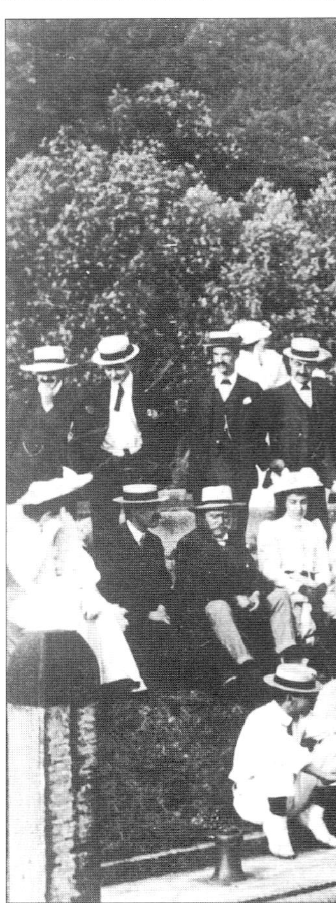

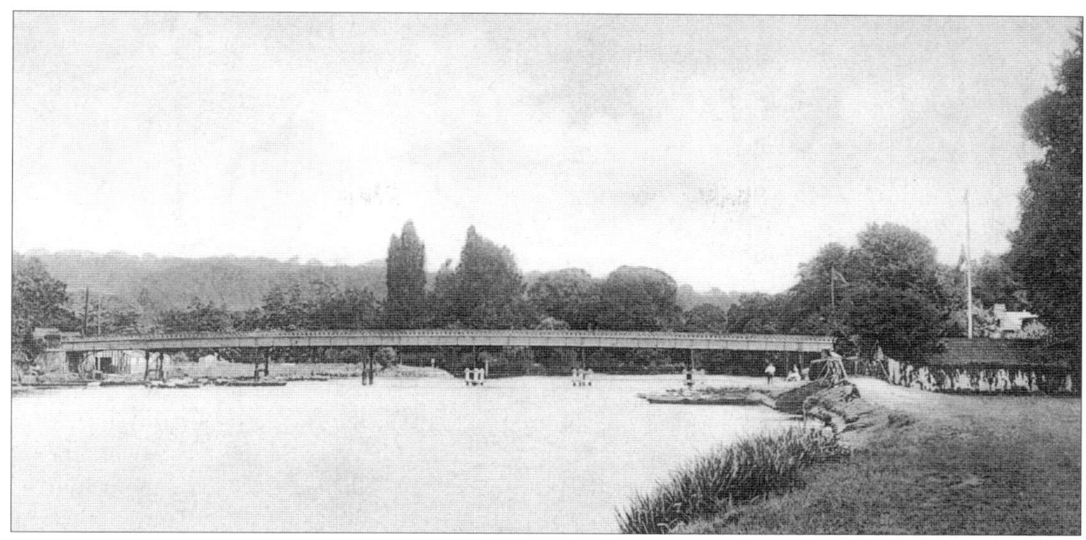

69 By 1840, a wooden bridge had replaced the ferry at Cookham and this, in turn, was superseded by a wrought iron bridge, which was opened in 1867. This early postcard view of Cookham Bridge, with its undivided back, probably dates from the first decade of the 20th century.

70 Smartly clad spectators line the lock side in this Edwardian postcard view of Cookham Lock, which was postally used on 13 August 1909.

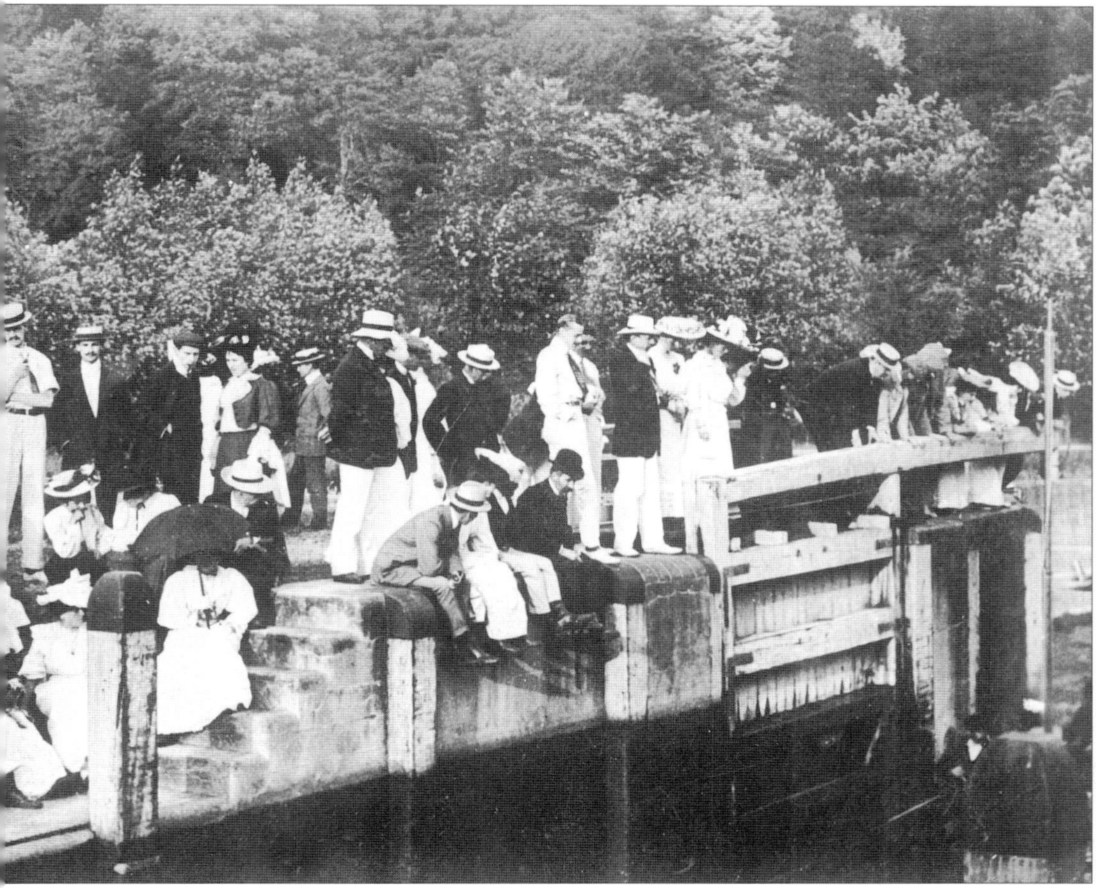

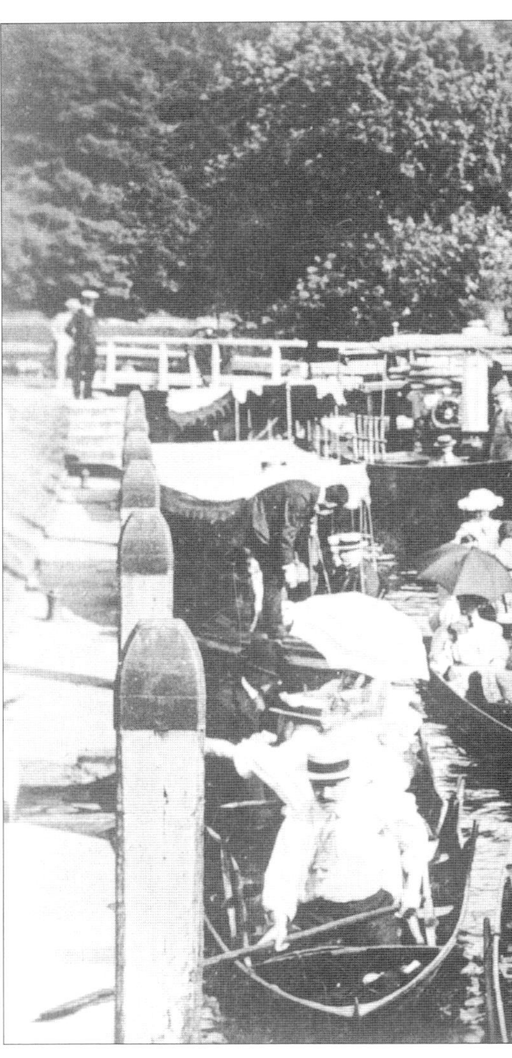

71 Rowing boats, punts and steamers were crowded into Cookham Lock when this postcard view was taken.

72 Boat rollers at Cookham Lock on an early postcard with an undivided back, which was postally used on 4 July 1904. The pencilled message at the side of the view reads, 'The trees in the background are part of Cliveden Woods. It has been like that for the last two miles.'

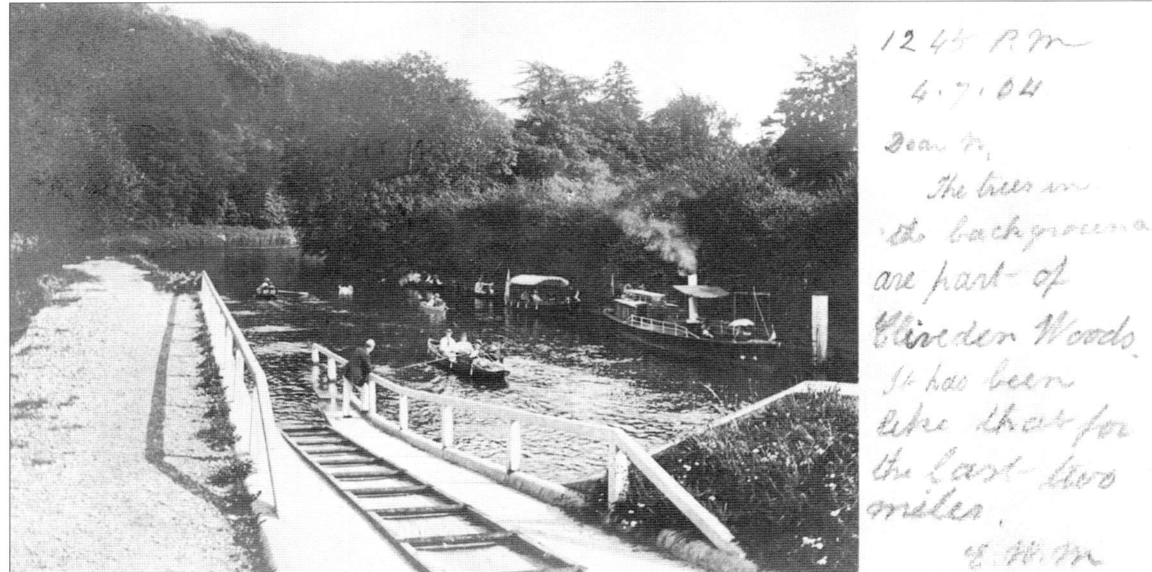

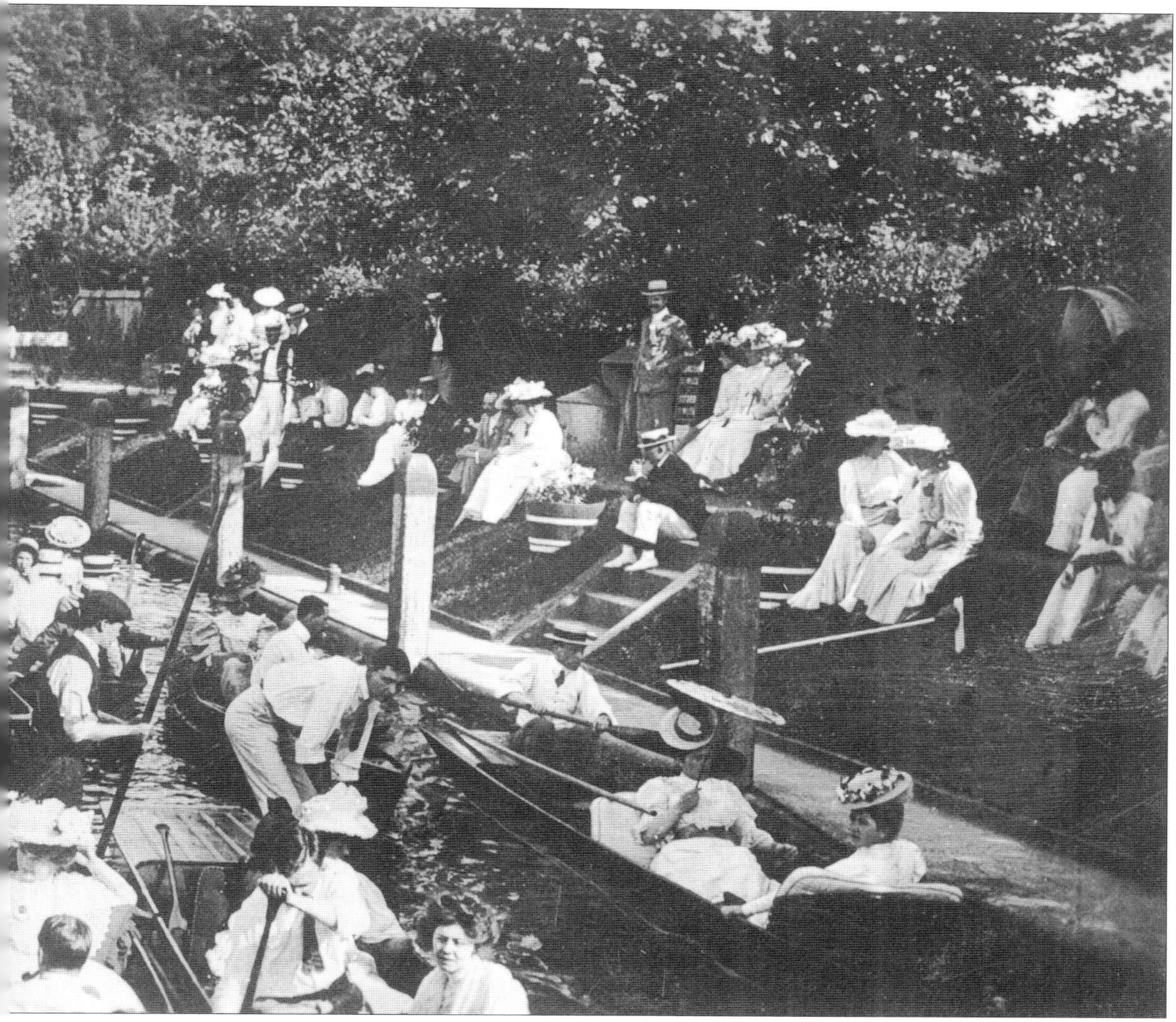

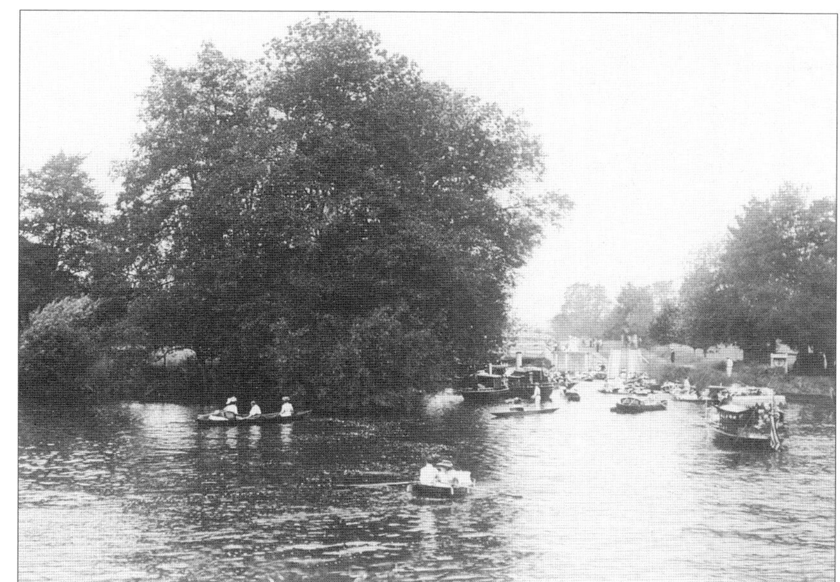

73 An Edwardian view looking upstream towards Cookham Lock, which was postally used on 15 August 1909. The boat rollers can be seen on the right of the lock. According to Peter H. Chaplin, in *Thames from source to tideway*, this boat slide was constructed in 1892 when Cookham Lock was lengthened.

Hedsor to Boveney Lock

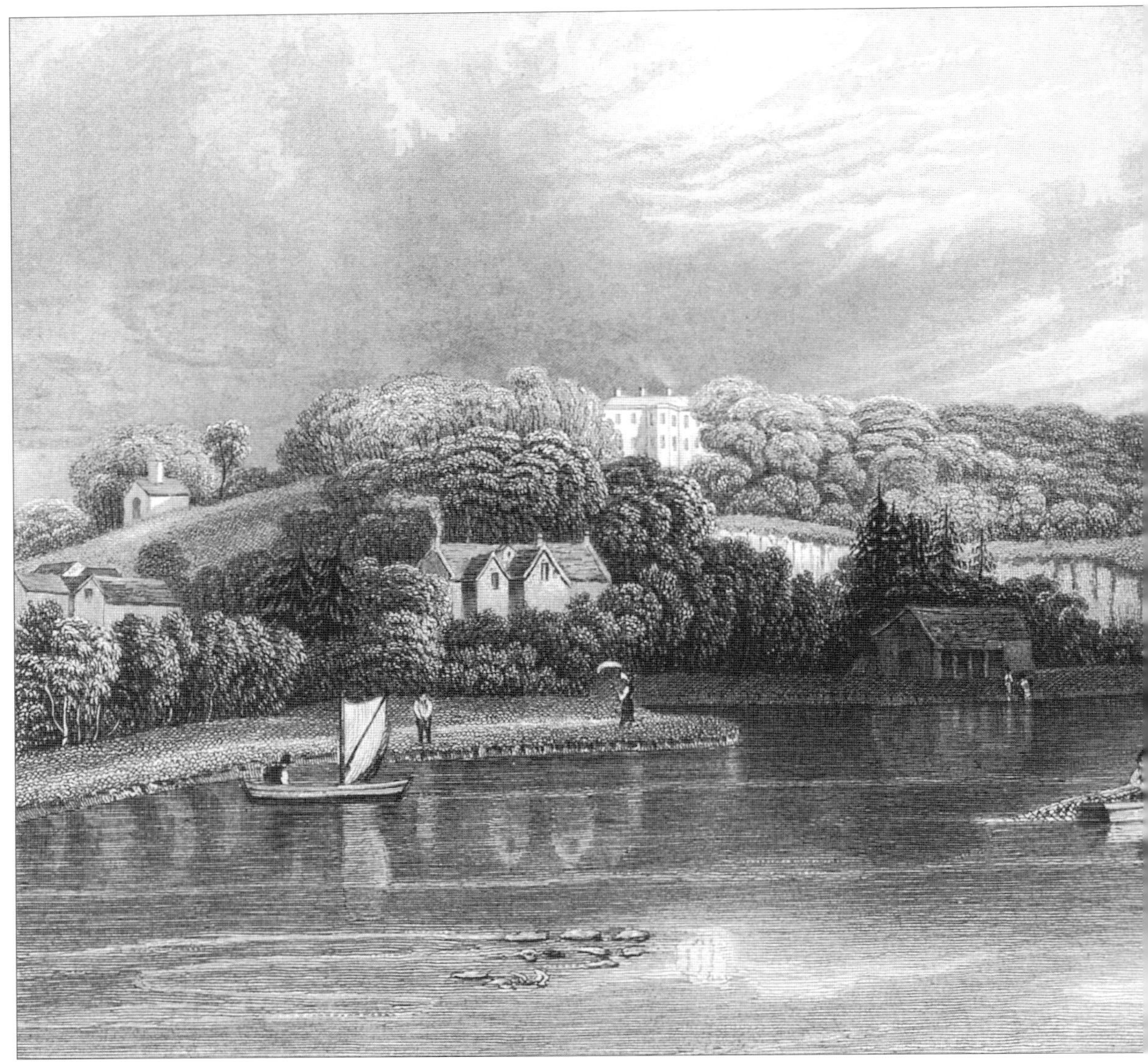

74 This engraving of Hedsor is from *Tombleson's Thames*. W.G. Fearnside described the location:

> The scenery now becomes extremely beautiful; the Hedsor heights rising from their chalky beds, with the hanging woods above, connected with the bolder and more richly variegated foliage of Cliefden. Hedsor church occupies a highly picturesque situation, embosomed in trees and placed on a hillock near the summit of the heights. Hedsor Lodge, the seat of Lord Boston, stands on a commanding eminence, overlooking some of the most picturesque parts of Berks and Bucks.

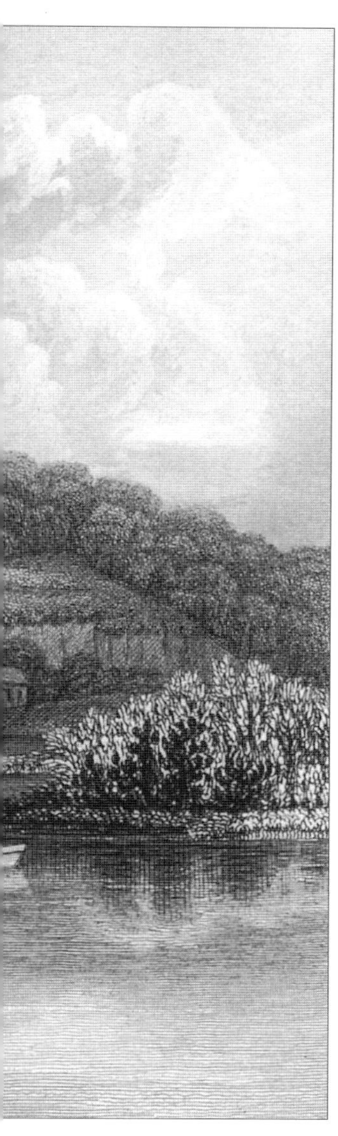

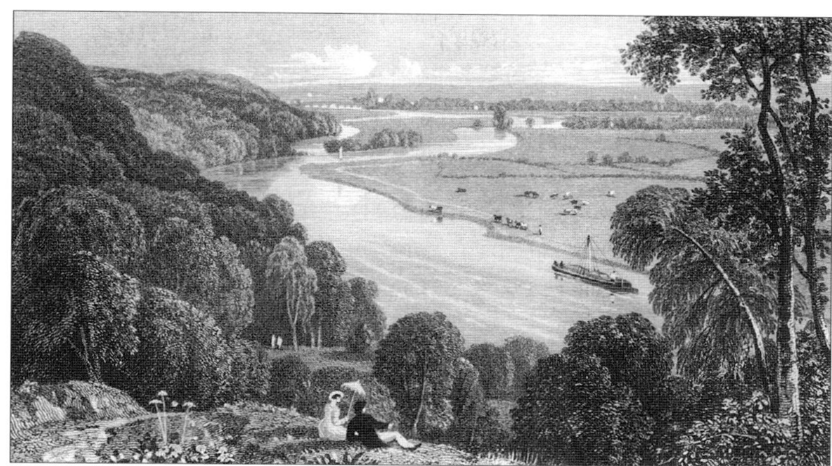

75 Published on 1 October 1814, this view, looking downstream from 'Cliefden', was drawn by W. Havell and engraved by W.B. Cooke. It was included in *Views on the Thames* by W.B. Cooke and George Cooke.

76 There were three ferries in the vicinity of Cookham. Fred S. Thacker noted that the Upper Ferry crossed from the Berkshire end of Cookham Bridge to the head of the lock cut, while the Hedsor or Lower Ferry crossed the tail of the weir stream. Lady or My Lady Ferry, the lowest of the three, crossed at the end of the towpath against the millstream. This early 20th-century view is of My Lady Ferry.

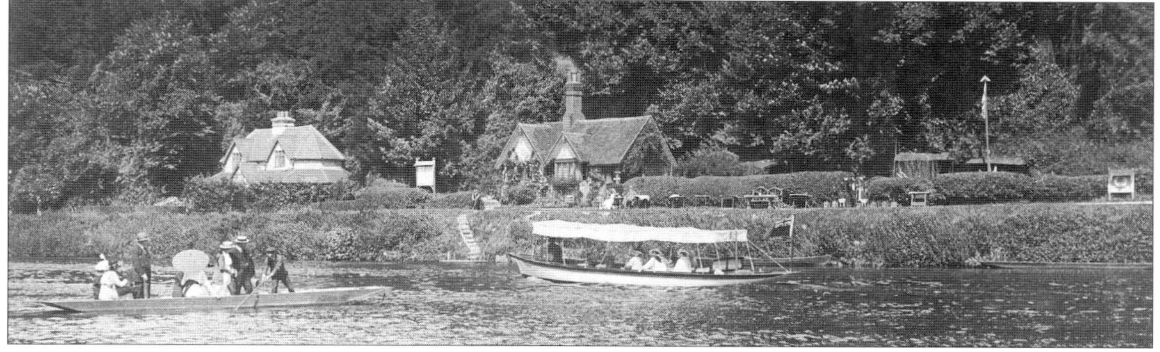

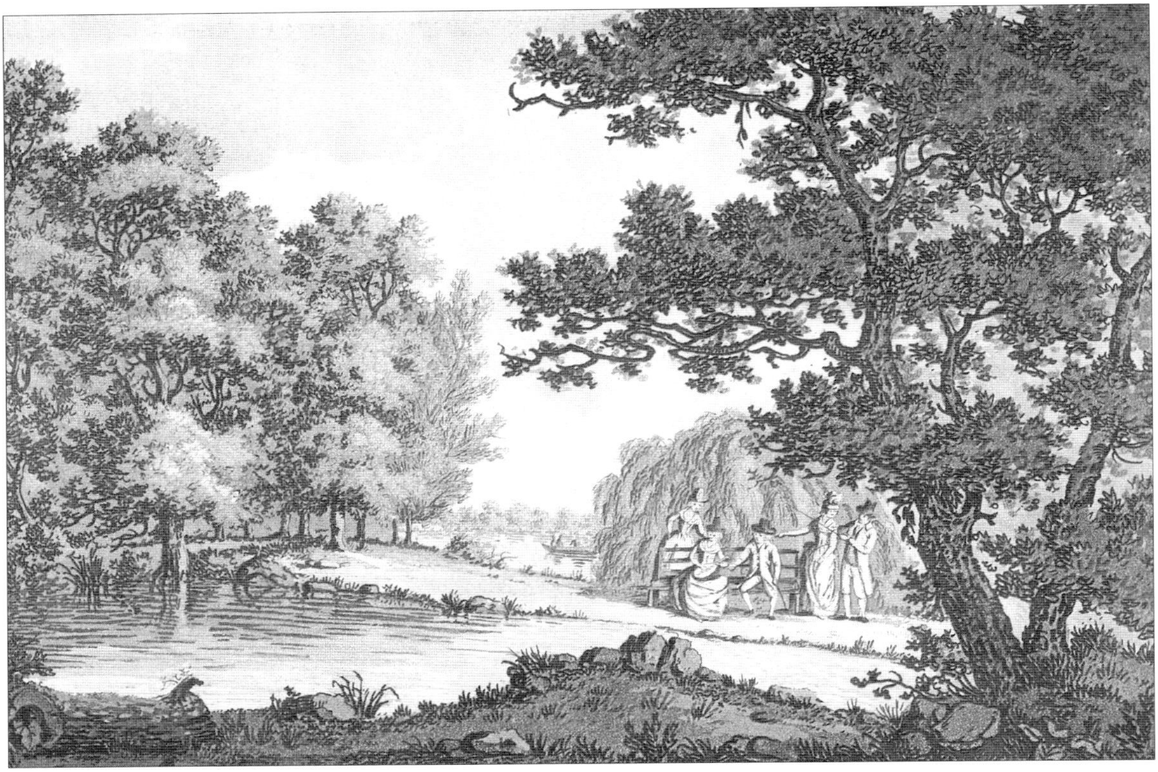

77 An aquatint entitled 'Cliefden Spring' from Samuel Ireland's *Picturesque Views on the River Thames*. Having mentioned Sir George Young's house, the author noted:

> A little below this house, at the foot of Cliefden Wood, rises Cliefden Spring, which by an easy descent forms a small, yet beautiful cascade, that gently murmuring over its gravelly bed, empties itself into the river Thames. To this charming retreat, (by permission of the Earl of Inchinquin, to whom it belongs) social parties frequently repair to take their repast beneath its cooling shade.

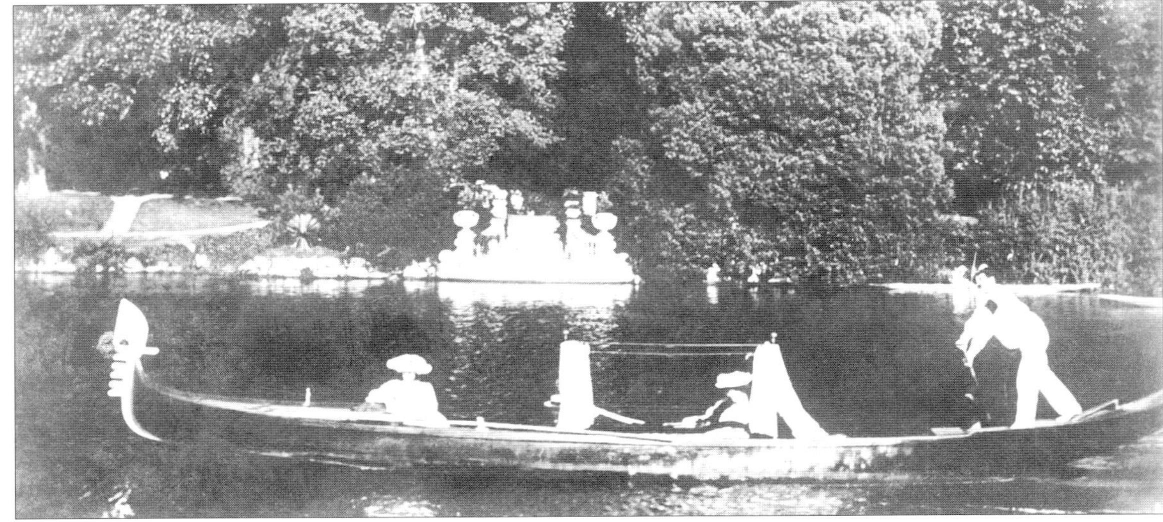

78 The gondola shown passing Cliveden Steps is likely to have been the one belonging to Mr C. Hammersley, who lived at Abney House, Bourne End, not far upriver from where this postcard view was taken. The postcard was postally used on 28 August 1907.

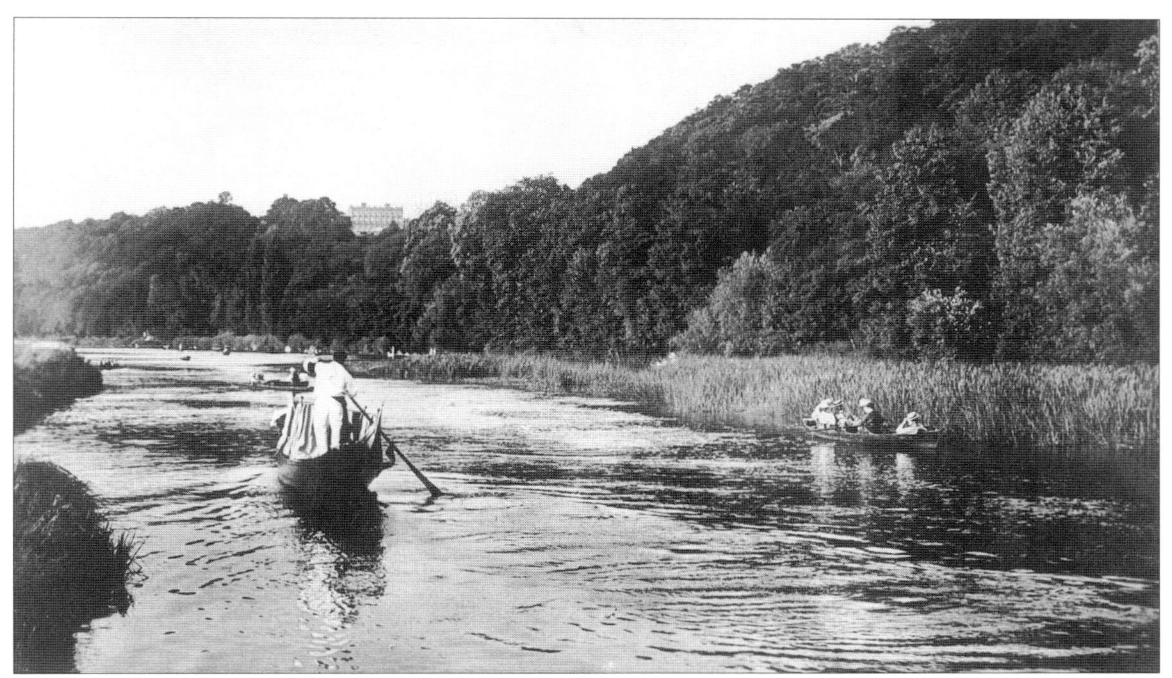

79 This postcard view of 'Cliveden House and Wood', which also features the gondola mentioned previously, was postally used on 11 September 1907.

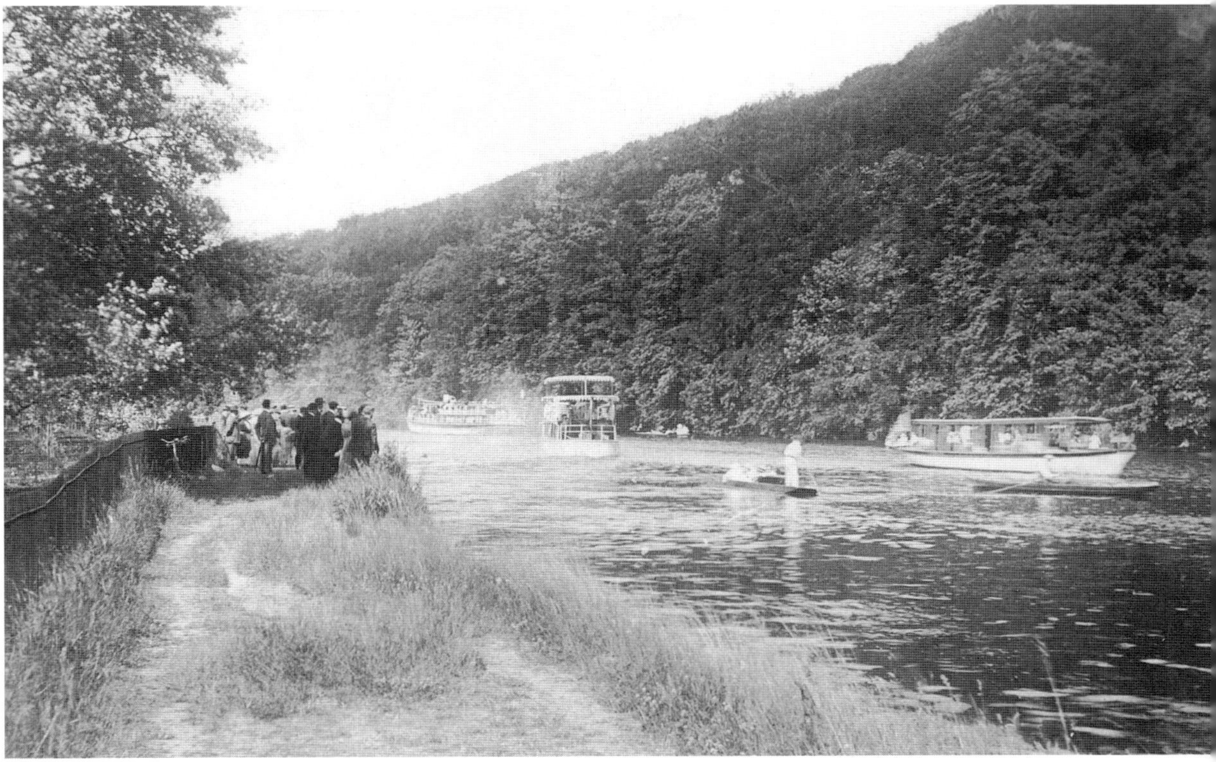

80 The message on the back of this postcard of Cliveden Reach noted that the view showed 'The grounds of our hospital from the river'. This was the Canadian Red Cross Hospital, which was built on the Cliveden estate and used during the First World War.

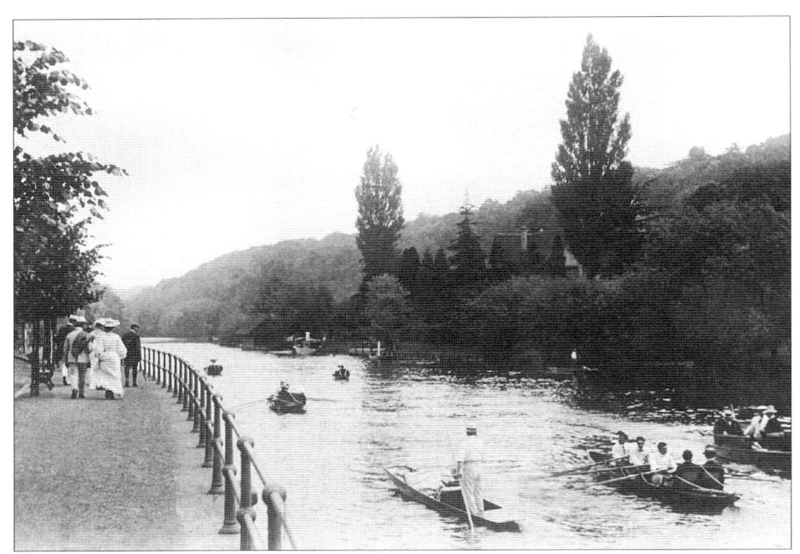

81 The pedestrians taking a stroll along Maidenhead Embankment were passed by a variety of pleasure craft when this view was taken in Edwardian times. Postally used on 24 December 1910, this postcard was sent as a Christmas card.

82 This Edwardian postcard shows a busy day at the Upper Lock Cut, Boulter's Lock, with scores of people lining the riverbank and numerous punters waiting for the lock.

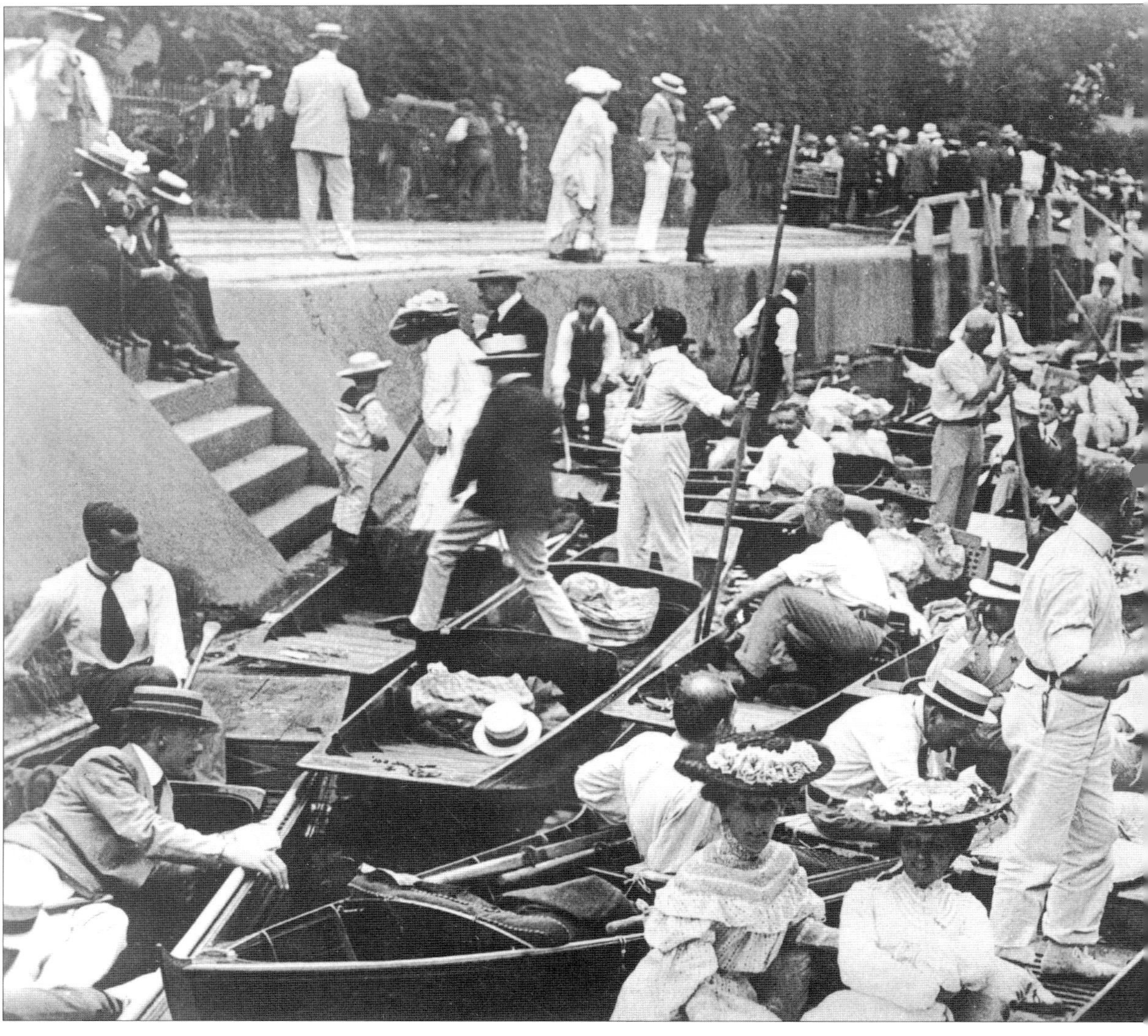

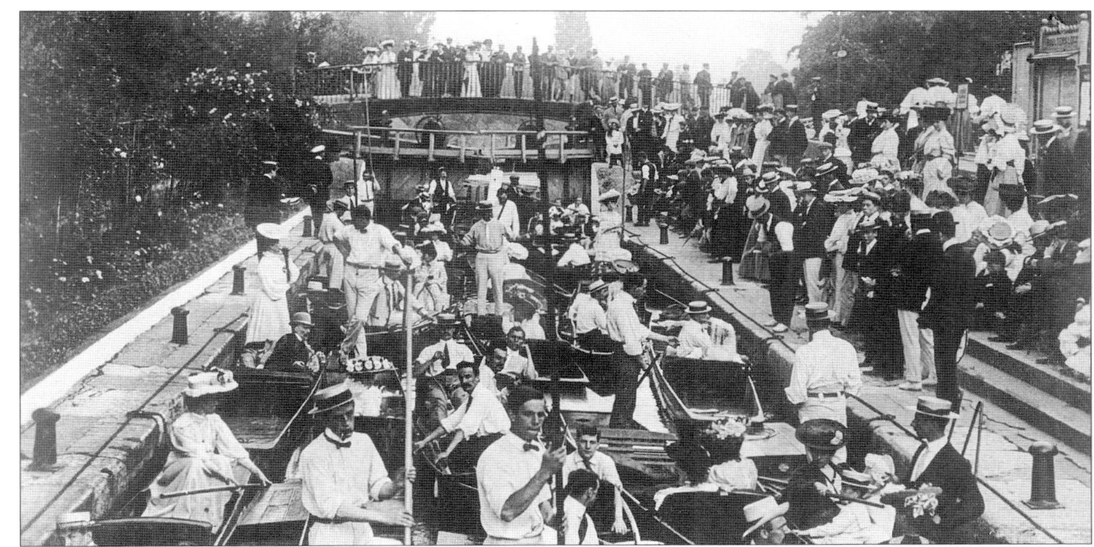

83 There was hardly any room to manoeuvre in the packed Boulter's Lock, when this view was taken in the early years of the 20th century. The postcard was postally used on 2 November 1907.

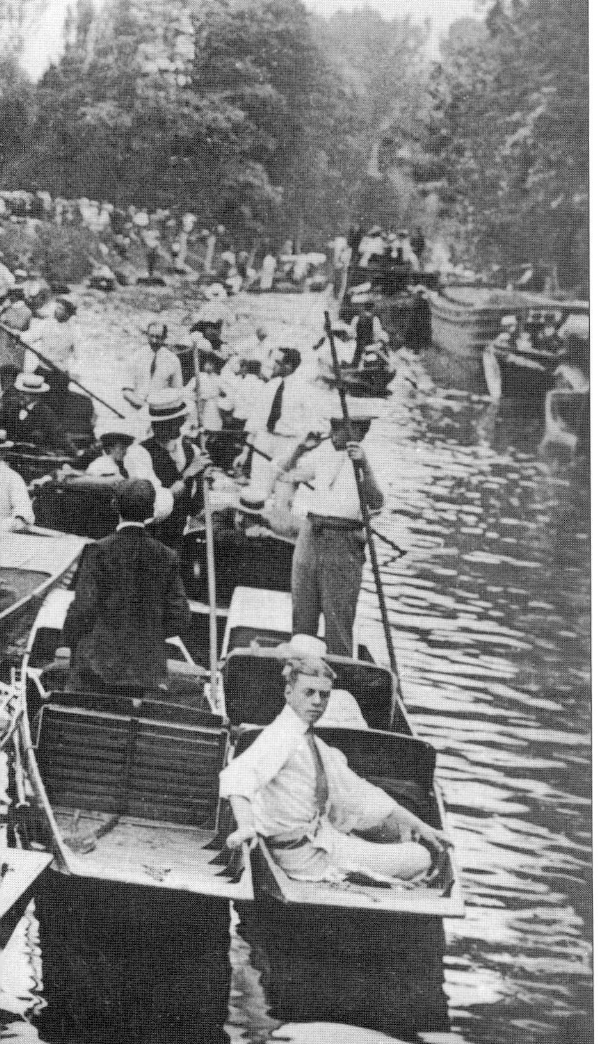

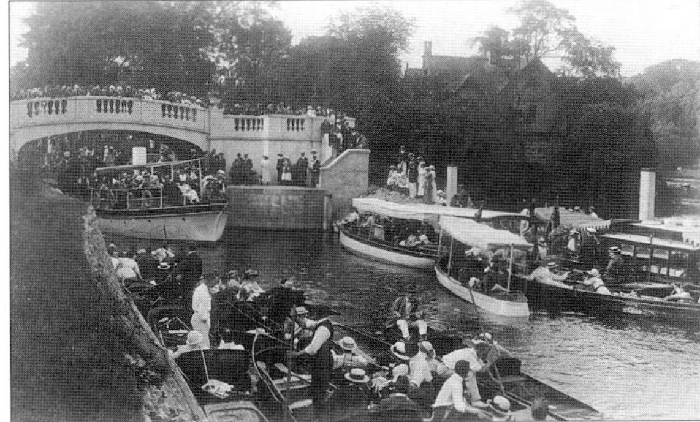

84 A busy scene outside Boulter's lock with one steamer just emerging from the lock, while other craft wait to go in. This view was postally used on 22 May 1913. In the same year, *Salter's Guide to the Thames* mentioned that many trains and scores of motors brought London visitors to Maidenhead. Before getting to Cliveden reach they all had to pass through the lock, which often had to deal with as many as a thousand boats and launches in a day.

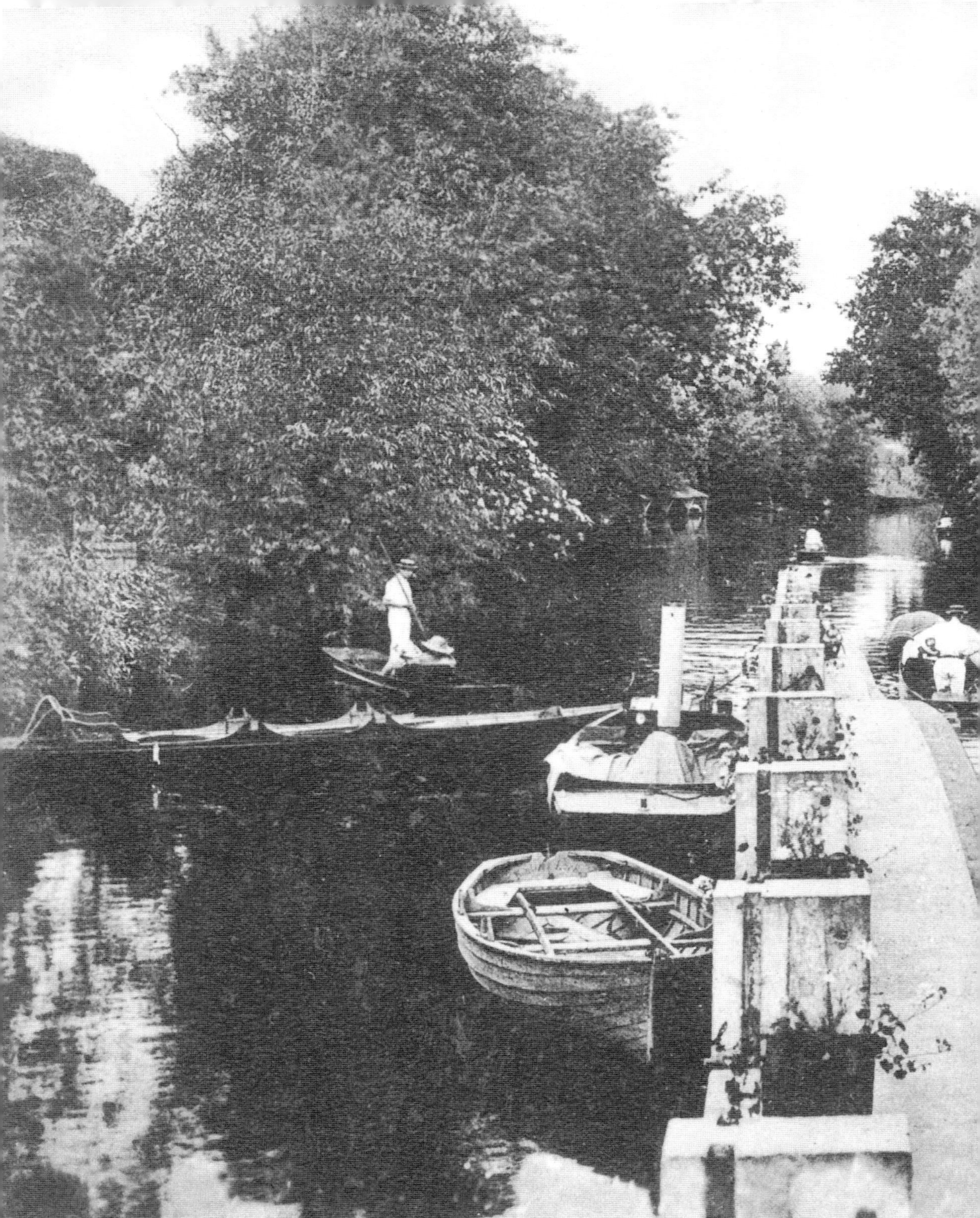

85 New Boat Transit, Boulter's Lock. *Salter's Guide to the Thames* of 1913 noted that a new large double lock was opened in June 1912, along with 'an efficient transporter for rowing boats, thus affording accommodation that has been lacking all too long.'

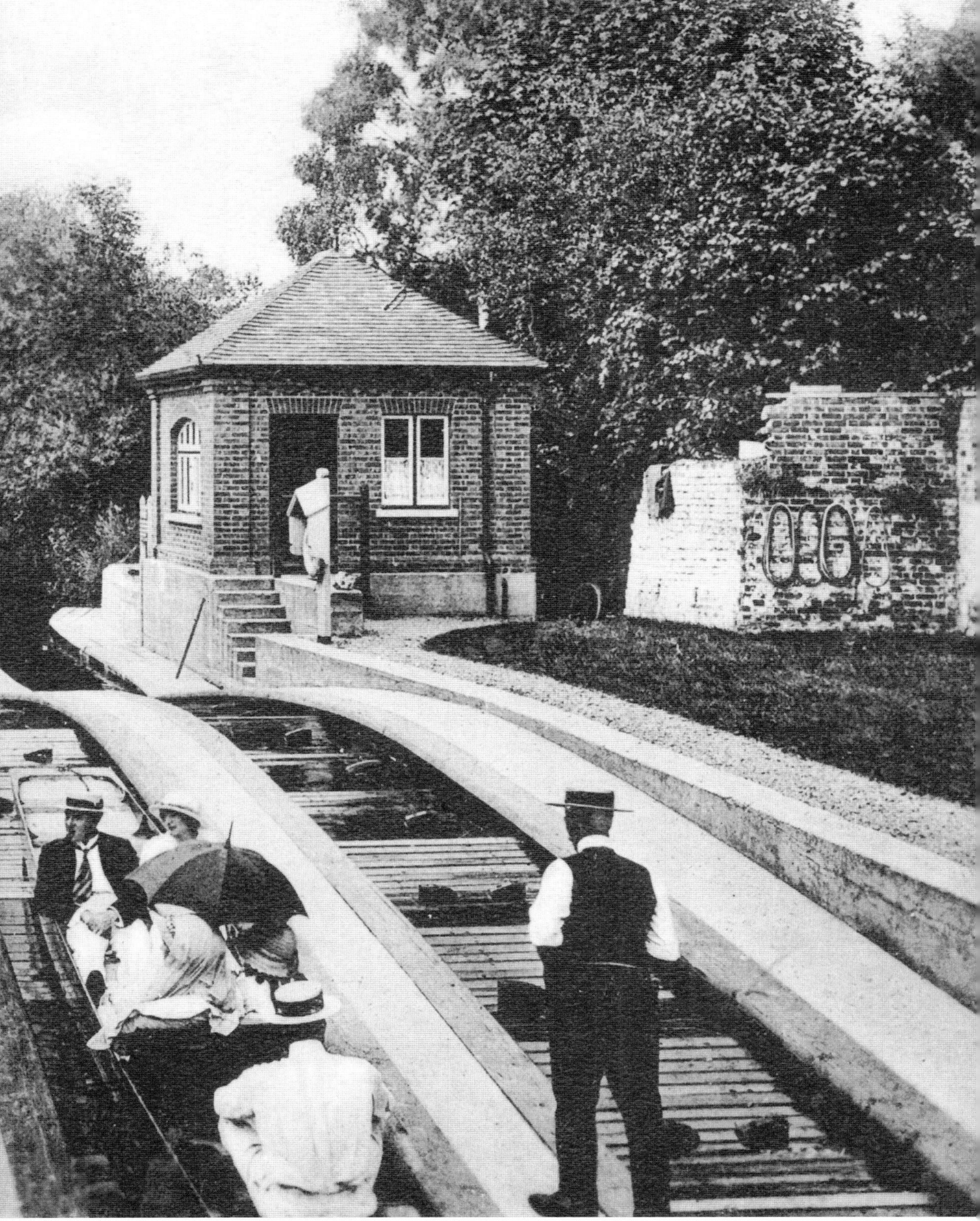

86 Taplow is on the east bank of the Thames. The brick-built *Oak and Saw* public house, with its bay windows, can be seen in this Edwardian postcard view of the village, which was postally used on 31 December 1908.

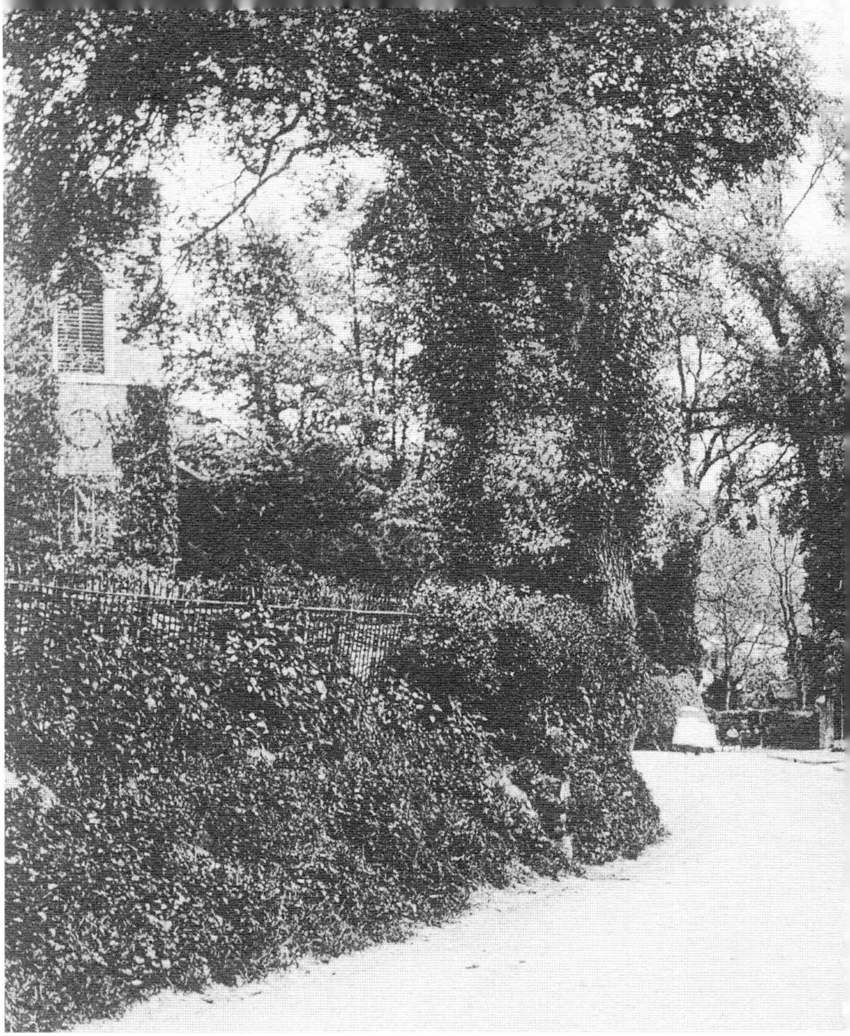

87 The once-renowned hotel called *Skindles*, situated on the upstream side of Maidenhead Bridge, was built on the site of an inn formerly known as the *Orkney Arms*. The hotel was named after a 19th-century proprietor whose surname was Skindle.

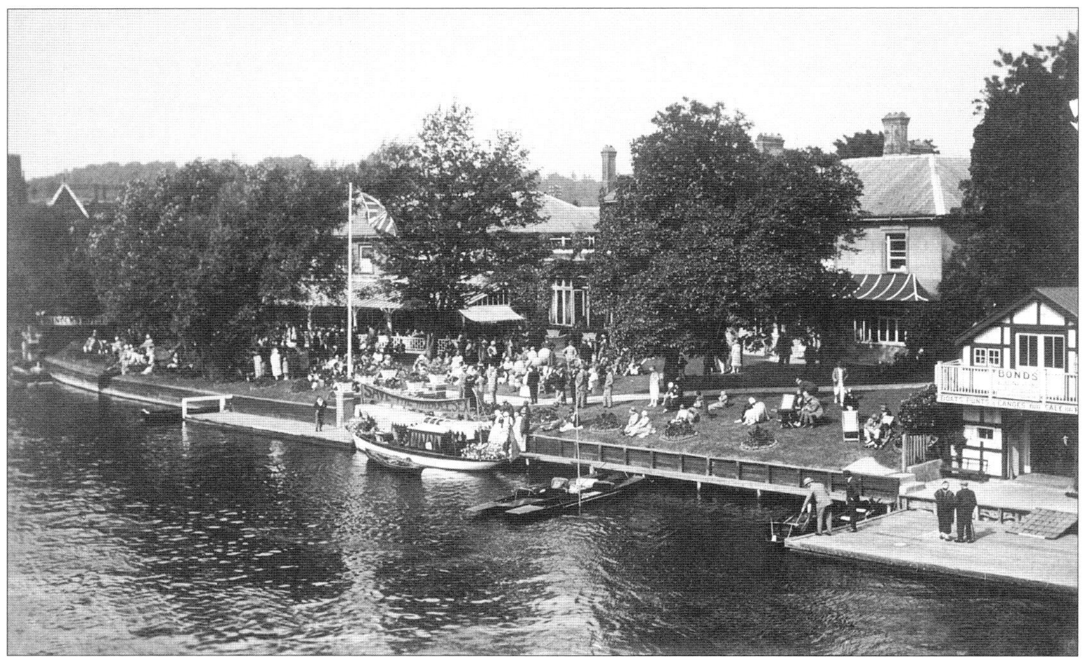

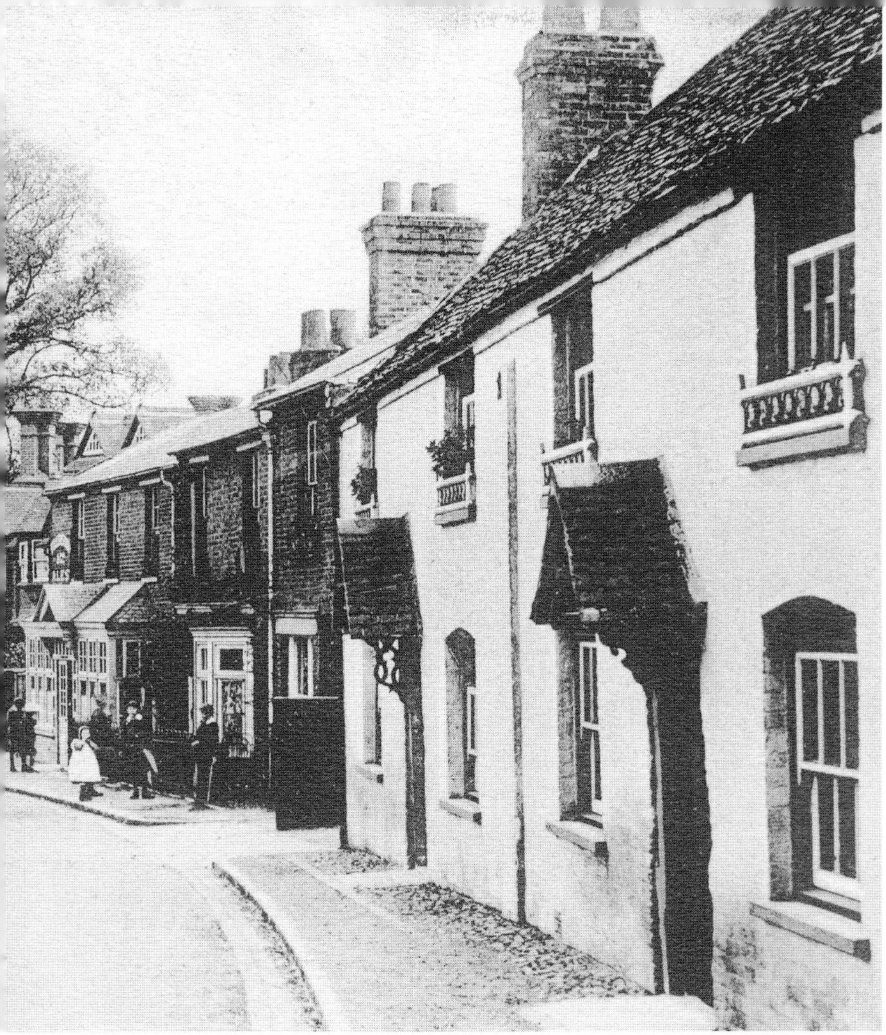

88 A view of the upstream side of Maidenhead Bridge showing a board advertising Bond's, which had launches, boats and punts for sale or hire.

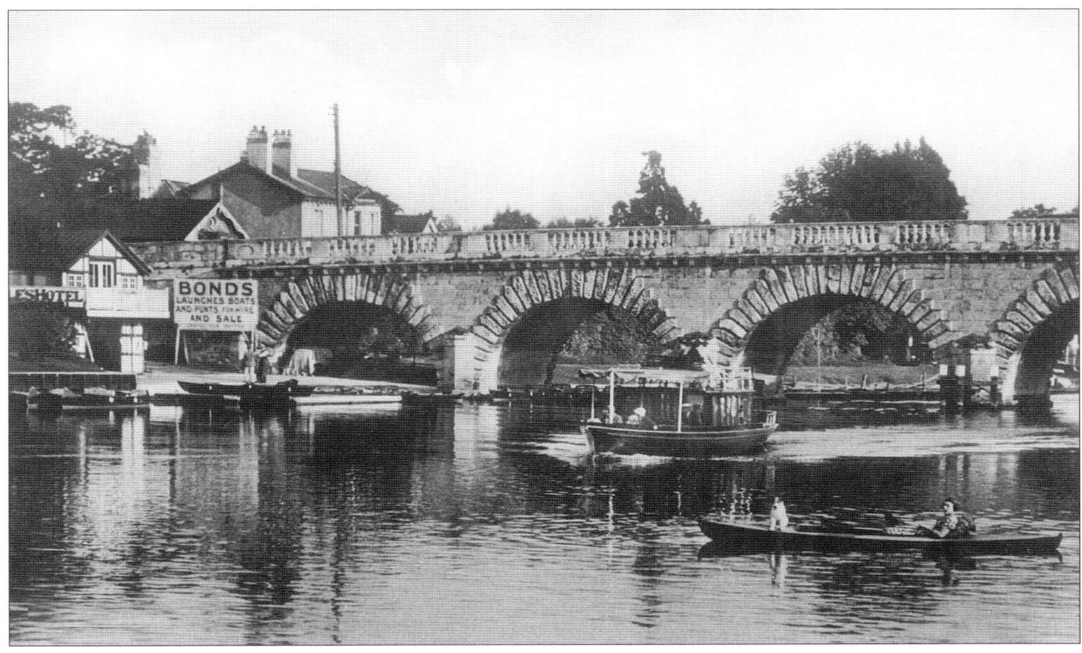

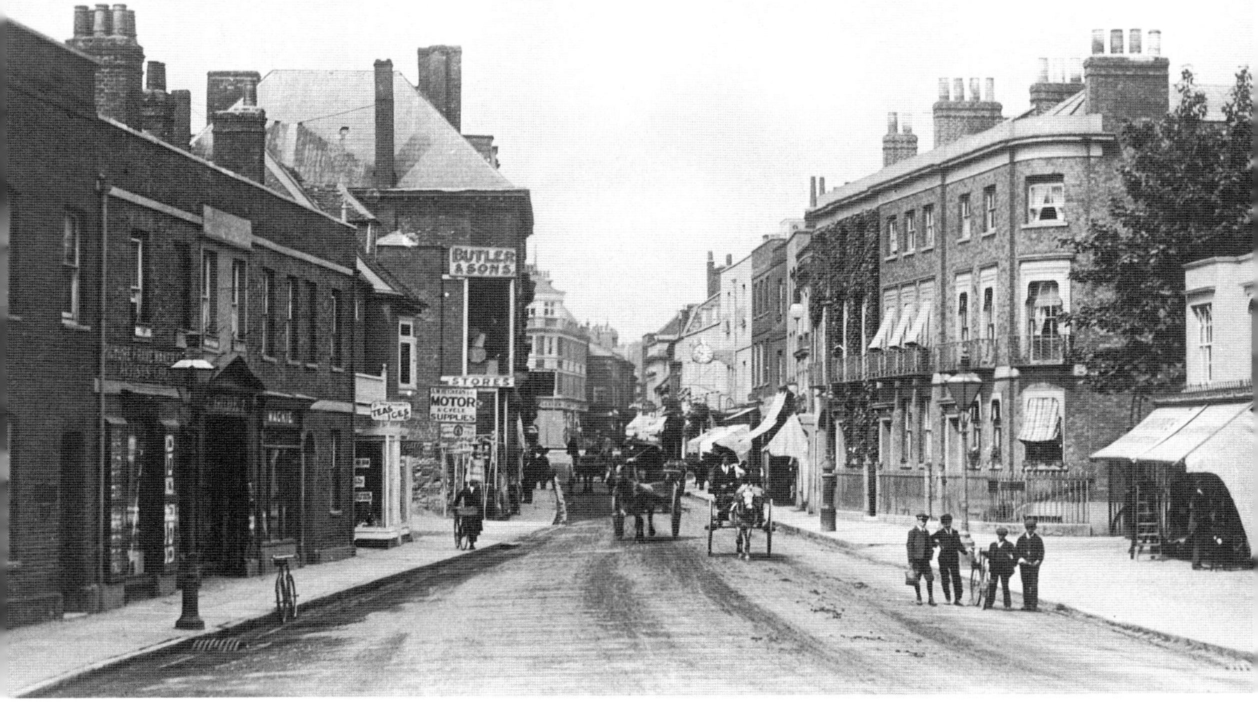

89 This postcard view of Maidenhead's High Street was postally used on 15 April 1909. On the right is the *Bear Hotel*, a long-established hostelry, which moved to this site in the 19th century. A figure of a bear stands over the entrance.

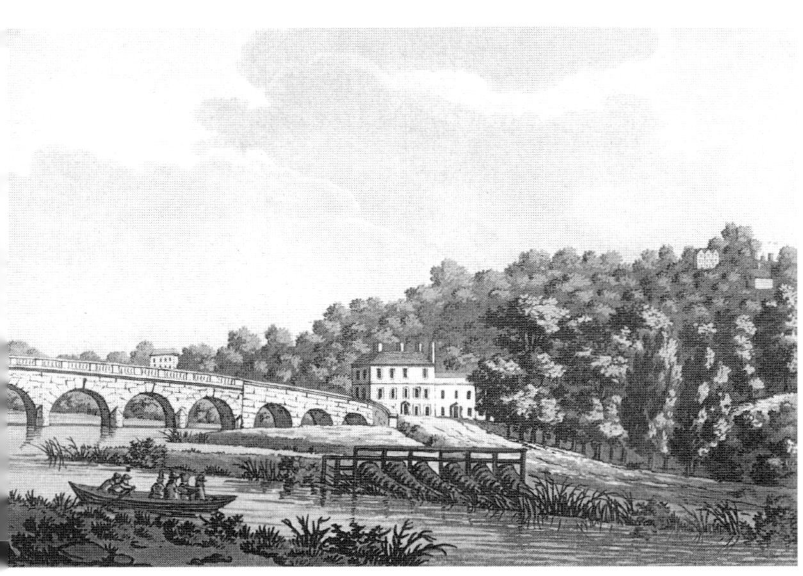

90 Samuel Ireland used this aquatint of Maidenhead Bridge in his *Picturesque Views on the River Thames*.

The handsome bridge at Maidenhead was constructed from a design of the late Sir Robert Taylor, and is a work of much merit. It is of stone, and consists of seven large semi-circular arches, with three smaller ones of brick at each end. It has been finished about nine years, at an expence of nineteen thousand pounds, independent of the purchase of lands contiguous, to render the work compleat.

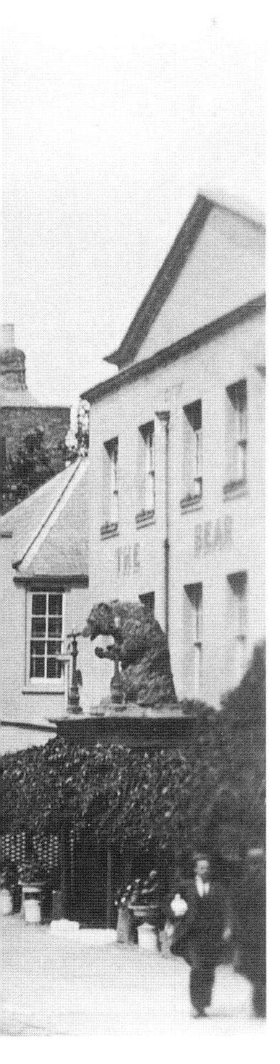

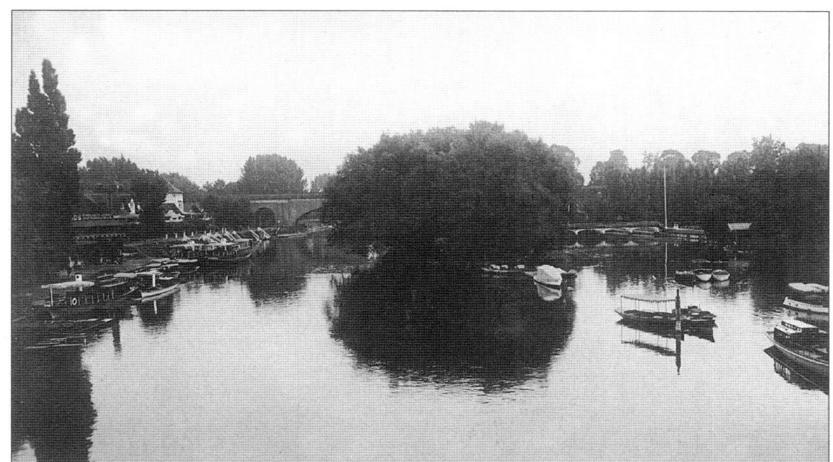

91 Looking downstream from the bridge, Maidenhead, *c.*1910-14. On the left can be seen the river launches operated from Maidenhead Bridge by boat builder J. Bond. In 1913, J. Bond had eight steam launches for hire, including the 101ft-long *His Majesty*, which was licensed to carry 306 passengers. The premises also operated at least 10 electric launches.

92 The Great Western Railway Bridge at Maidenhead, with its two semi-elliptical arches over the Thames, was designed by Isambard Kingdom Brunel. Completed in 1838, these were the widest and flattest arches in the world, each spanning 128ft with a rise of just over 24ft. The bridge featured in the famous painting by J.M.W. Turner entitled 'Rain, Steam and Speed — The Great Western Railway', which was exhibited at the Royal Academy in 1844. It is also renowned for the echo in its arch across the towpath, known as the Sounding Arch. Widened between 1890 and 1893, the railway bridge carries four lines of track.

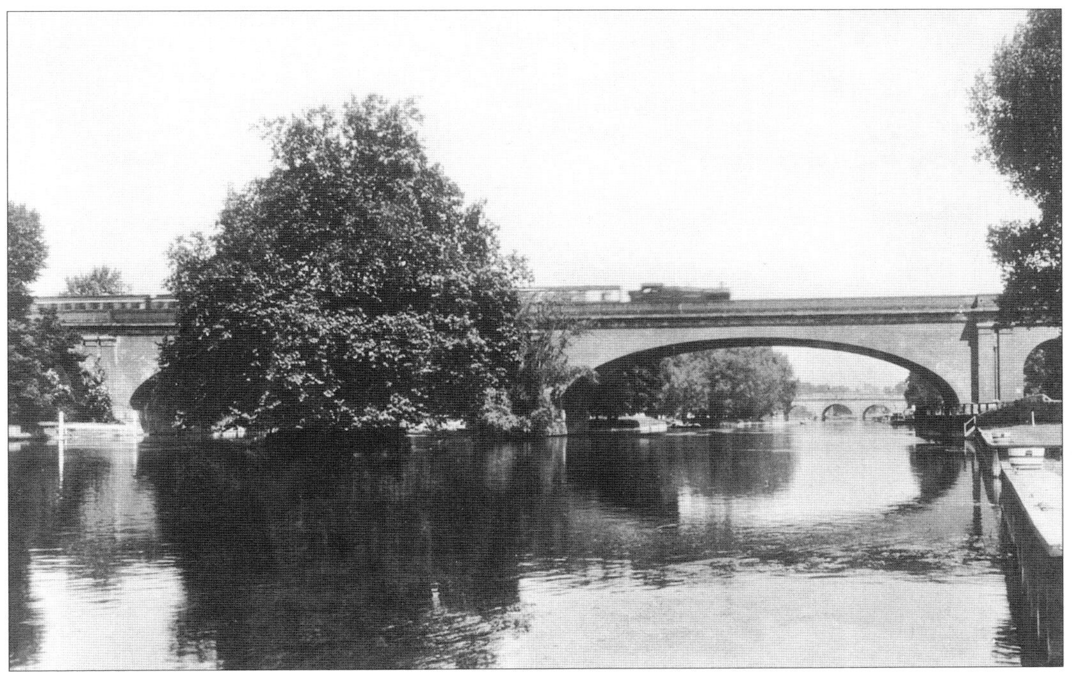

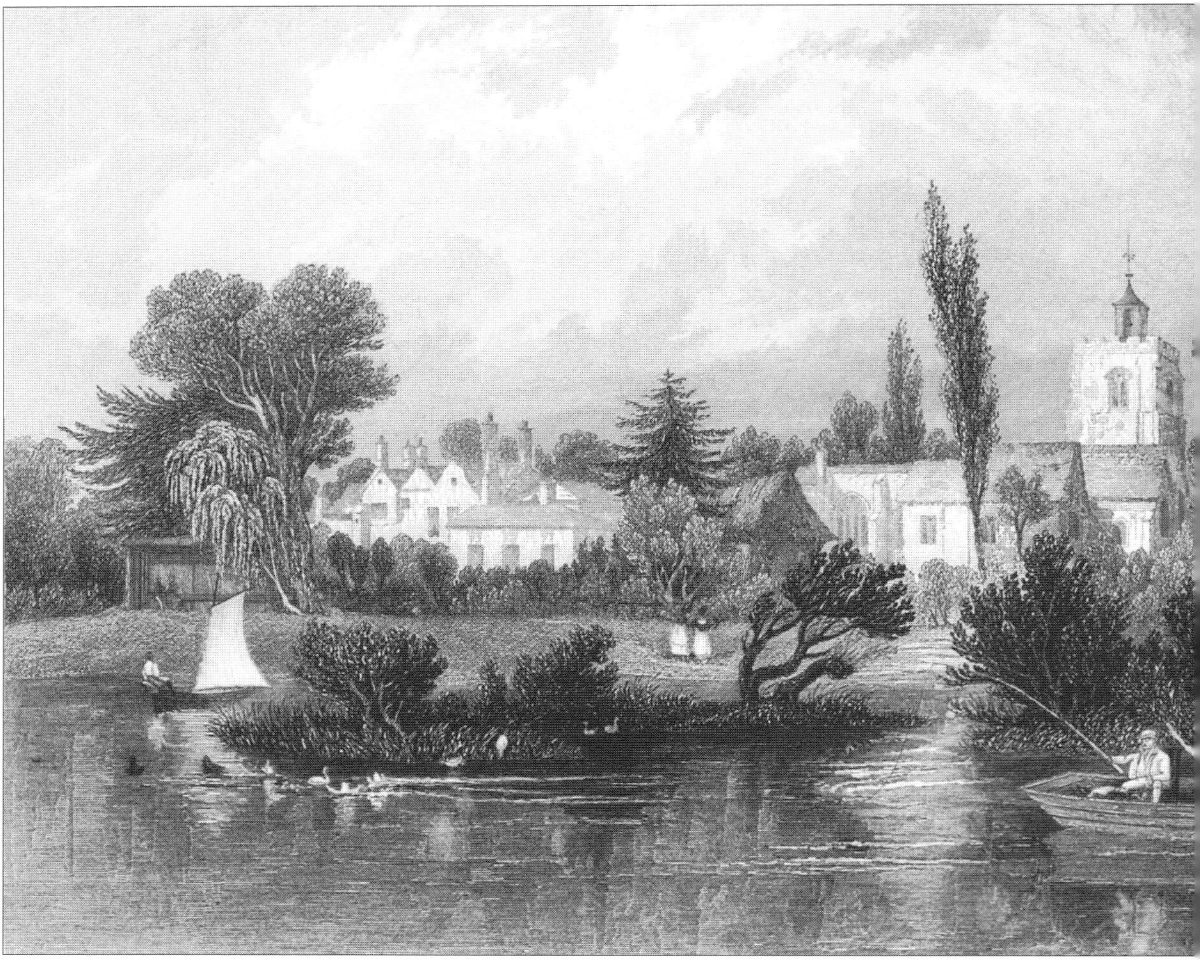

93 An engraving of Bray from *Tombleson's Thames, c.*1834. W.G. Fearnside commented:

> Bray has, however, been rendered memorable by the accommodating conscience of one of its early vicars ... who possessed the benefice in the reigns of Henry VIII, Edward VI, and queens Mary and Elizabeth; having become twice a papist and twice a protestant; and when reproached for his want of moral principle, which allowed him to alter his creed in accordance with the different political changes of the times, replied, that he governed himself by what he thought a very laudable maxim, never, on any terms, to part with his vicarage.

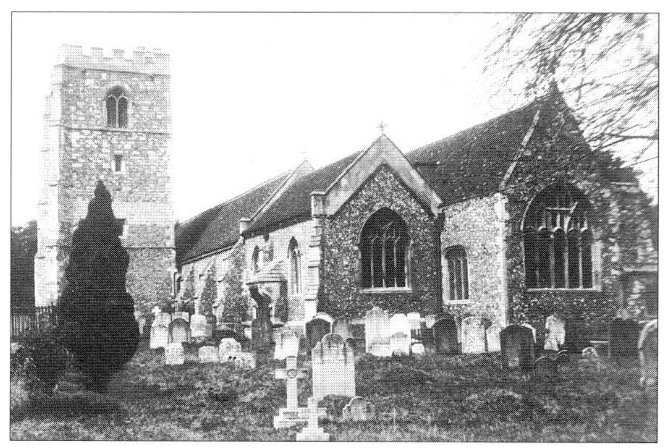

94 St Michael's Church at Bray dates from the 13th century, while its large battlemented tower was erected in the 14th century. Inside the church is a monument to the founder of Bray's Jesus Hospital, William Goddard, and his wife.

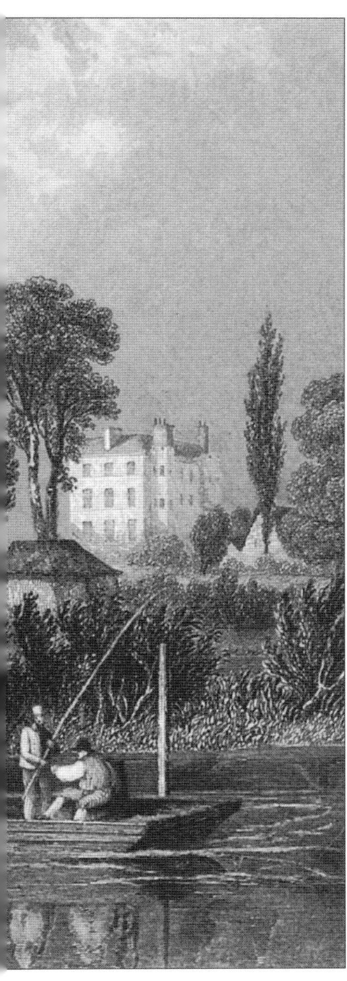

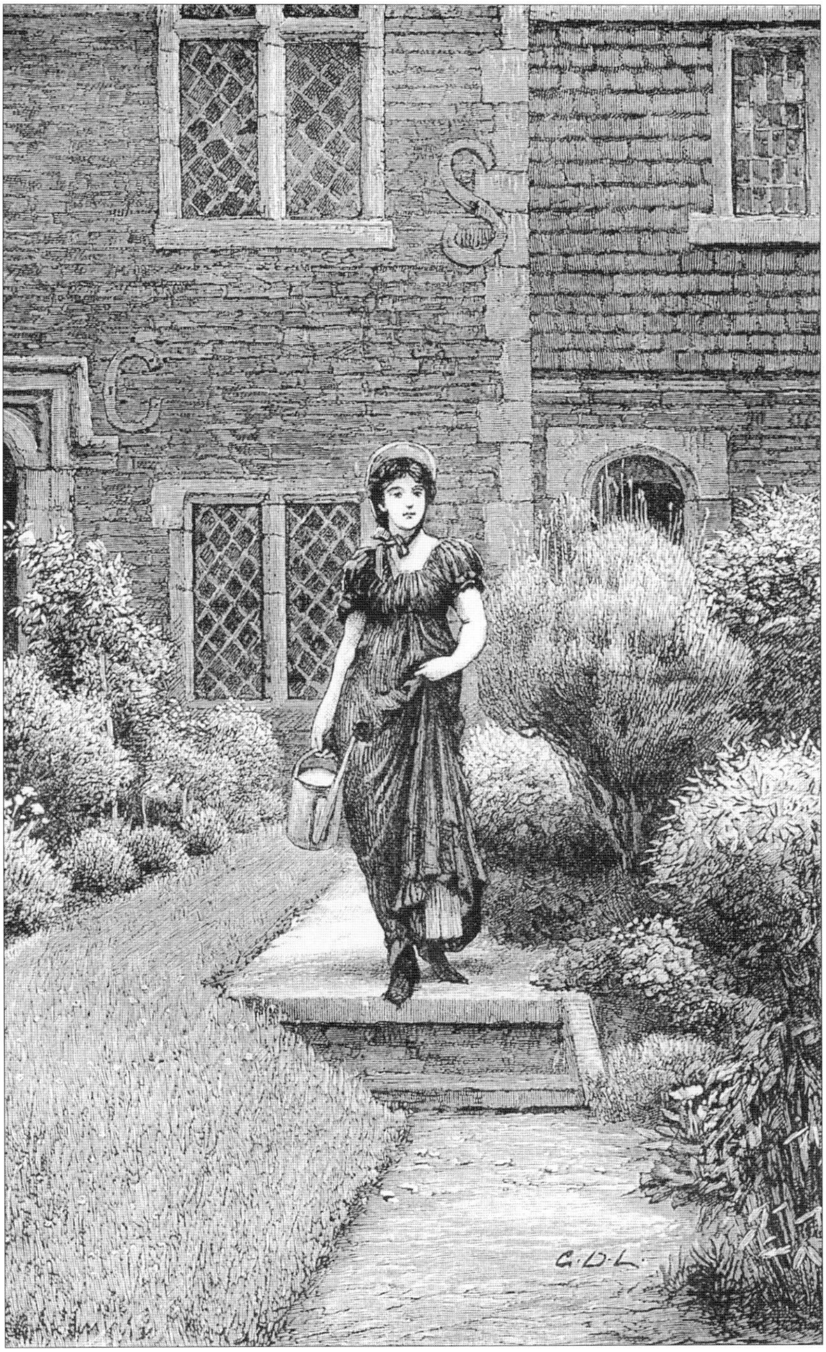

95 George D. Leslie included this illustration of the Chaplain's Garden, Jesus Hospital, Bray, in *Our River* and remarked:

> The most interesting thing at Bray, however, is Jesus Hospital, which was endowed by William Goddard, a free brother of the Fishmongers' Company, A.D. 1628. The front is a long building of red brick, with a narrow slip of trim garden separated from the road by a low wall ... Passing inside you find yourself in a fine quadrangle, with a broad path up the middle leading to the ivy-grown chapel, with its picturesque weathercock.

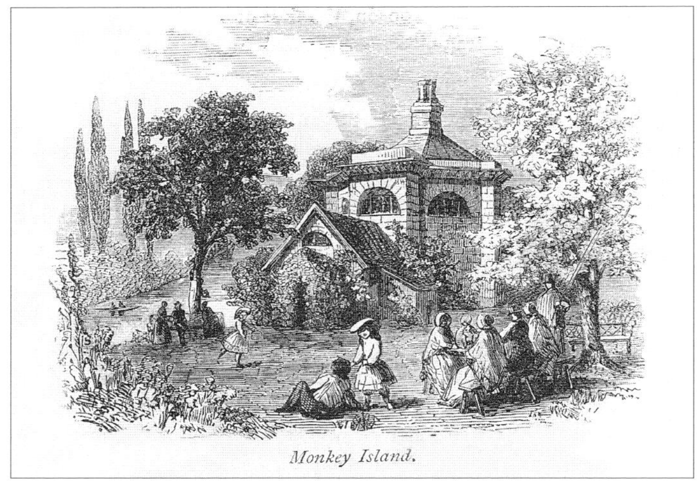

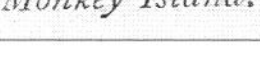

96 An illustration of Monkey Island from *The Book of the Thames* by Mr and Mrs S.C. Hall. The authors wrote,

> Soon after leaving Bray we step ashore at 'MONKEY ISLAND': the fishing-lodge built here by the third Duke of Marlborough is now a 'house of entertainment;' and the grounds, although limited in extent, are famous for 'picnics' in the summer seasons.

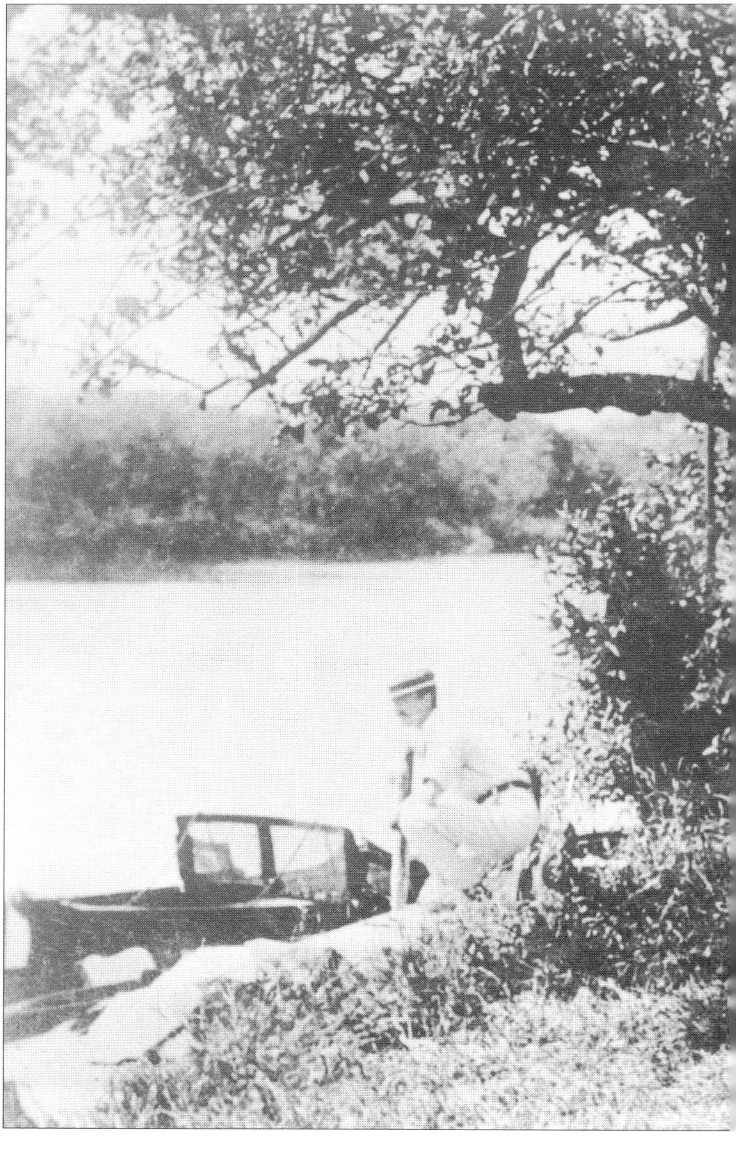

97 Camping on Boveney Island in Edwardian times. One of the campers was looking along the river, while his two companions were involved in the business of shaving when this photograph was taken.

98 Peter H. Chaplin, in *Thames from source to tideway*, noted that proposals were made for a lock at Boveney in 1836, but it was not until November 1838 that the lock was in use. This illustration of Boveney Lock was included in *The Book of the Thames* by Mr and Mrs S.C. Hall. A new lock was built in a different position here in 1898 and the old lock was converted into a boatslide.

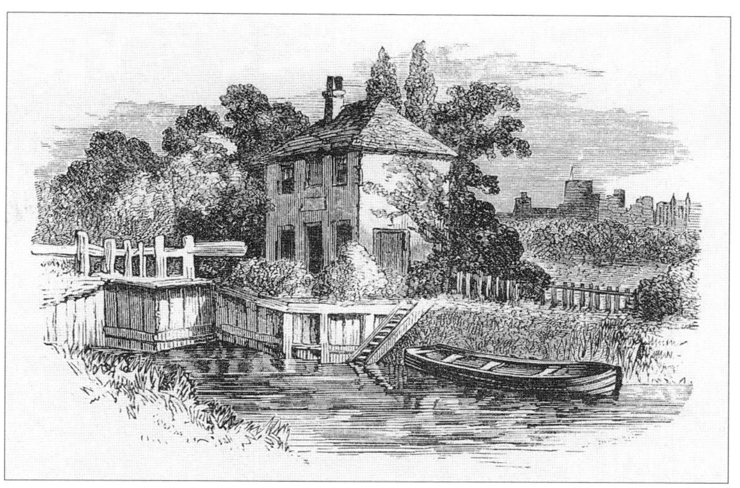

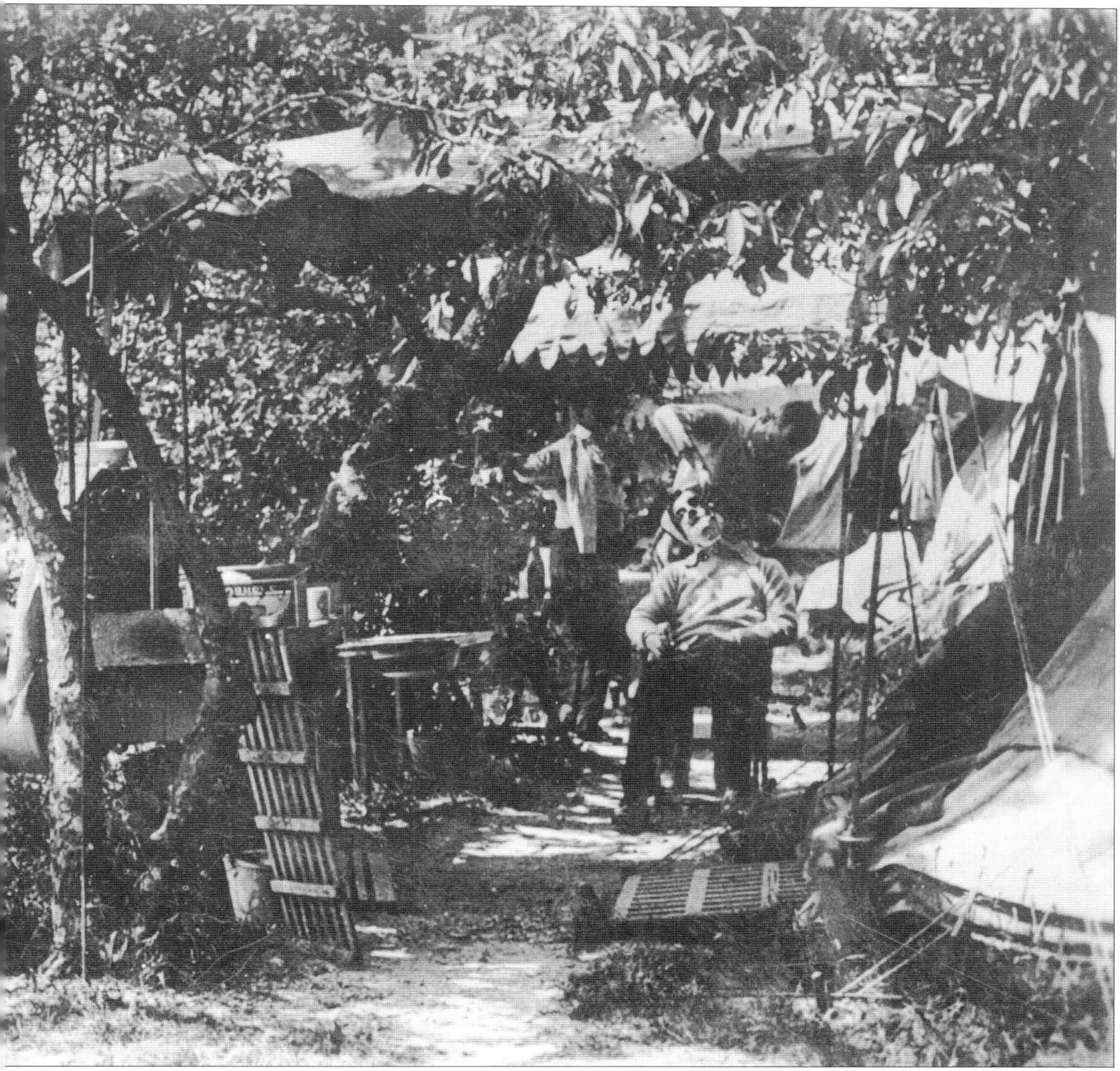

Windsor to Bell Weir

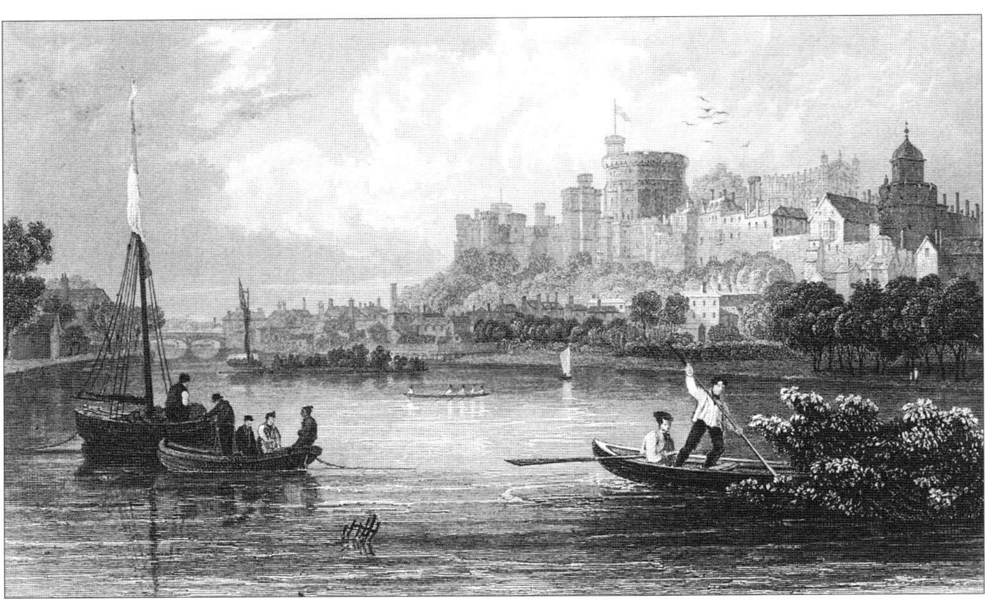

99 Windsor Castle from *Tombleson's Thames*, *c*.1834. W.G. Fearnside remarked, 'As we approach the celebrated town, the castle becomes more and more a distinct and imposing object, until ... the various parts of this regal and splendid building are blended into one rich architectural mass, rising from the town, and displaying simultaneously its extent and magnificence.'

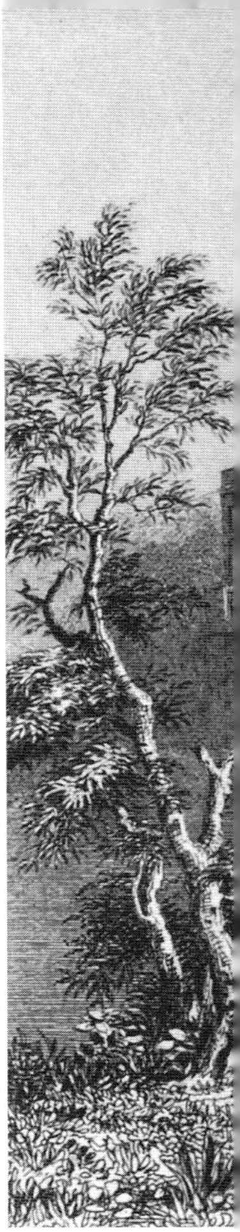

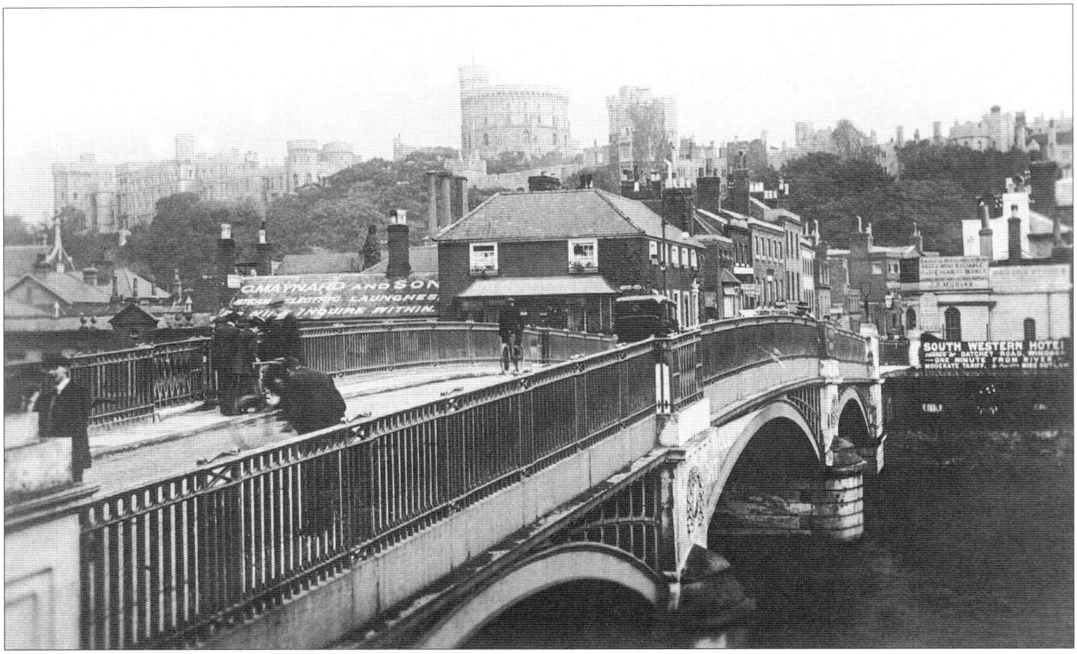

100 Windsor Castle from the bridge, *c*.1910-14. The sign on the roof of the premises next to the bridge advertises C. Maynard and Son, steam electric launches.

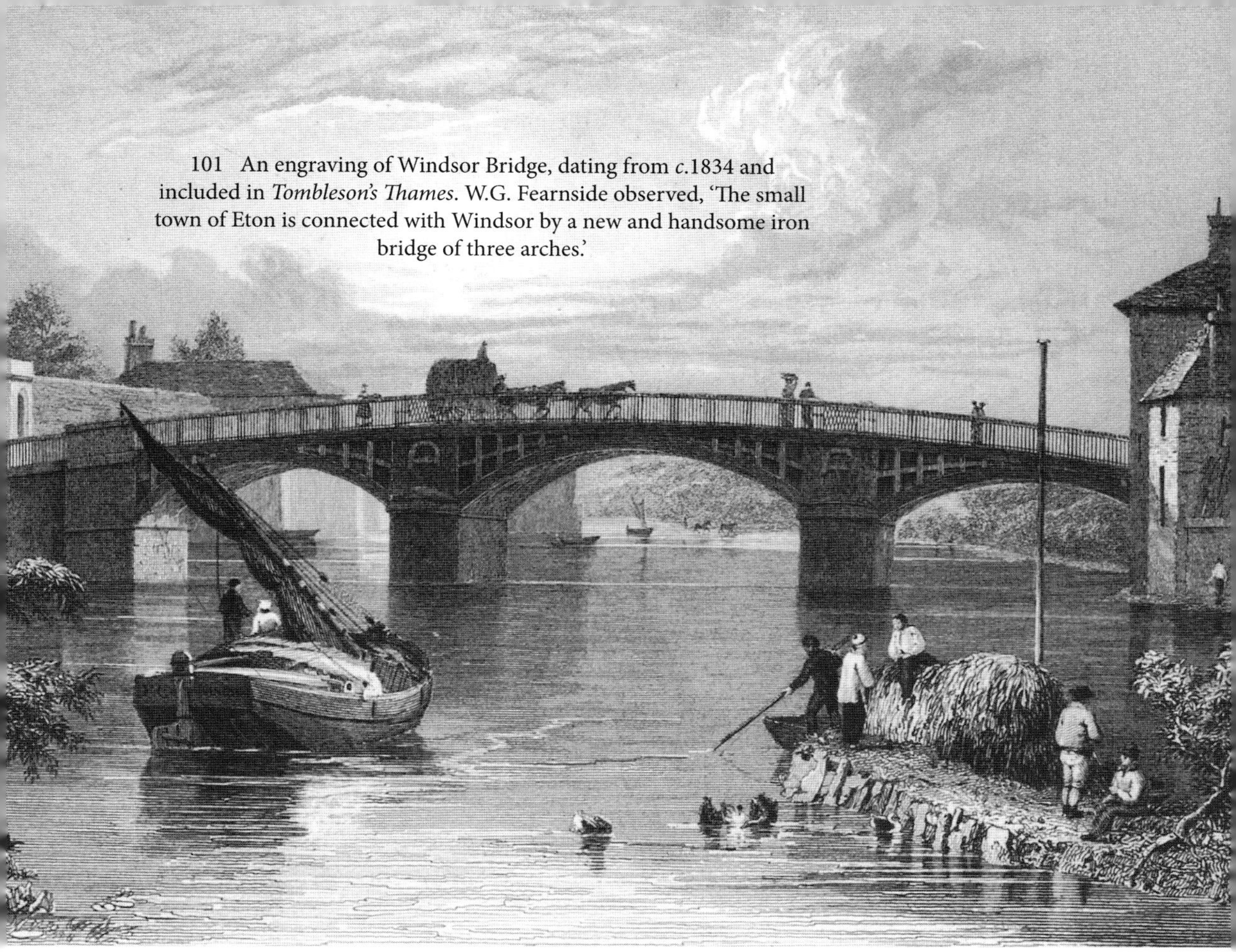

101 An engraving of Windsor Bridge, dating from *c.*1834 and included in *Tombleson's Thames*. W.G. Fearnside observed, 'The small town of Eton is connected with Windsor by a new and handsome iron bridge of three arches.'

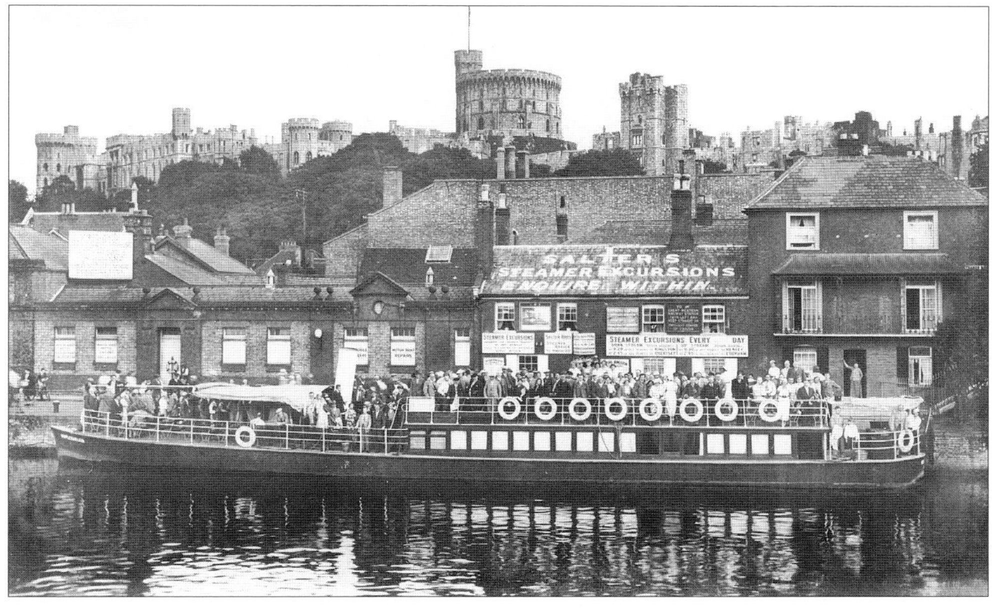

102 Salter's steam launch, *Mapledurham*, Windsor. The advertisement on the front of Salter's steamer office shows that there were excursions downstream to all places to Kingston, leaving at 9.20 a.m., and to all places to Chertsey, leaving at 2.45 p.m. Excursions upstream to all places to Henley left at 9.30 a.m., and for all places to Cookham the departure time was 2.45 p.m.

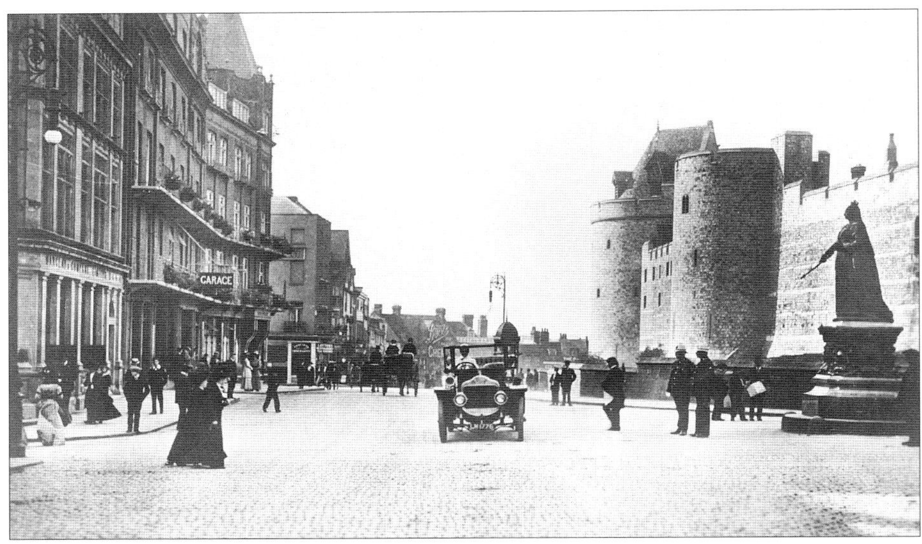

103 High Street, Windsor, *c.*1910-14. On the extreme right is a statue of Queen Victoria erected in 1887 to commemorate the Golden Jubilee of the monarch. In the background is the Curfew Tower.

104 This view of Church Street, Windsor, looks towards Henry VIII's Gateway at Windsor Castle.

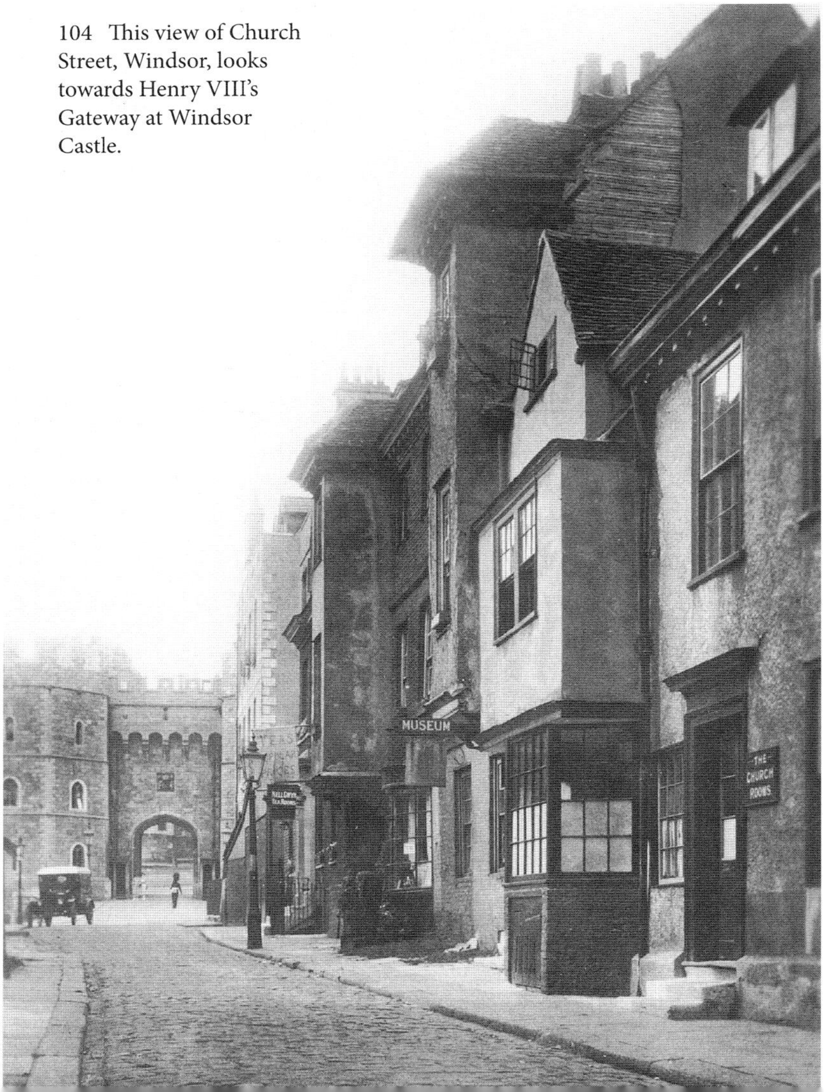

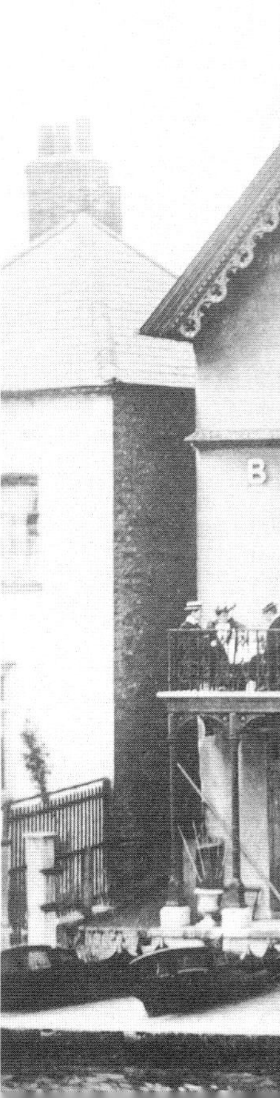

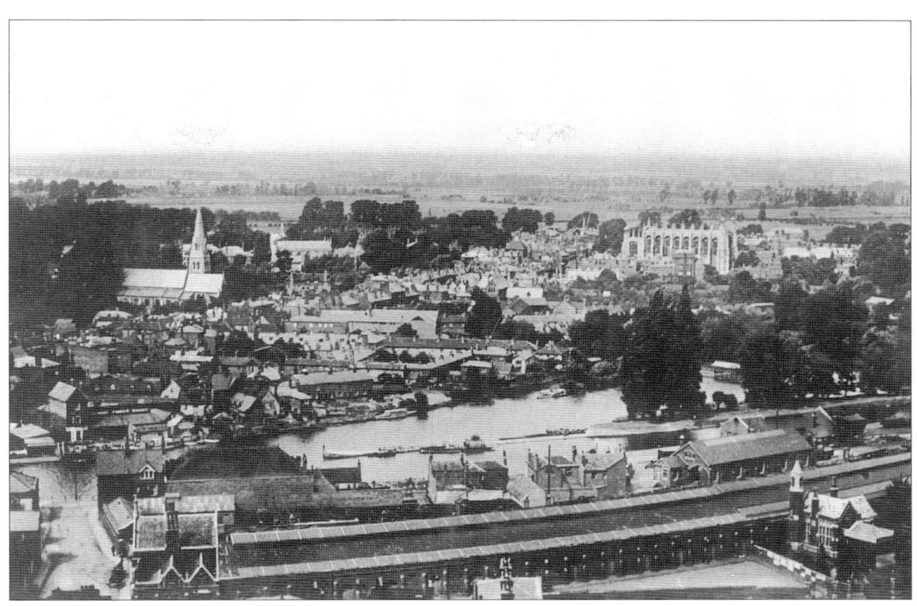

105 An early 20th-century view of Eton from Windsor Castle showing one of Windsor's two railway stations in the foreground. This is the riverside station, built by the London and South Western Railway. In the background, the church of St John the Evangelist is on the left, while Eton College is on the right.

106 *Bridge House Hotel*, High Street, Eton, was immediately opposite Windsor Quay where the Oxford and Kingston and other steamers landed. In the early 20th century, when this view of the hotel was taken, it was advertised as being 'within three minutes' walk of Eton College' and 'an easy drive from Ascot and Virginia Water'. A sign for boats to let can be seen below its balcony where visitors are taking refreshment. Gilbert Russell was listed as proprietor of the hotel in directories of 1907 and 1915.

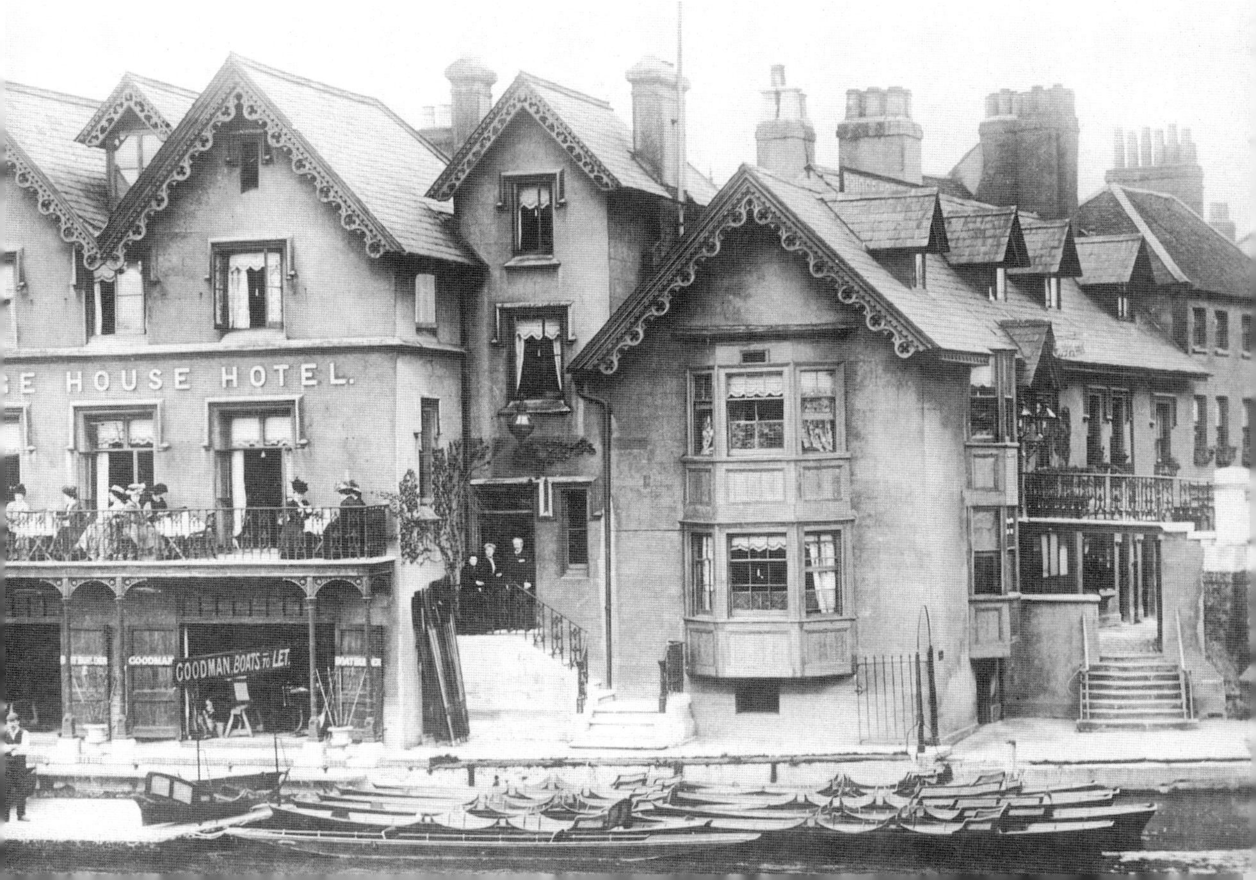

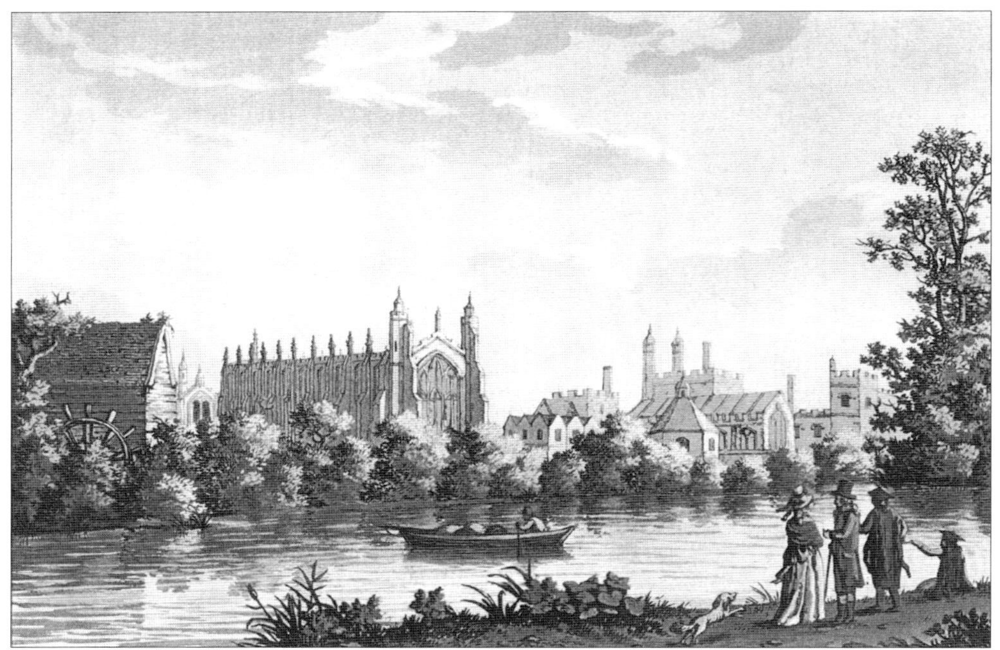

107 This aquatint of Eton College appeared in Samuel Ireland's *Picturesque Views on the River Thames* with the comment, 'Eton College, that noble seminary of learning, has every advantage from situation which the luxuriant hand of nature could bestow. The valley in which it stands is healthy and fertile, and happily calculated for the residence of youth.'

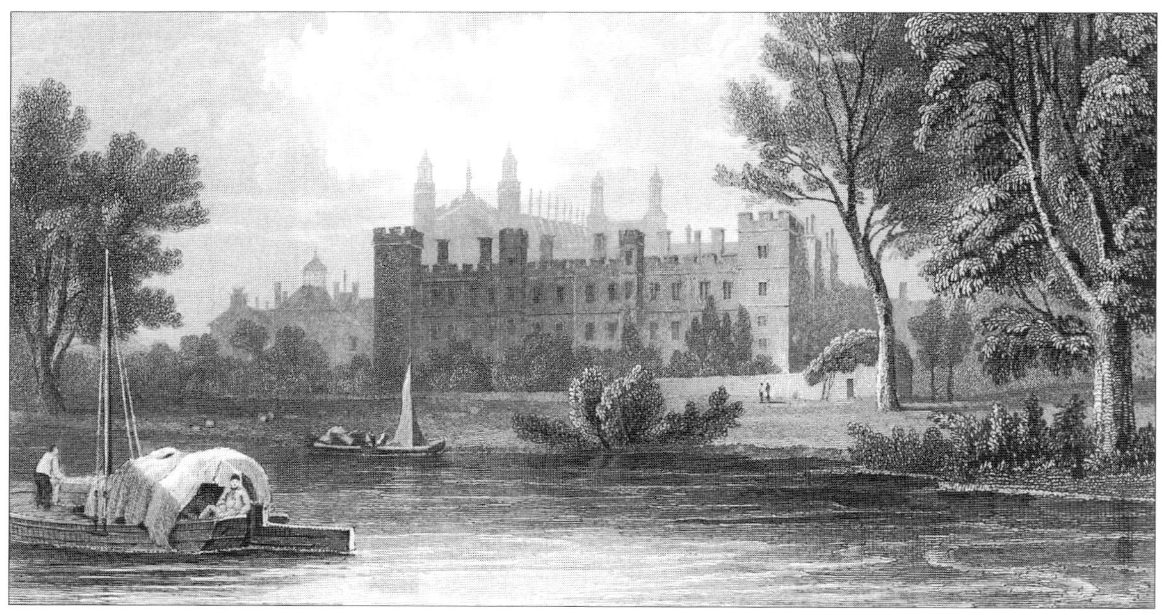

108 An engraving of Eton College from *Tombleson's Thames*, dating from *c.*1834. W.G. Fearnside noted:

> The college was founded by Henry VI, in 1440, and contains at present on its establishment a provost, vice-provost, six fellows, a master, under master, assistant, seventy king's scholars, seven lay-clerks and ten choristers. The chapel, constructed in all the elegance of gothic architecture, forms an interesting and beautiful object on the Buckinghamshire side of the river.

109 An aquatint of Windsor Castle from Samuel Ireland's *Picturesque Views on the River Thames*. The author observed:

> From every point in which the noble Castle of Windsor is viewed, it affords beauties peculiar and interesting. The north view annexed has an ample share of those beauties, as it comprises the most extensive range of buildings, and those best massed and adapted, from the size of this undertaking, to give some idea of the magnitude of the whole.

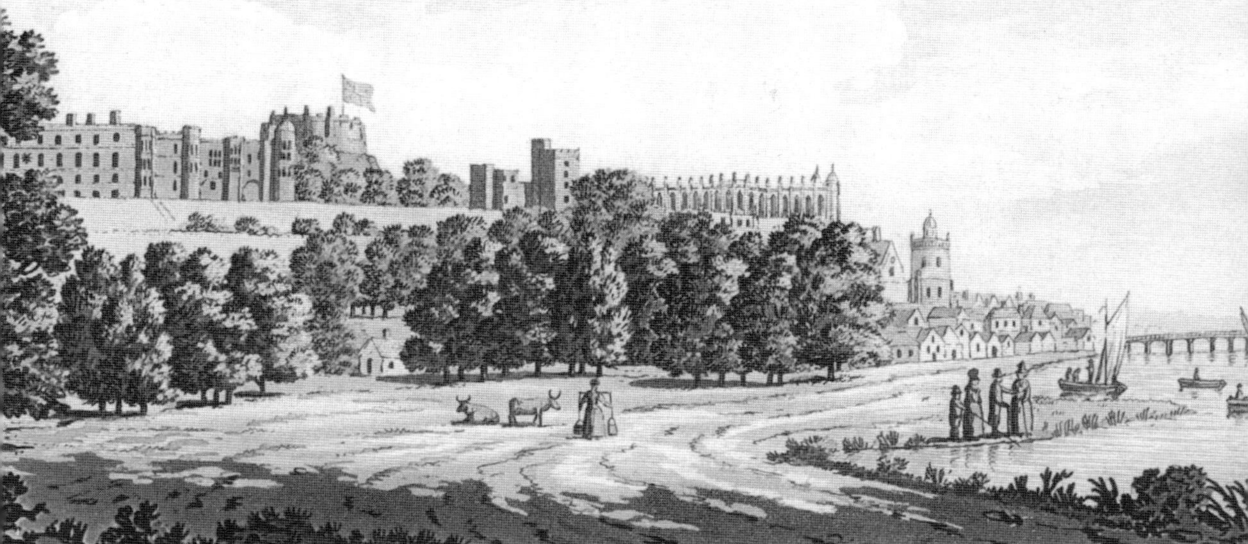

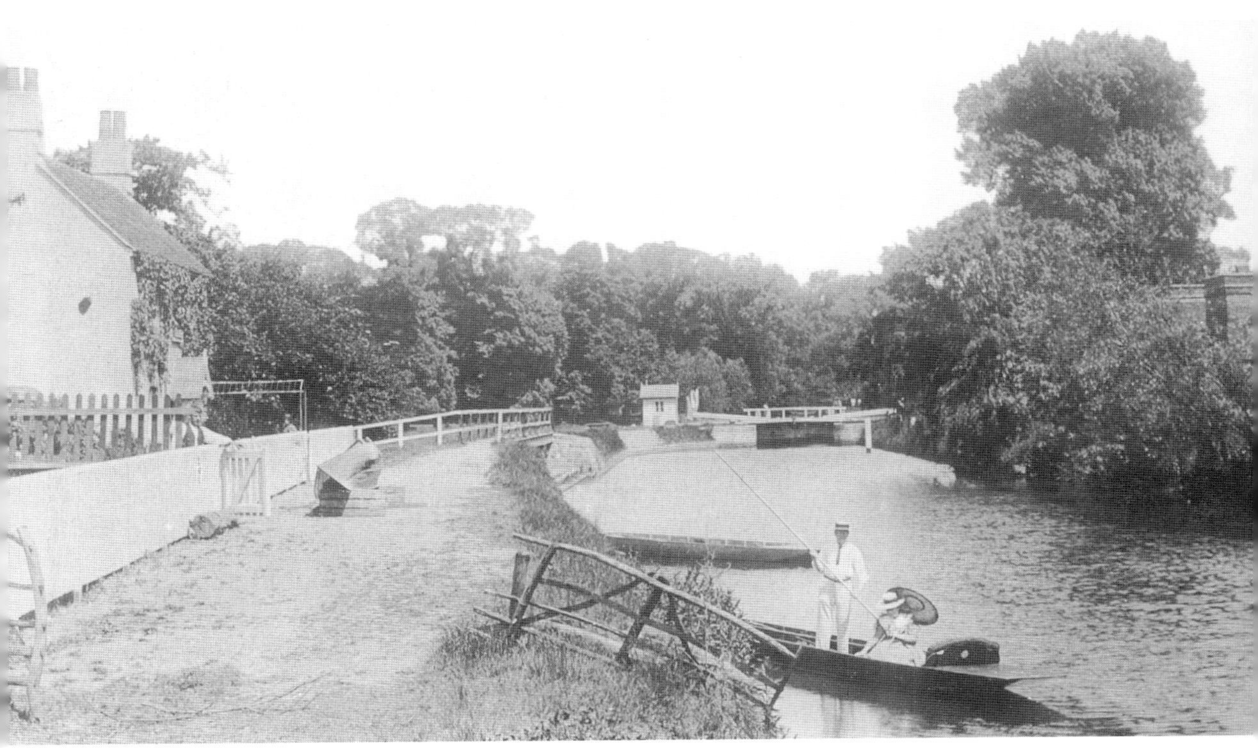

110 This Edwardian postcard shows the lock at Windsor in the background. Romney Lock was originally built in 1797. Being in a poor state, it underwent reconstruction in 1869 and was rebuilt in 1979-80.

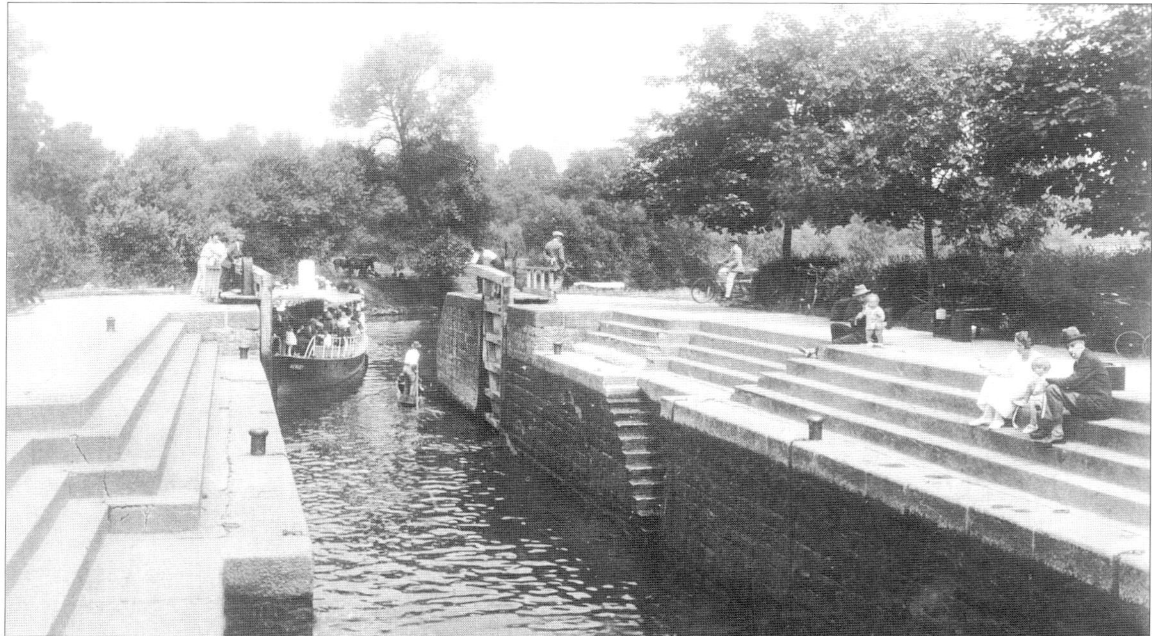

111 Visitors to the Thames often whiled away time at the locks watching the steamers, punts and rowing boats. The sender of this postcard of Romney Lock wrote, 'We are spending the weekend at Windsor ... We are now sitting by the lock fishing, but have not yet been on the island for tea.'

112 Datchet Bridge was replaced in the mid-19th century by Victoria Bridge and Albert Bridge. This engraving of Datchet Bridge, dating from *c*.1834, was included in *Tombleson's Thames*. W.G. Fearnside described the bridge as 'a substantial wooden structure, with nine arches on stone piers'.

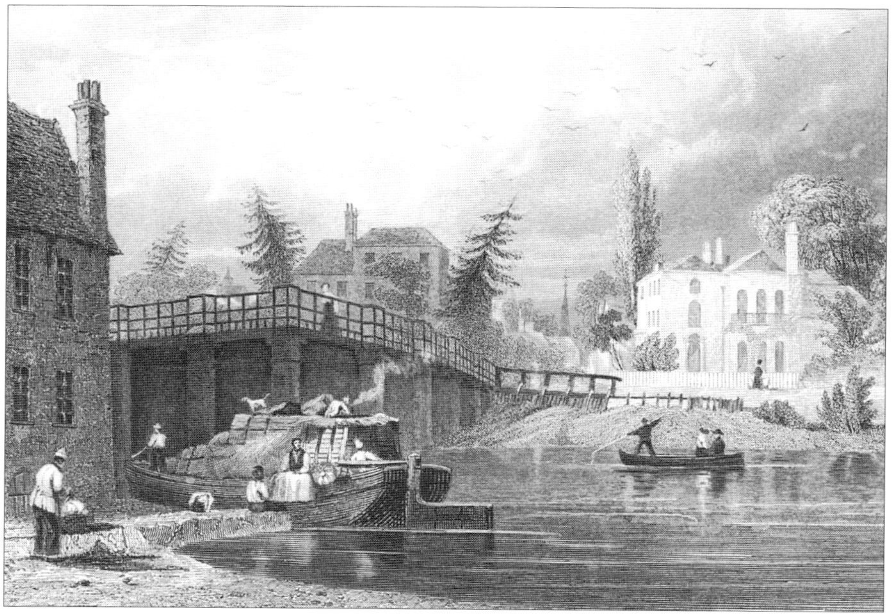

(Right) 114 Datchet, 1900s. The Princess of Wales and her children were photographed by the river as they were about to board a launch.

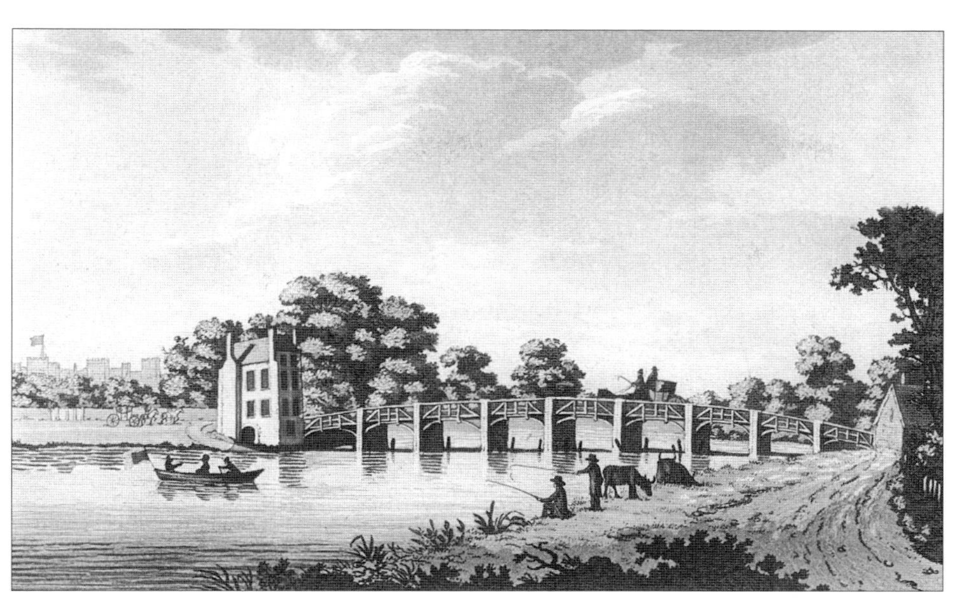

113 An aquatint of Datchet Bridge from *Picturesque Views on the River Thames*. The author noted, 'On the approach to Datchet, the wooden bridge has a light appearance from every point of view; but it is decaying so fast as to become dangerous, though it has not been built above fifteen or sixteen years.'

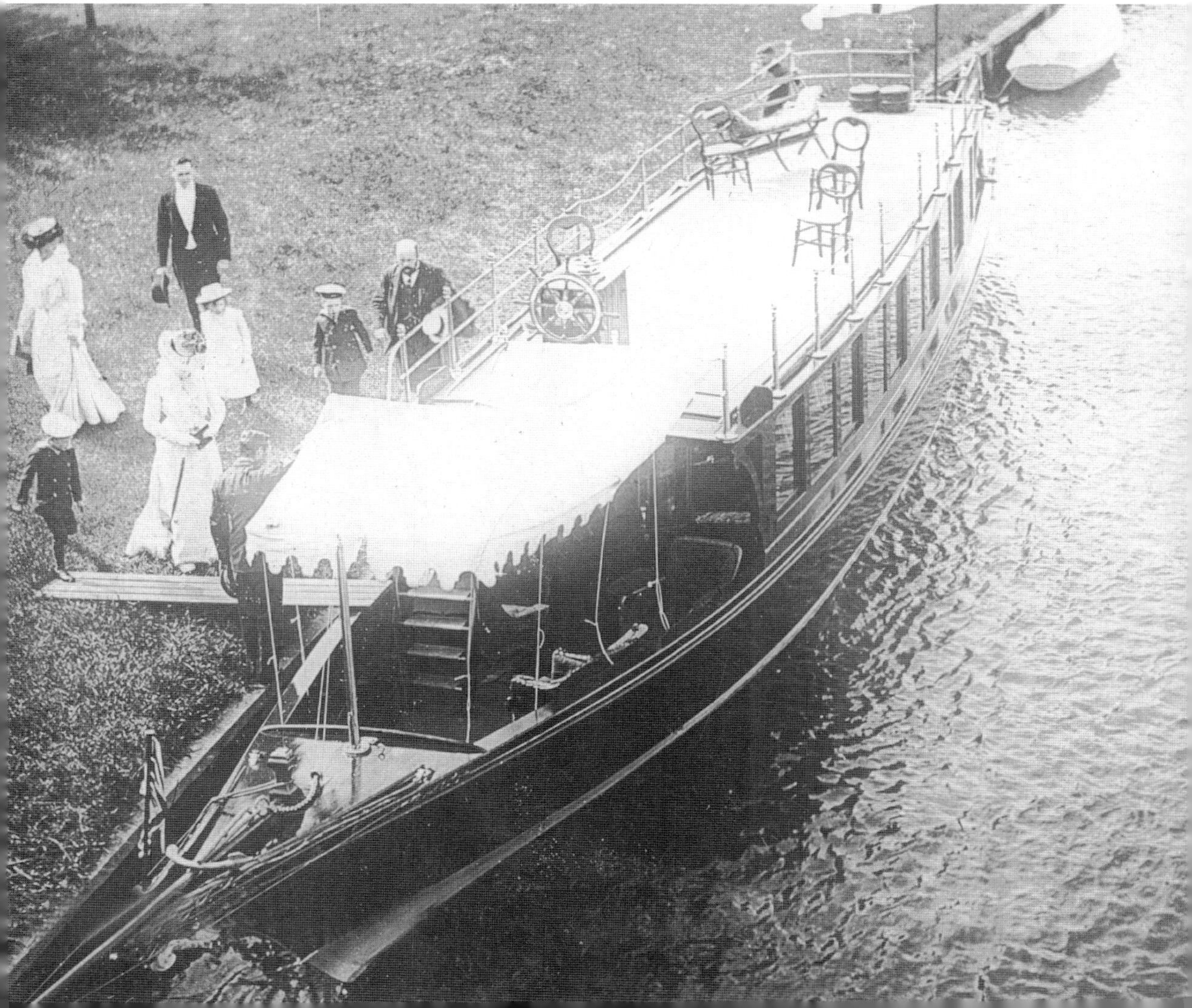

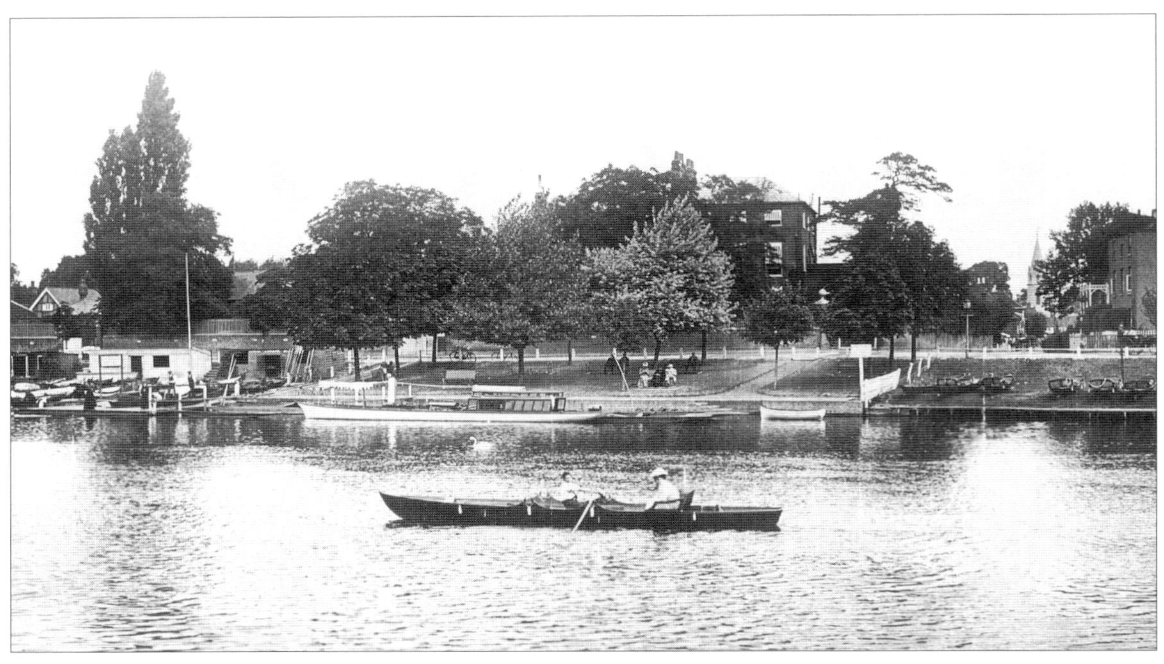

115 In past times, the railway brought crowds of visitors to Datchet at weekends. Here, they enjoyed themselves by and on the river. This Edwardian view of the riverside at Datchet dates from *c*.1906-10.

116 The Reach, Datchet. On the right of this postcard view, which was postally used on 14 July 1915, is a sign with the words LUMDSEN, LANDING and HOTEL. In 1911, George Lumsden was a boat proprietor at Datchet along with Fenn & Burfoot and Mrs Georgina Swain.

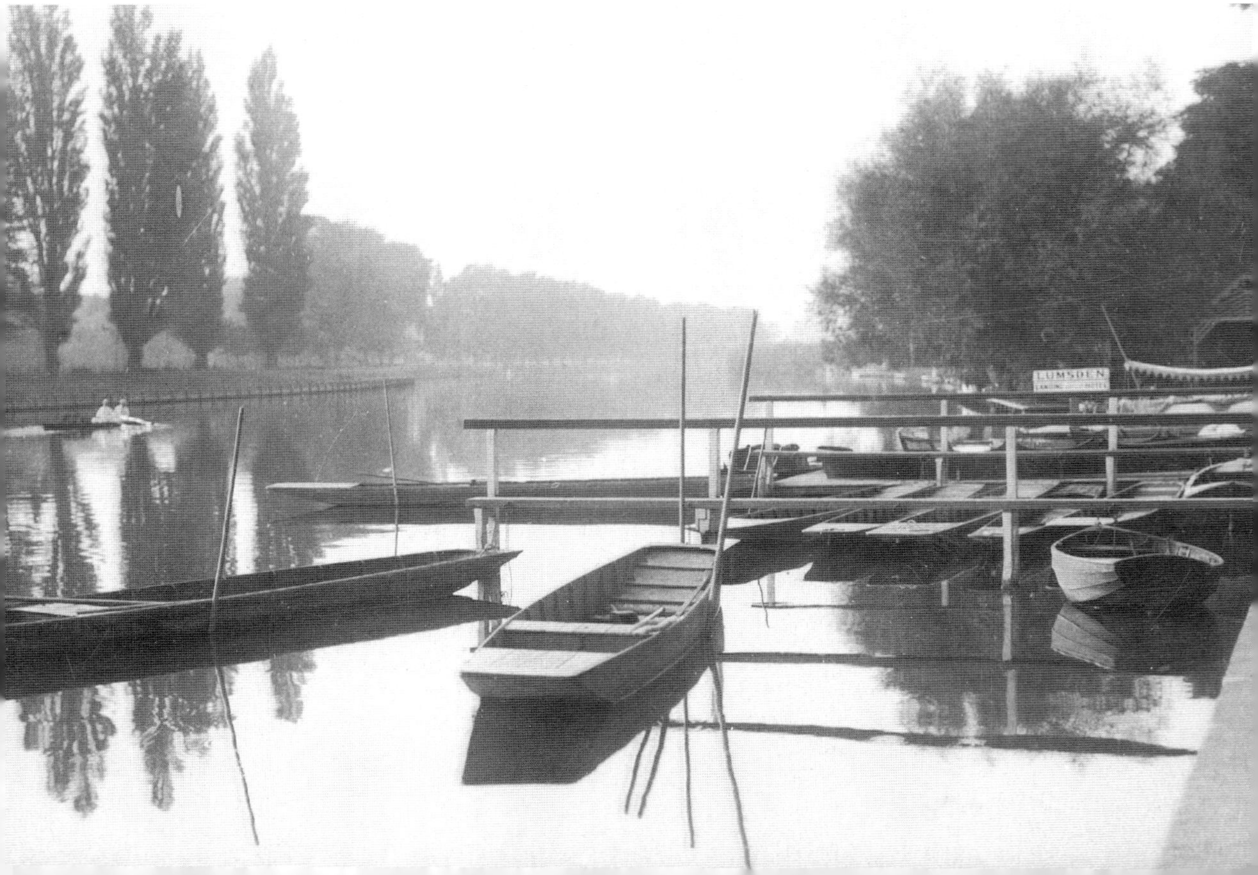

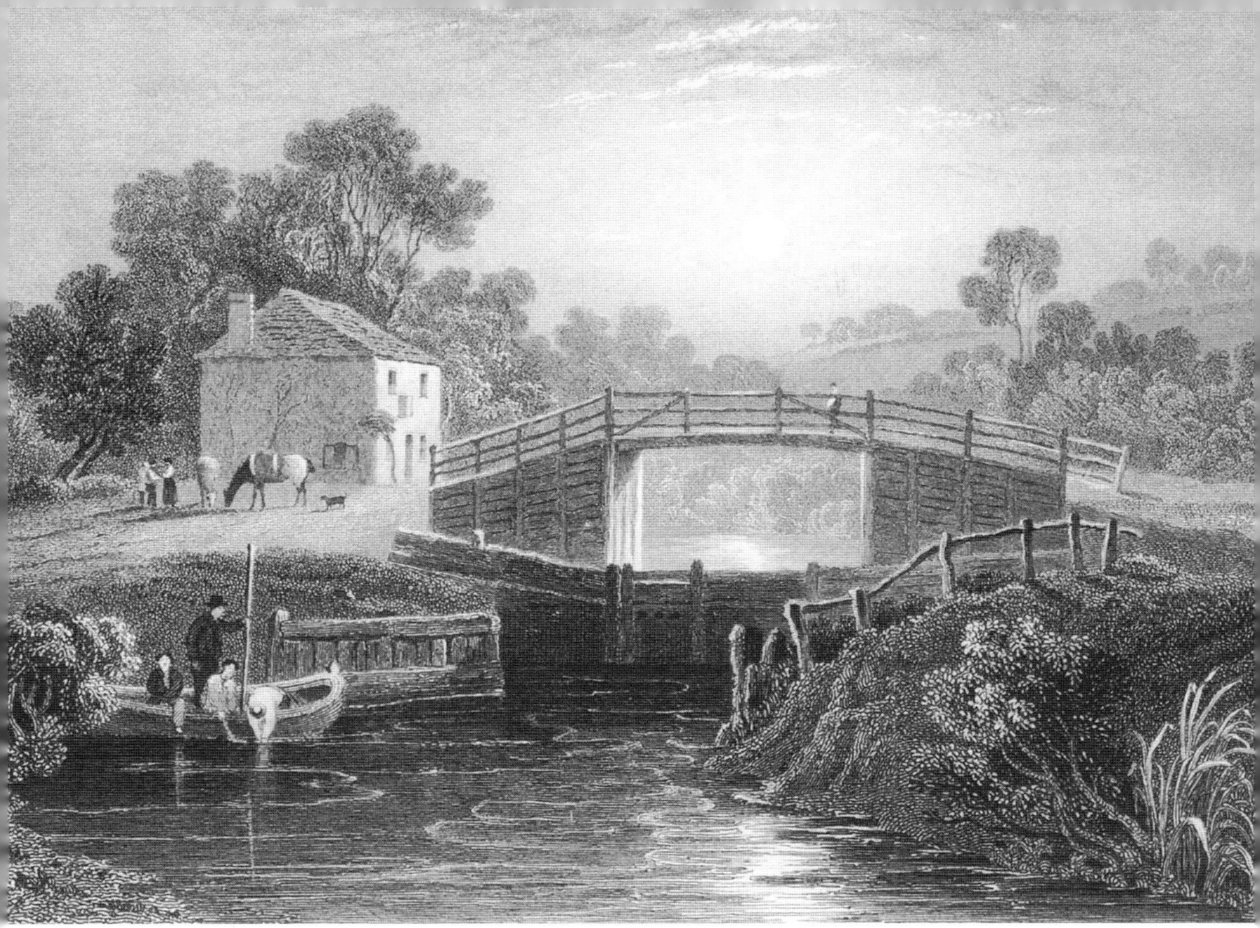

117 Old Windsor Locks, an engraving from *Tombleson's Thames*, *c*.1834. Fred S. Thacker, in *The Thames Highway Volume II: Locks and Weirs*, observed that the site of this lock had the name of 'Top of Caps', but he was unable to explain the derivation. He noted that the first boat went through the lock on 27 September 1822 and that Henry Hyde was the first lock keeper, earning £3 10s. each month.

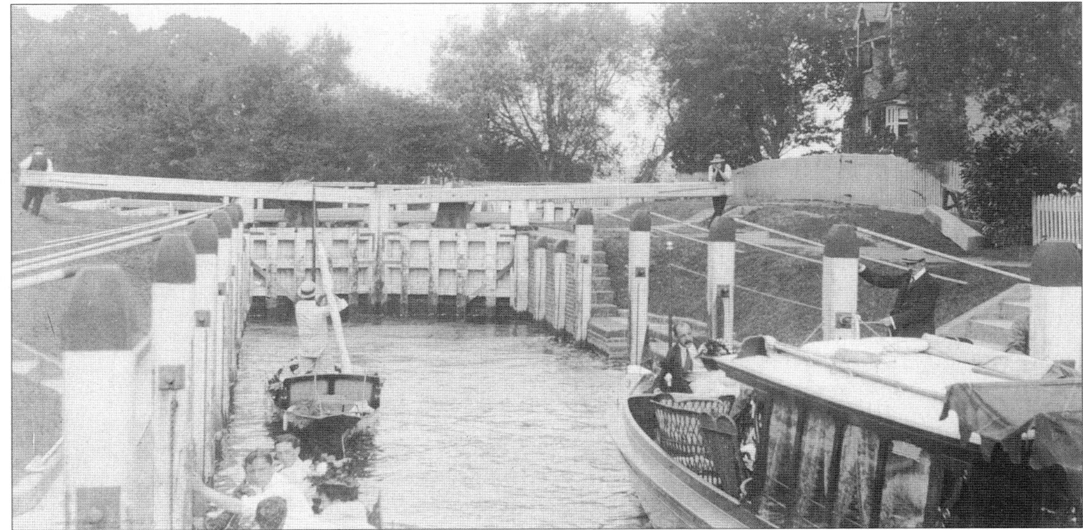

118 Old Windsor Lock was rebuilt in 1889 and reconstructed again in 1953. This postcard view of the lock was postally used on 7 July 1910.

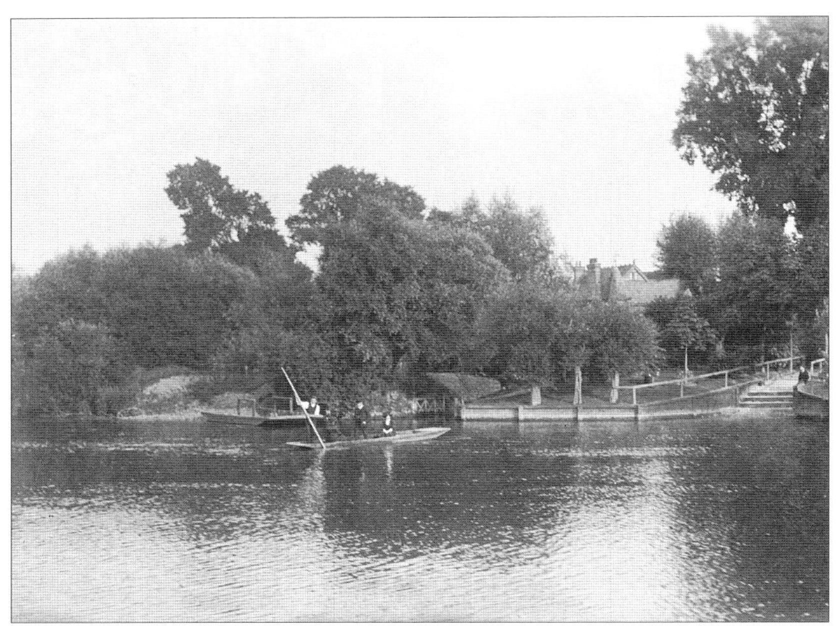

119 The Old Ferry House, Wraysbury, *c.*1912. Another name for Wraysbury, a Buckinghamshire parish and a village on the north bank of the Thames, was Wyrardisbury.

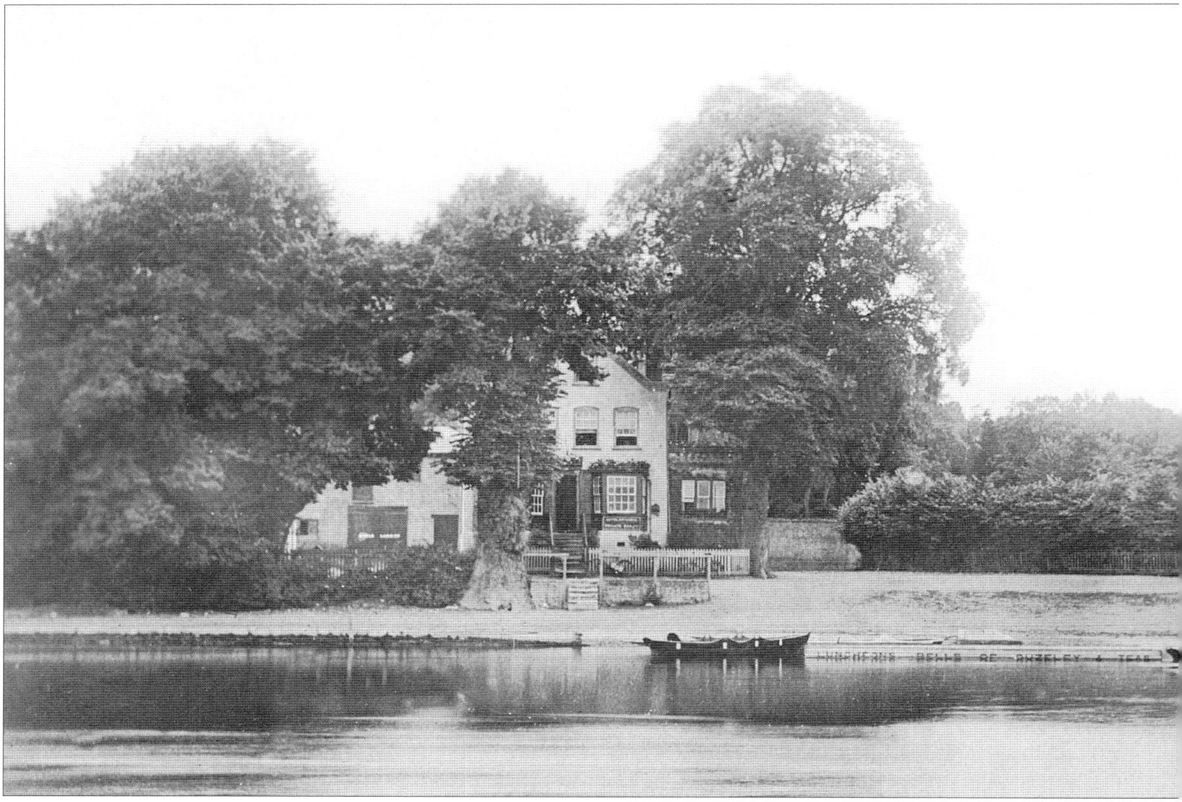

120 The *Bells of Ouseley, c.*1912. The name of this old inn is said to have originated from the time when the nearby monastery of Ouseley was closed during the Dissolution of the Monasteries. Legend has it that the monks hid their bells in the river near the inn. Another tradition is that, at full moon and depending on the direction of the wind, the chimes of the five bells of Ouseley may be heard. The inn shown in this early 20th-century view was destroyed by a bomb during the Second World War and was replaced by a mock-Tudor half-timbered building.

121 This illustration of Magna Carta Island, dating from 1859, was included in *The Book of the Thames* by Mr and Mrs S.C. Hall who commented:

> In the island which forms so charming a feature in the landscape, the Harcourts have built a small Gothic cottage — an altar-house, so to call it. It contains a large rough stone, which tradition, or fancy, describes as that on which the parchment rested when the king and the barons affixed their signatures to 'the Charter.'

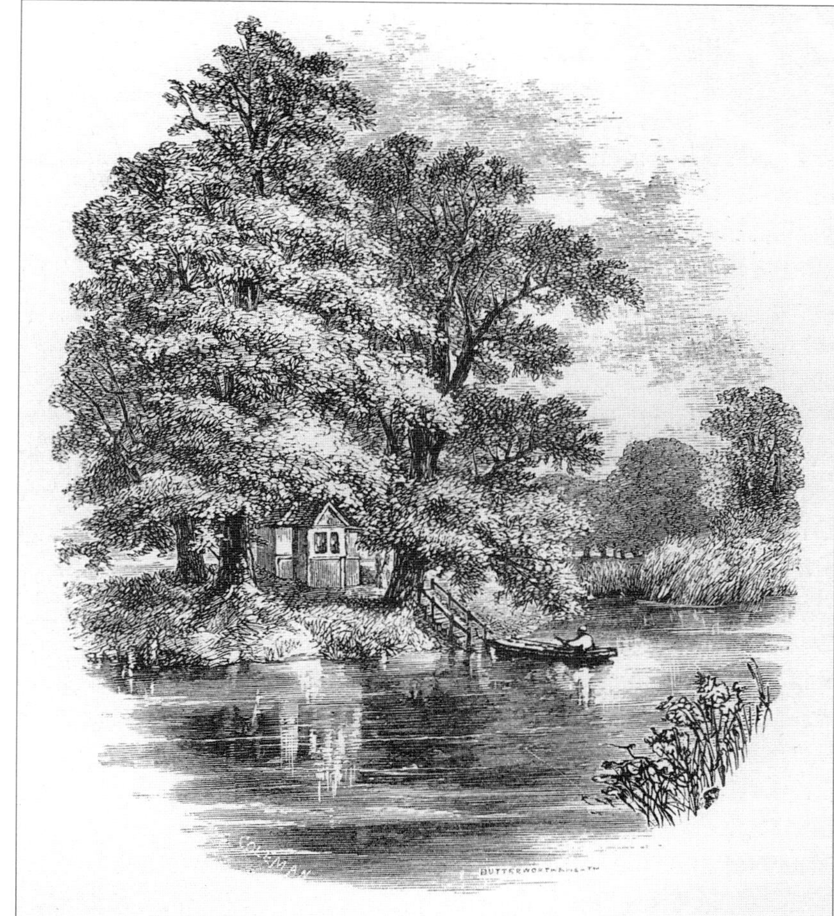

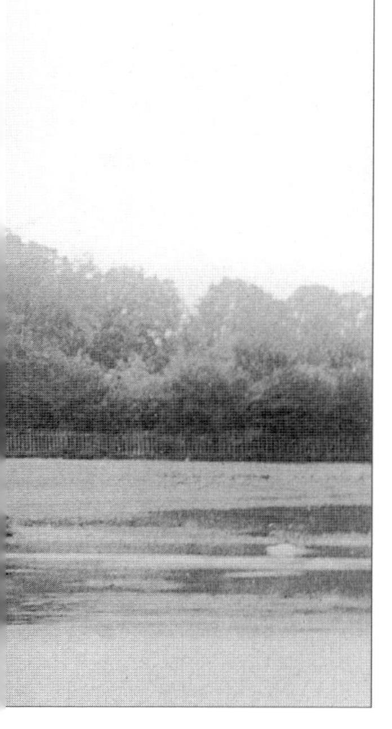

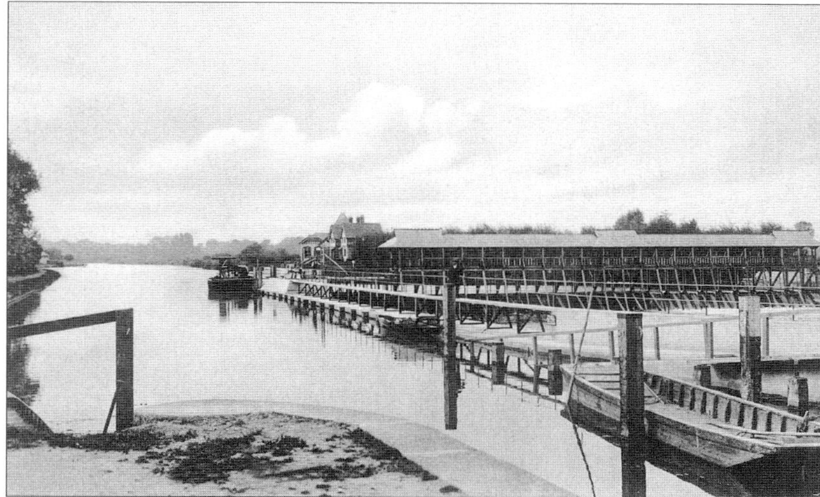

122 Fred S. Thacker, in *The Thames Highway Volume II: Locks and Weirs*, noted that the lock at Bell Weir was opened in the winter of 1817-18, the cost of the weir being about a quarter of the outlay for the work, which was altogether around £6,650. He added that both lock and weir were rebuilt during 1867-8 and that 'a new weir, a little above the old one had been completed in 1904'.

Staines to Hampton Court Palace

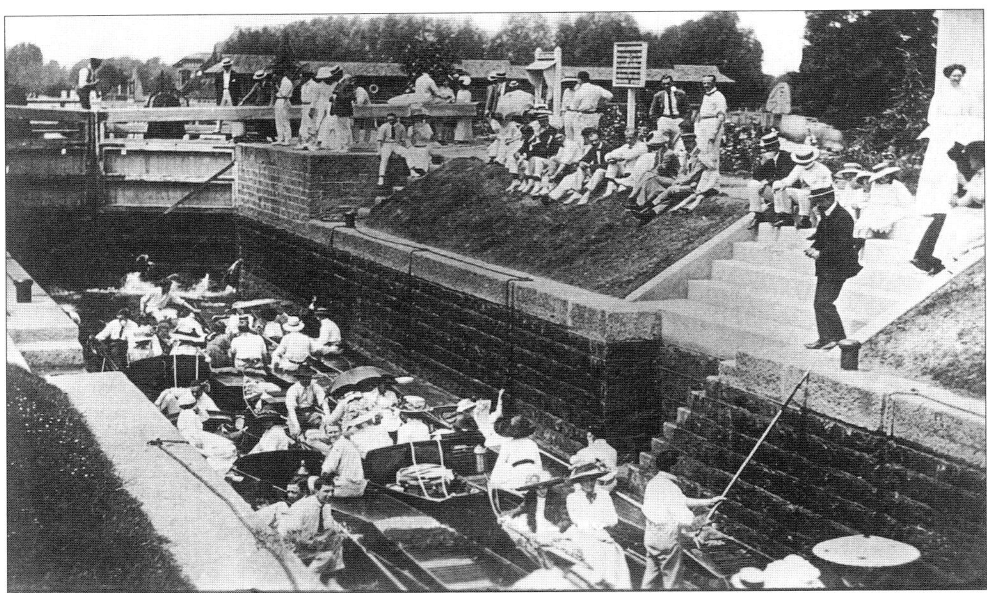

123 A busy scene at Bell Weir Lock in the early 20th century. Fred S. Thacker remarked that the lock was equipped with rollers about 1907.

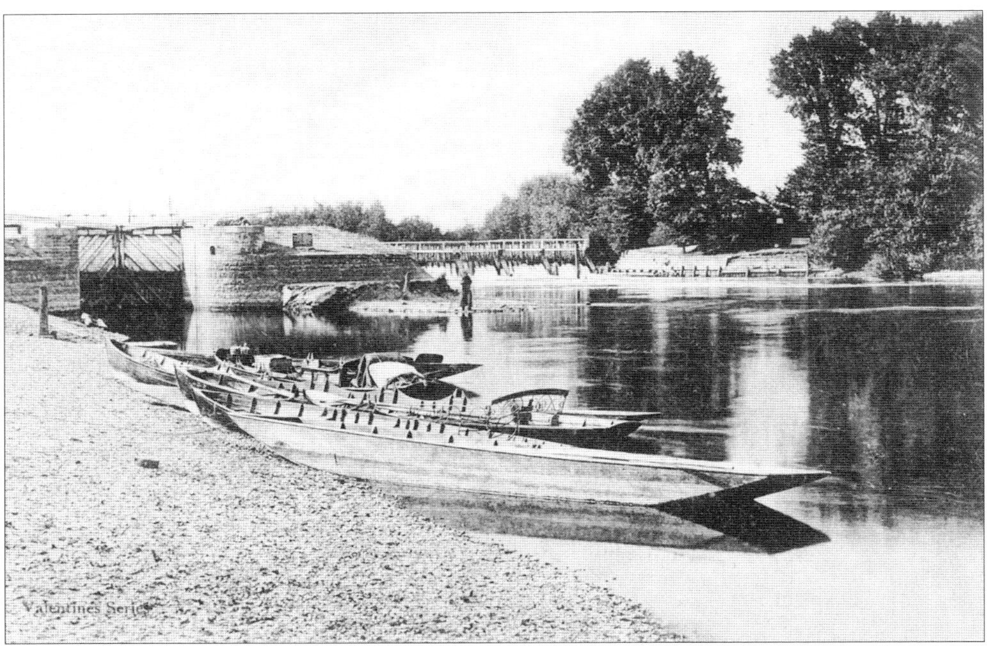

124 The *Angler's Rest Hotel*, below the lock at Bell Weir and just out of view in this picture, was a venue for boating, tourist and fishing parties and here boats were let and housed. In 1913, the inclusive charge for accommodation at the hotel was 8s. 6d. per day, with weekly terms from two guineas according to room.

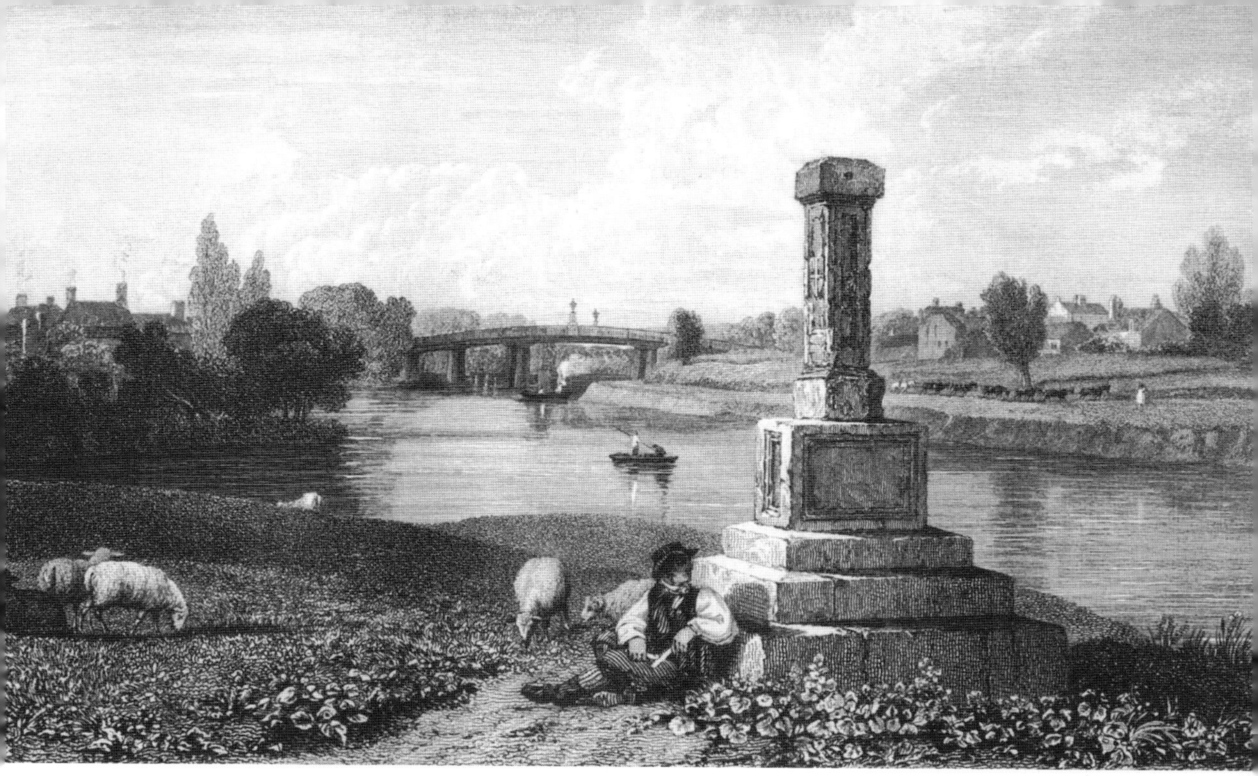

125 The London Stone at Staines, from *Views on the Thames* by W.B. Cooke and George Cooke. The caption reads, 'STONE AT STAINES marking the western boundary of the jurisdiction of the City of London on the River Thames.' The engraving was published on 1 November 1821 by W.B. Cooke, 9 Soho Square, London.

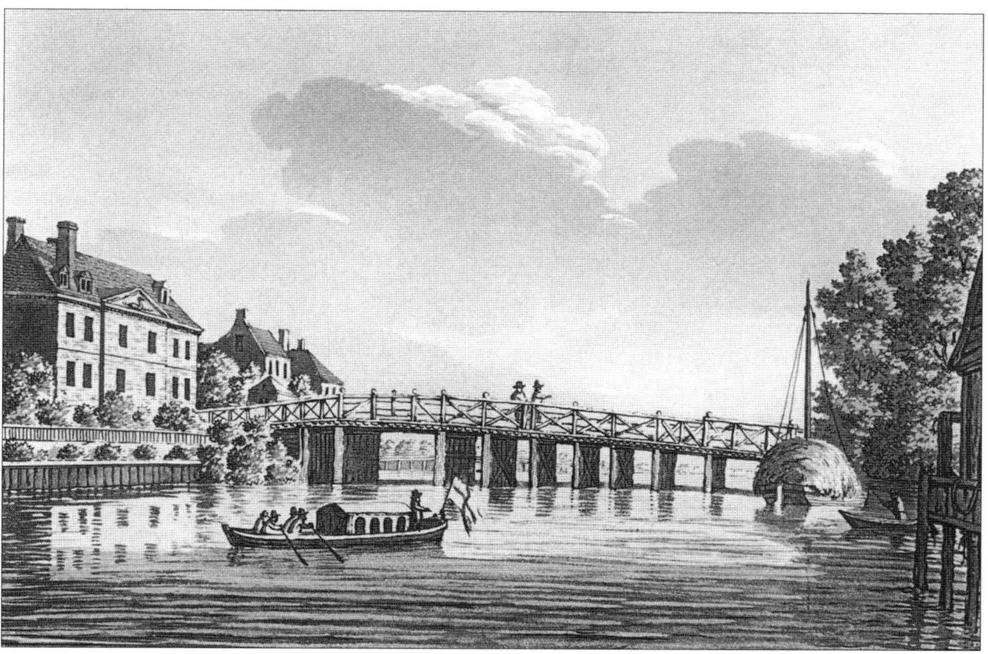

126 Samuel Ireland used this aquatint of Staines Bridge in his *Picturesque Views on the River Thames*. He remarked, 'Its ancient decayed wooden bridge, I am happy to find, is shortly to be removed, and will receive an elegant substitute of stone, from a design of the ingenious Thomas Sandby, Esq. R. A. whose plan has already been approved by the Commissioners.'

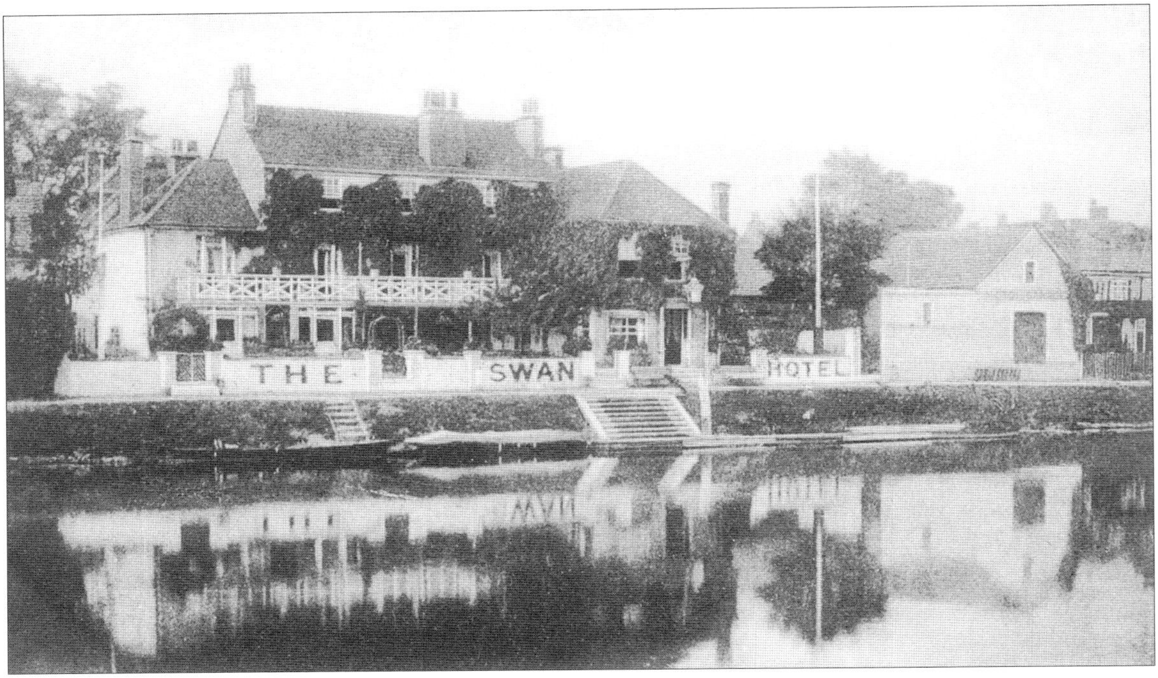

127 The *Swan Hotel*, on the downstream side of Staines Bridge, dates from at least the early 17th century. The name of Samuel Pepys, the famous 17th-century diarist, is linked with this riverside inn as he often frequented it. This early 20th-century view of the establishment was taken at the time when Frederick Ping was proprietor.

128 This postcard showing camping at Penton Hook was postally used on 6 August 1904.

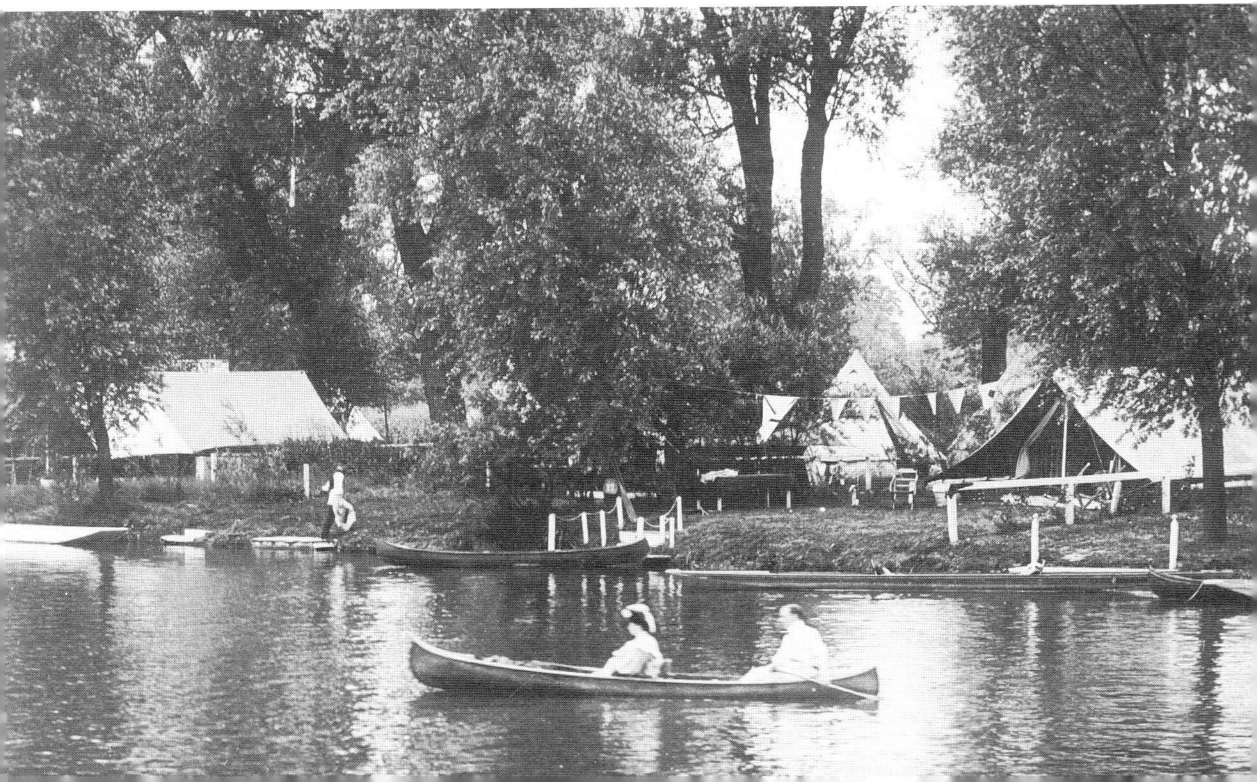

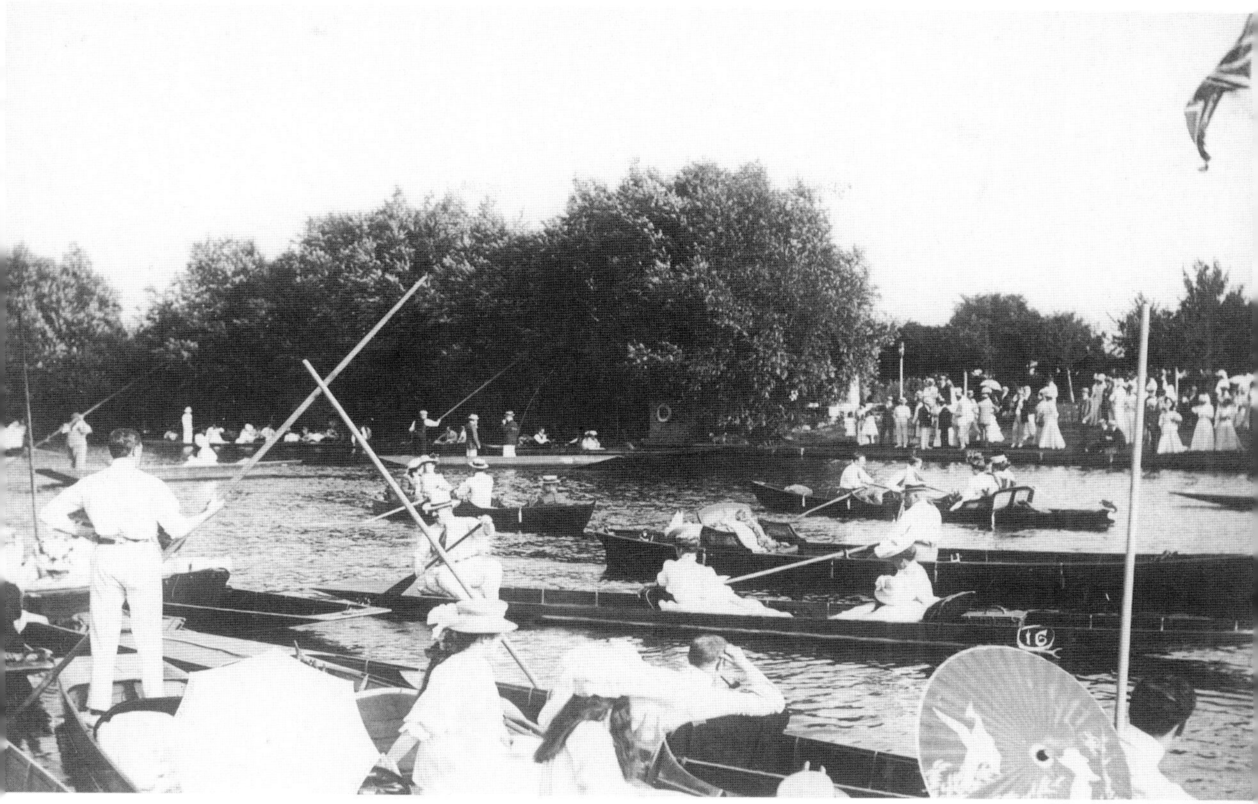

129 The Penton Camp Club was established in Edwardian times. It held a regatta in the summer, which included punting. This postcard view shows the Penton Camp Club Regatta of 1907.

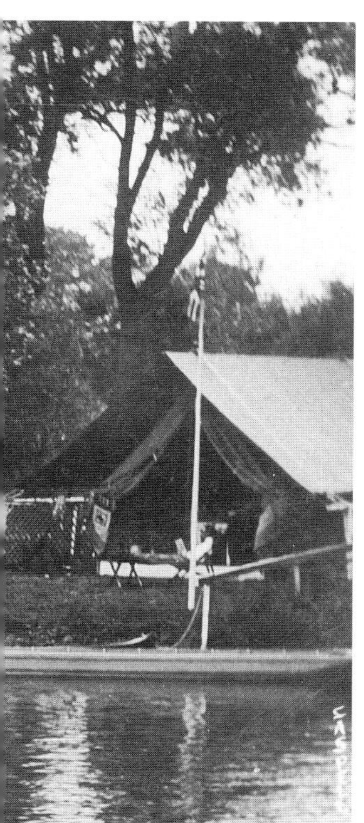

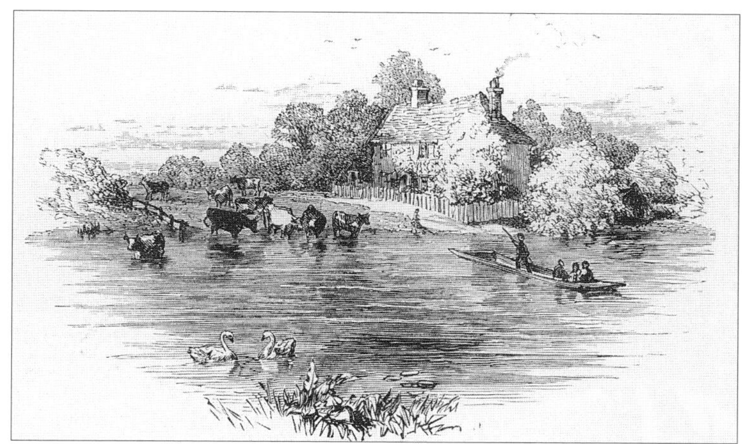

130 This illustration of Laleham Ferry is from *The Book of the Thames* by Mr and Mrs S.C. Hall, who observed:

> From Penty-Hook there is nothing to interest the voyager until he reaches the pretty FERRY at LALEHAM. He may, if he pleases, step ashore at the clean and neat ferry-house here pictured, and either dine on the bank, or in one of the small rooms, to which access is readily obtained.

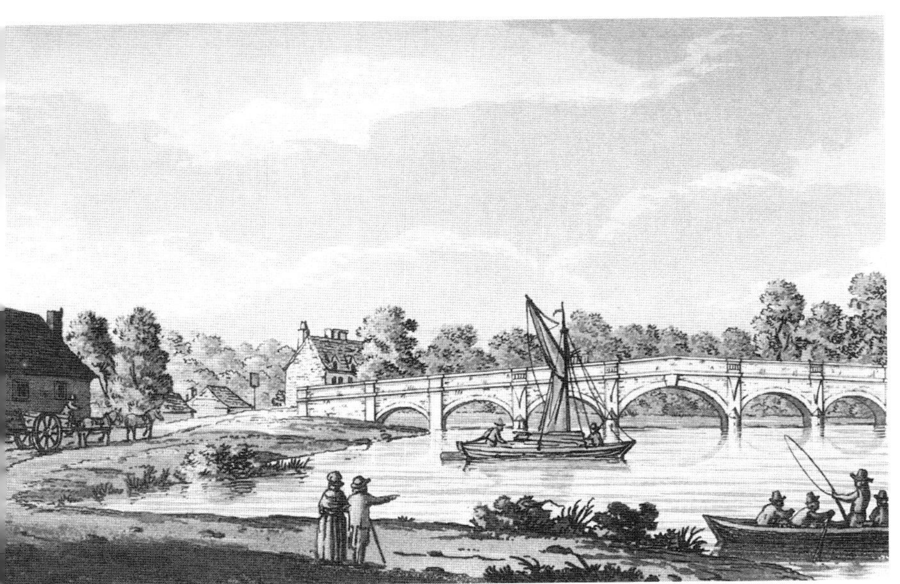

131 An aquatint of Chertsey Bridge from *Picturesque Views on the River Thames* by Samuel Ireland, who wrote:

> Chertsey Bridge is a handsome plain structure, begun in 1780, and finished in 1785, under the direction of Mr. Payne, the architect, whose works make no inconsiderable figure on the Thames. It consists of seven arches, each formed of the segment of a circle. It is built of Purbeck stone, at an expence of about thirteen thousand pounds, which falls equally upon the counties of Surrey and Middlesex. The original contract was for seven thousand five hundred pounds.

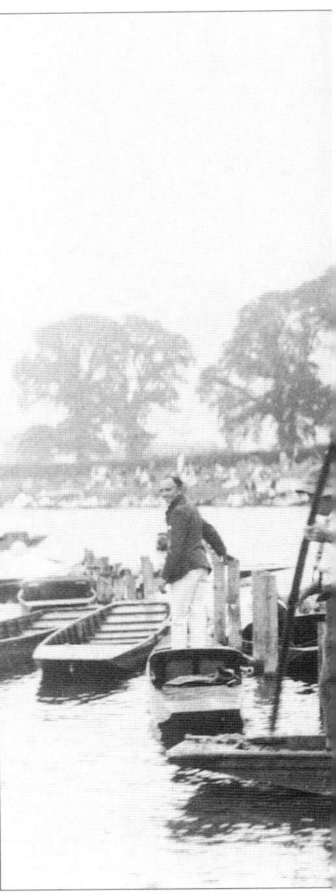

132 A crowd on the riverbank watch the racing during the Amateur Punting Championship of 1920 held at Shepperton.

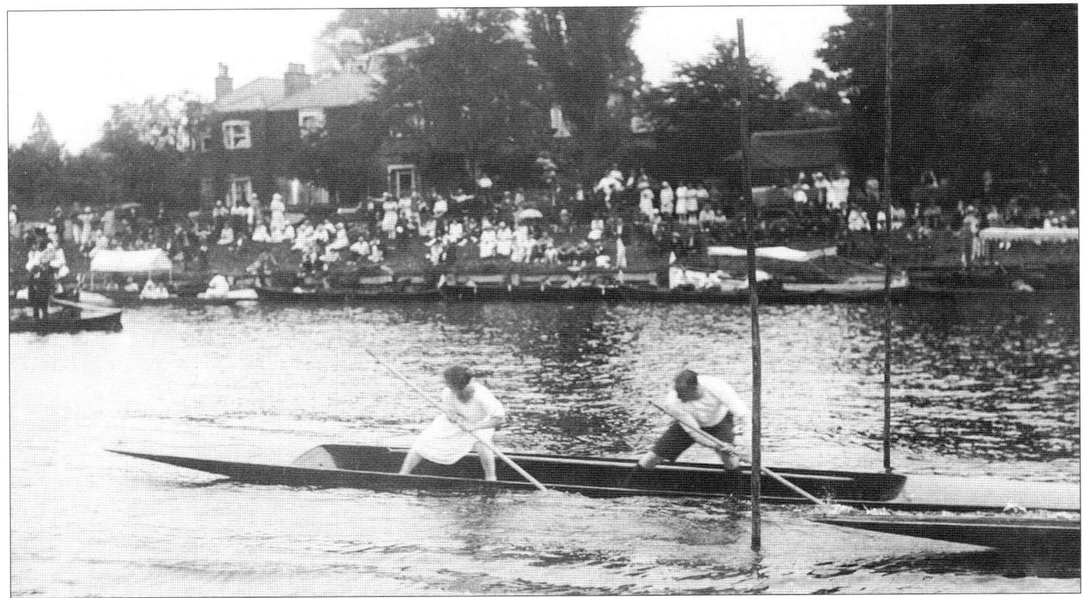

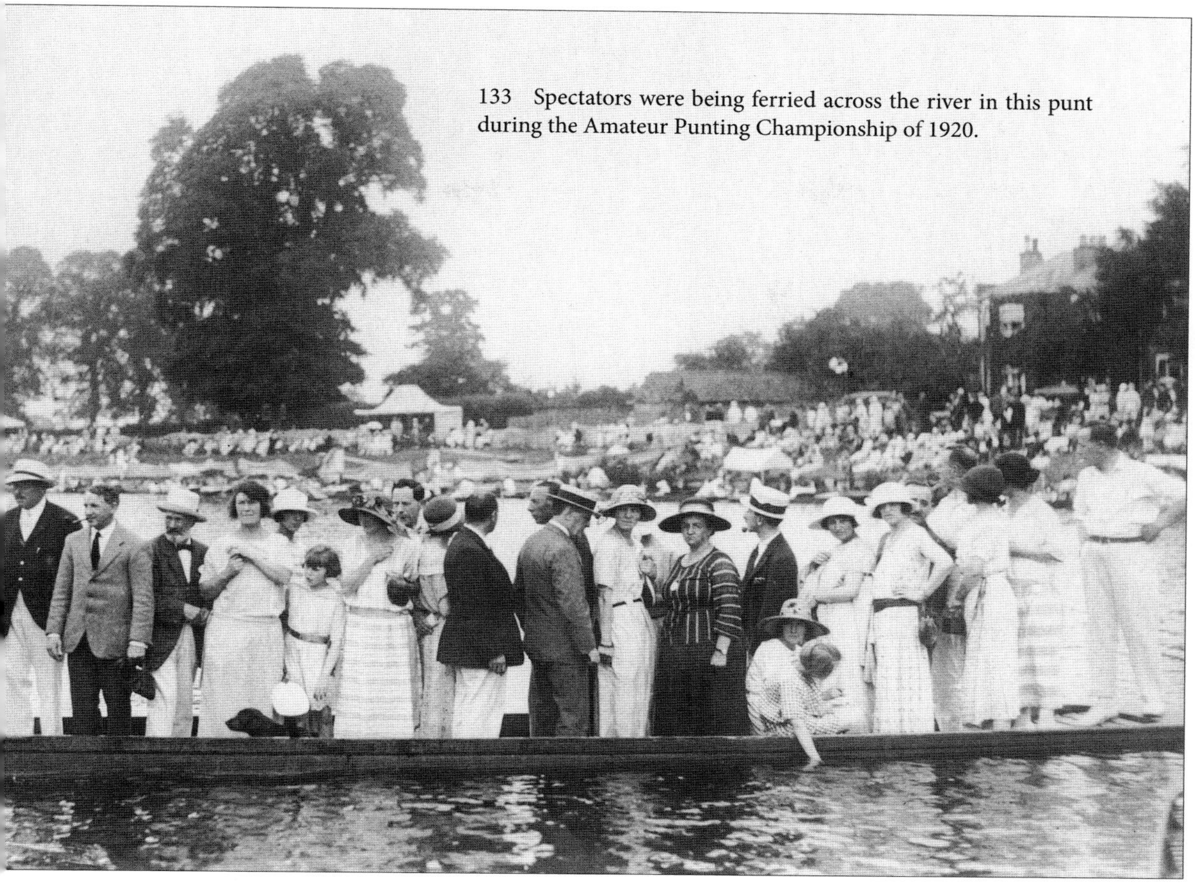

133 Spectators were being ferried across the river in this punt during the Amateur Punting Championship of 1920.

134 In the background of this riverside view is the church of St Nicholas at Shepperton. Signs at the water's edge are for G. Purdue, Boat builder, and for the *King's Head Hotel*, a centuries-old inn, said to have been visited by Charles II and Nell Gwynne. This postcard was postally used on 17 September 1909.

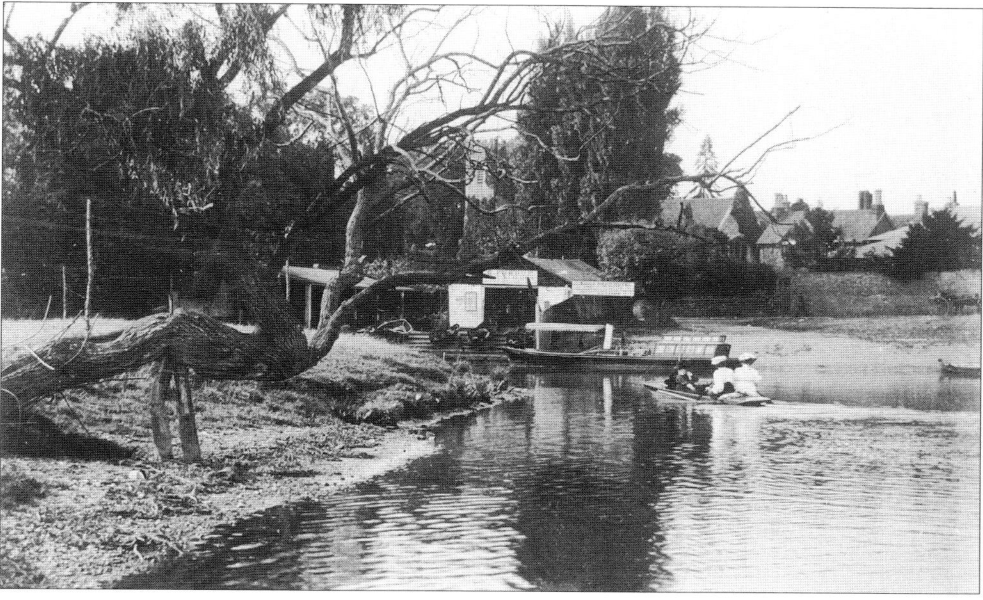

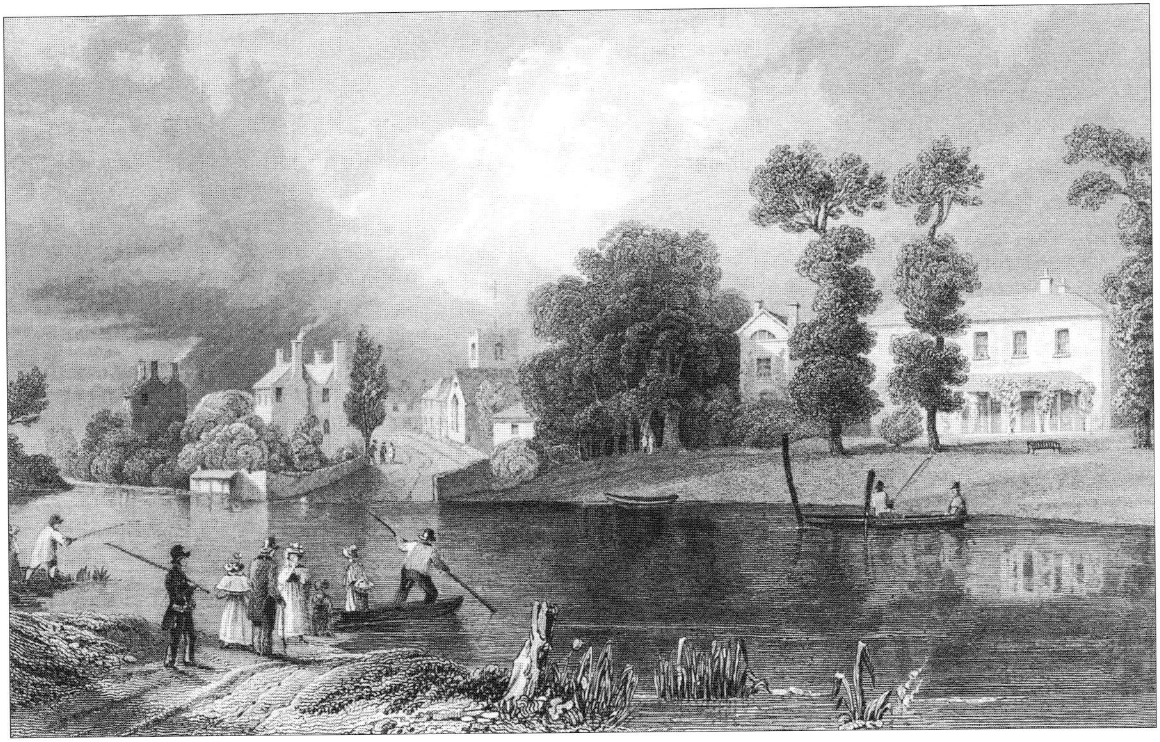

135 An engraving of Shepperton from *Tombleson's Thames*, dating from *c.*1834. W.G. Fearnside noted, 'we pass the village of Shepperton on the left, where, at the parsonage house, the learned Erasmus spent many of his earlier days with his preceptor, William Grocyn, the then incumbent'.

136 *Red Lion*, Lower Halliford, Shepperton. In *The Thames from the Towpath* (1938), E.K.W. Ryan described Lower Halliford, with its pretty cottages and houses shaded by giant elms, as 'one of the gems of the river'.

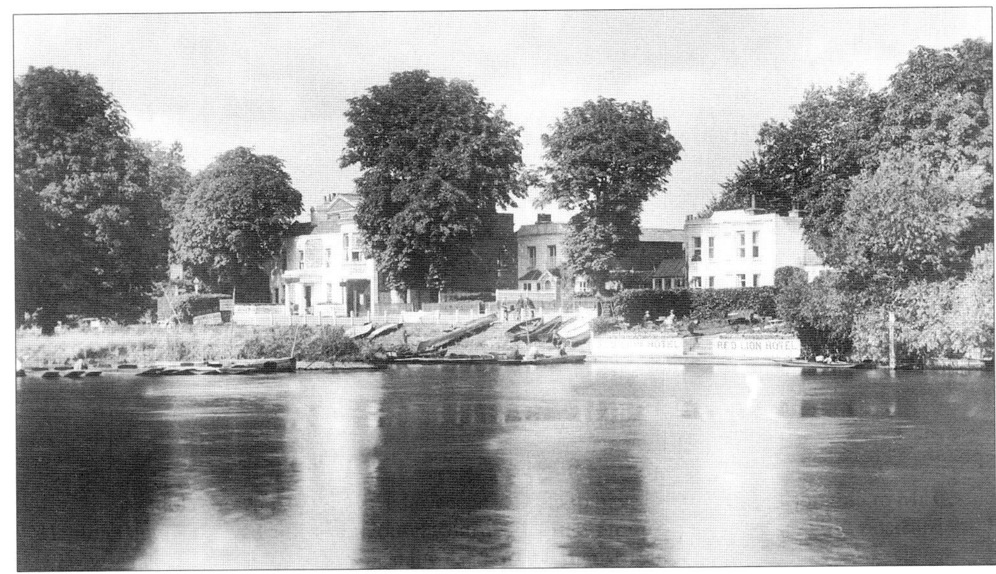

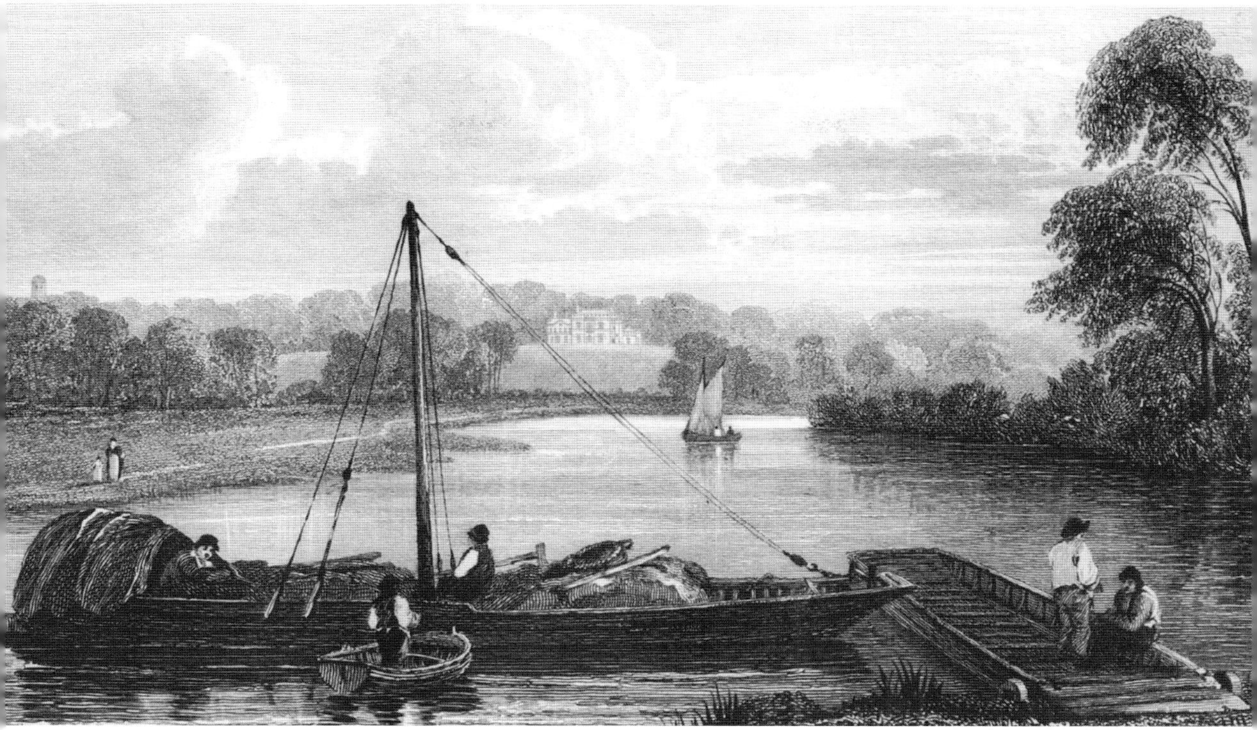

137 This illustration from *Views on the Thames*, drawn by S. Owen and engraved by W.B. Cooke, is entitled 'OATLANDS. Seat of H.R.H. The Duke of York'. It was published on 1 January 1817 by W.B. Cooke, 12 York Place, Pentonville.

138 An engraving of Walton Bridge from *Tombleson's Thames*, dating from *c*.1834. W.G. Fearnside stated, 'Walton Bridge, which was erected in 1787, is composed of four broad arches across the river, and seven over the land, to which are annexed 15 arches, continuing the main road over the meadows. The rustic village of Walton is prettily situated, a short distance from the river.'

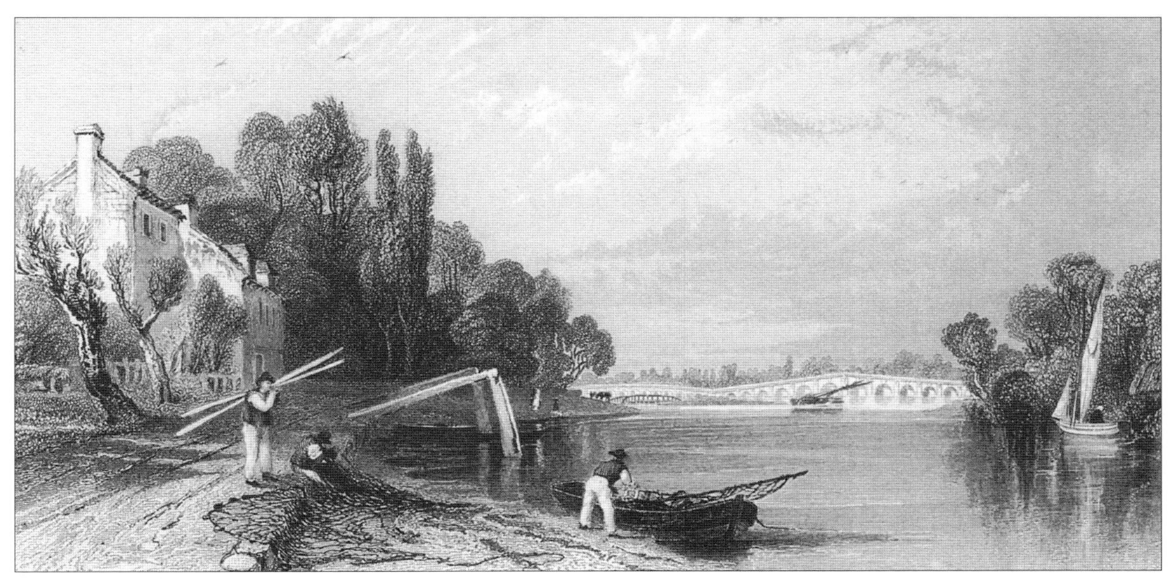

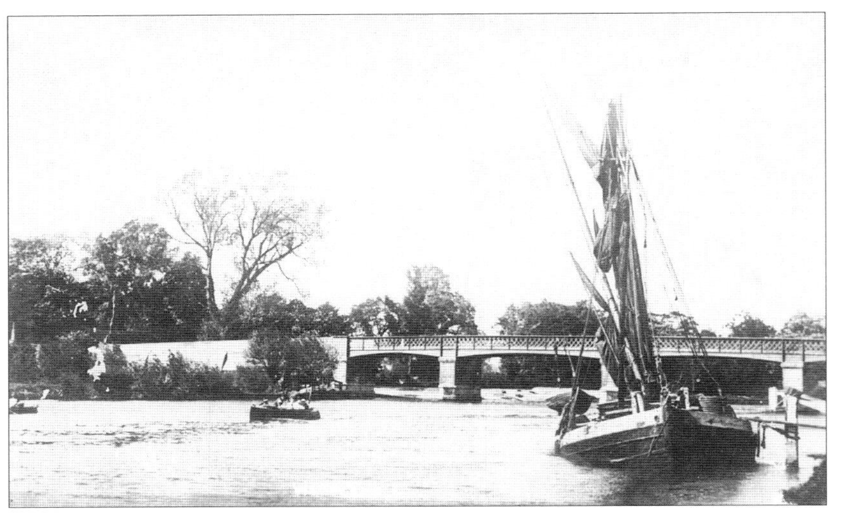

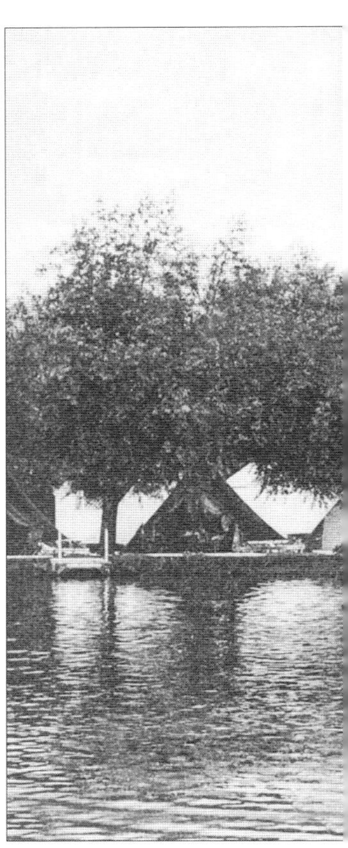

139 In 1859, two of the arches of Walton Bridge collapsed. The bridge was eventually replaced, in 1864, by the iron girder bridge, which is shown in this early 20th-century view. The 19th-century bridge was damaged during the Second World War and a temporary bridge has been in place since 1953. In recent years, the latter has been used by pedestrians and cyclists, while another temporary bridge, opened in 1999, is used by vehicles.

140 Church Street, Walton-on-Thames, in the early years of the 20th century. Vernon Burton, grocer, Adam Charles Bell, clothier, and F. Warren & Co., coal merchants, were among the tradespeople listed here in *Kelly's Directory of Surrey* for 1913.

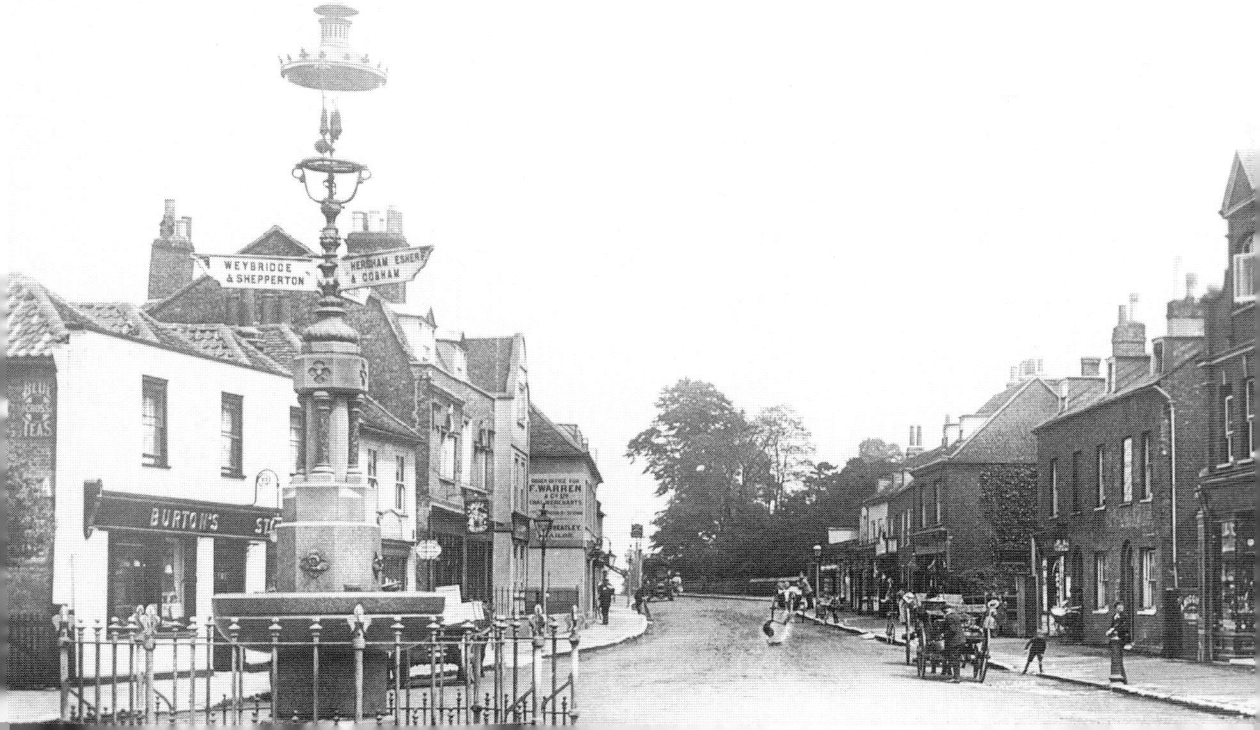

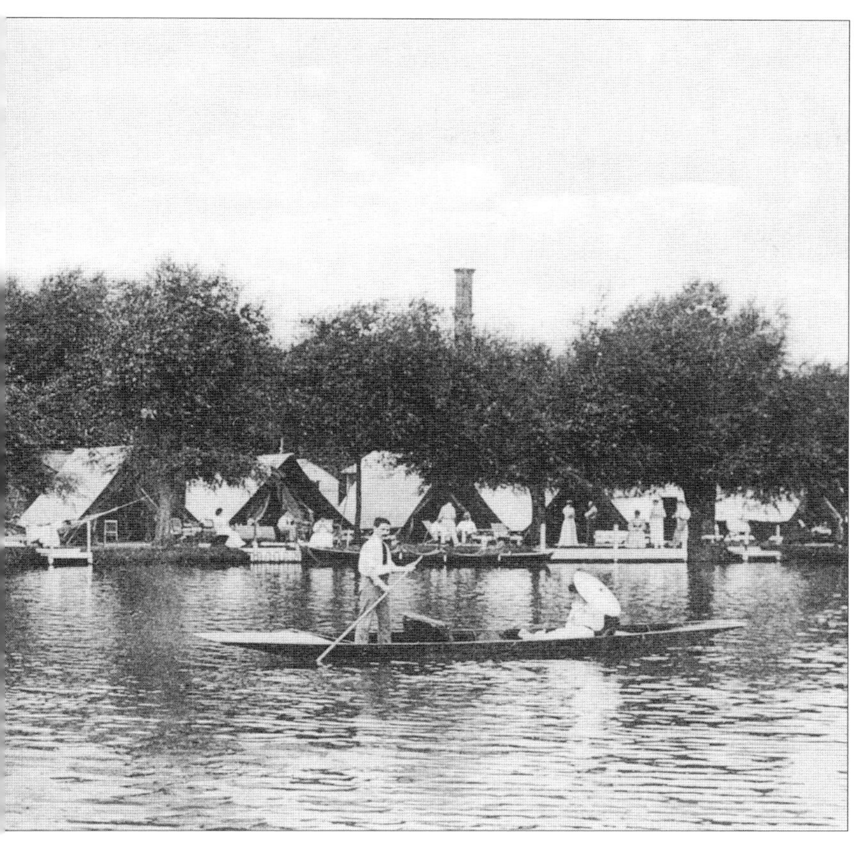

141 The Thames Camping and Boating Association camp site at Walton-on-Thames, *c.*1912. Writing nearly four decades later, Paul Gedge, in *Thames Journey*, mentioned that rows of little wooden huts and heavy tents of the 'explorer' type were at this site along Walton Reach. He noted that the names of some of these huts included 'WELKUM INN—PHALLINN—NO CUSS IN'.

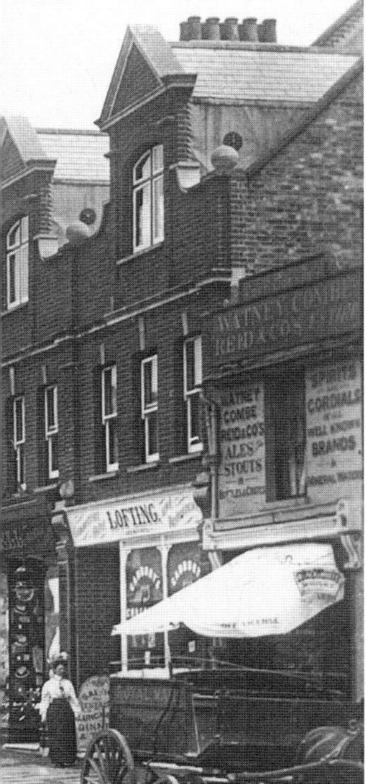

142 Sunbury Locks from *Tombleson's Thames*, *c.*1834. Fred S. Thacker, in *The Thames Highway Volume II: Locks and Weirs*, noted that a lock at Sunbury was first suggested in 1805, but it was not until 1809 that a modified scheme was proposed, which was eventually realised. He added that Sunbury Lock was 'ready for traffic on 6 February 1812'. By the 1850s, the lock was in a dilapidated condition and was rebuilt at the tail of the cut. It was reconstructed again in 1886 and a new lock was made in 1925 alongside the old one.

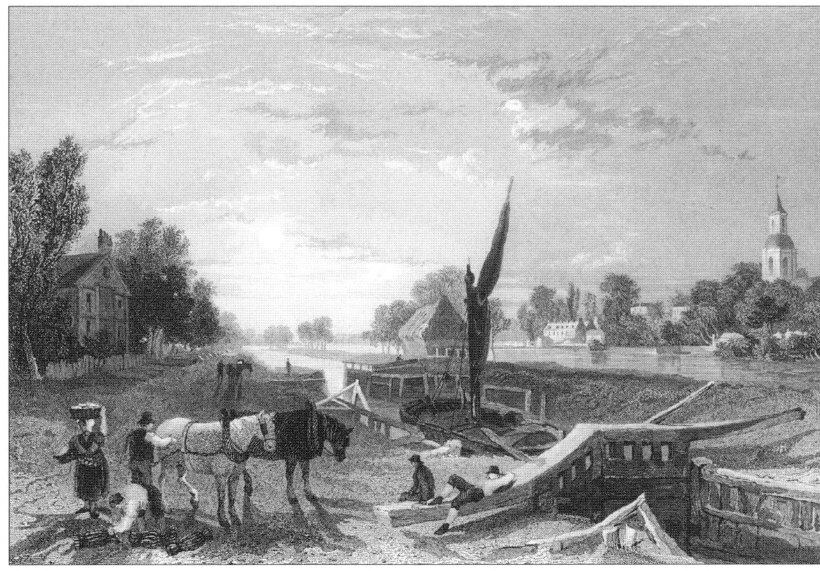

143 Peter H. Chaplin, in *The Thames from source to tideway*, noted that in 1866 Sunbury Lock was provided with boatslides to enable small boats to pass without the lock being opened. The lock and rollers at Sunbury are shown on this Edwardian postcard, which was postally used on 10 September 1906.

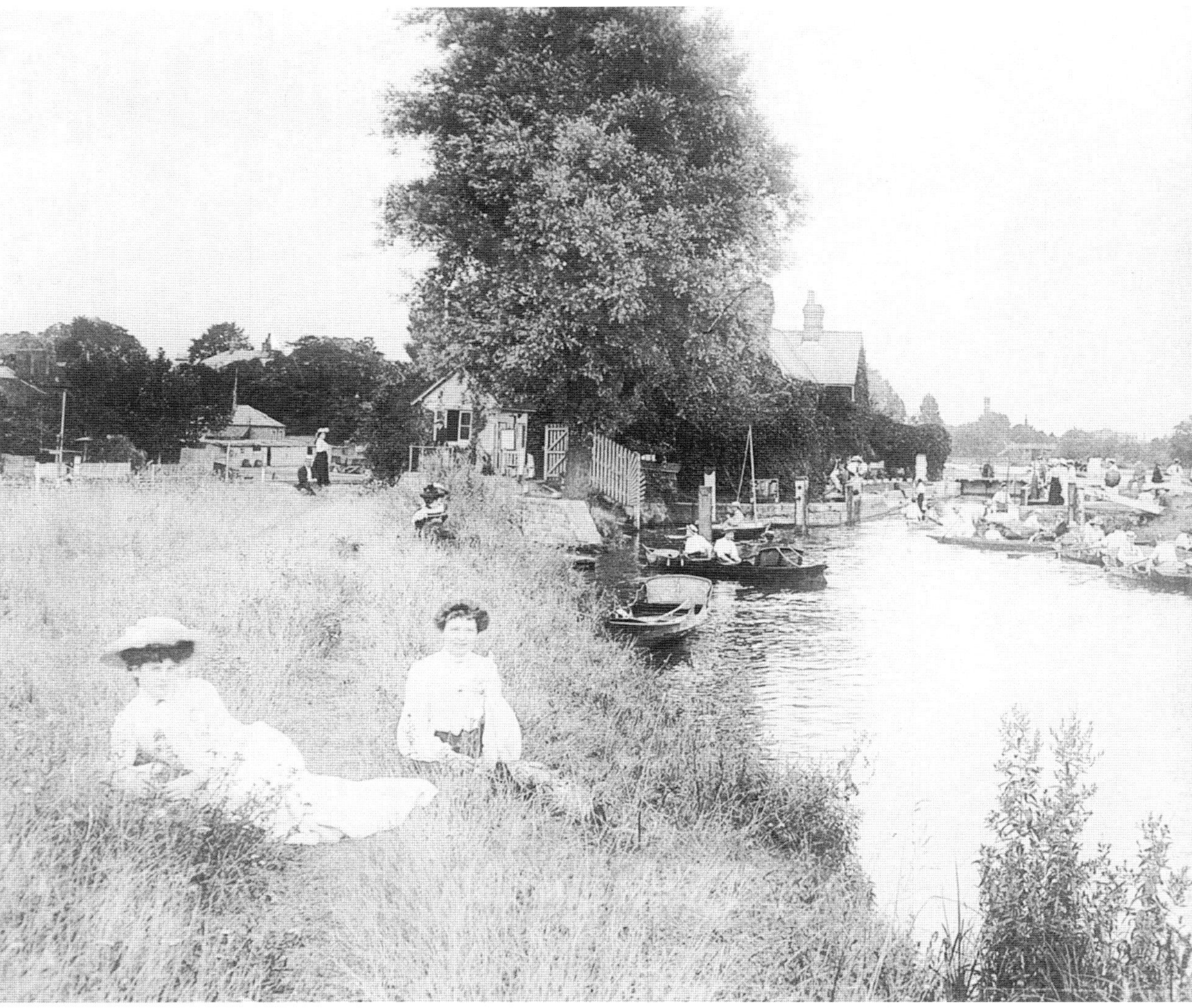

(Top right) 144 The ferry at Sunbury crossed the weir stream to the boathouse on the lock island.

(Centre right) 145 Erected in 1831, St Mary's Church at Hampton, which replaced an earlier building, is a landmark on the riverside. Peter H. Chaplin, in *The Thames from source to tideway*, observed that the materials for rebuilding the church were brought by barge.

(Bottom right) 146 An engraving of Garrick's Villa from *Tombleson's Thames*, *c.*1834. W.G. Fearnside described the scene, 'The river … laves with its limpid waters the lawn of Hampton-House, the delightful villa of the late David Garrick. On the verge of the Thames he erected a small but elegant temple, dedicated to Shakespeare and placed within it a statue of the "immortal bard" by Roubillac.'

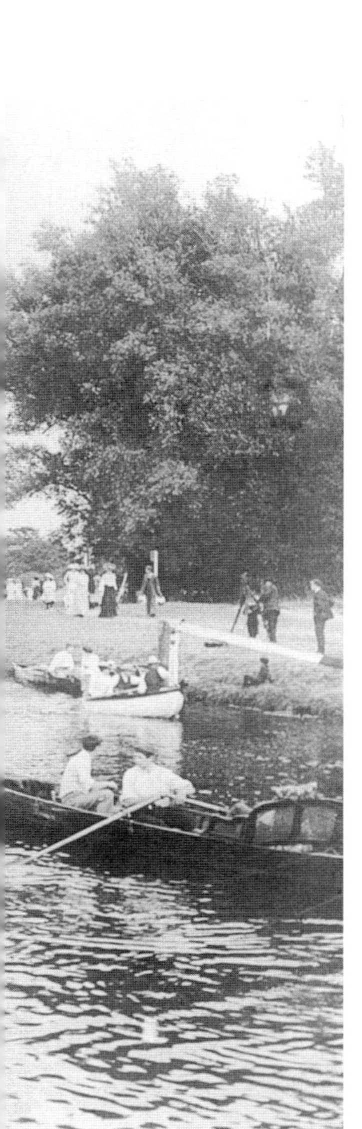

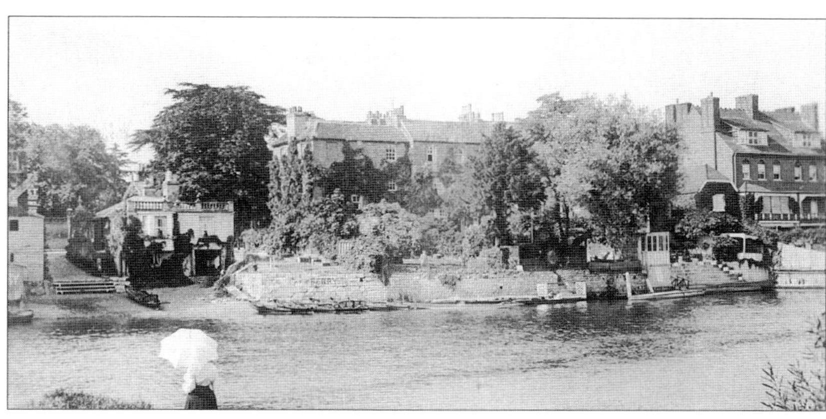

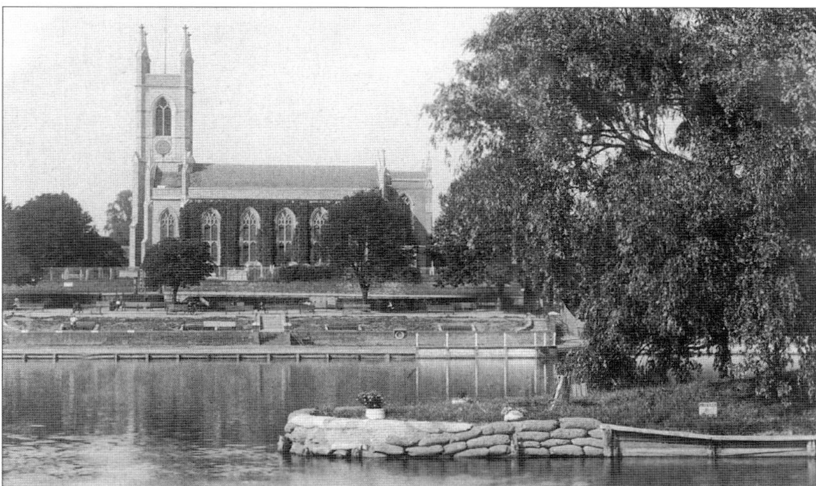

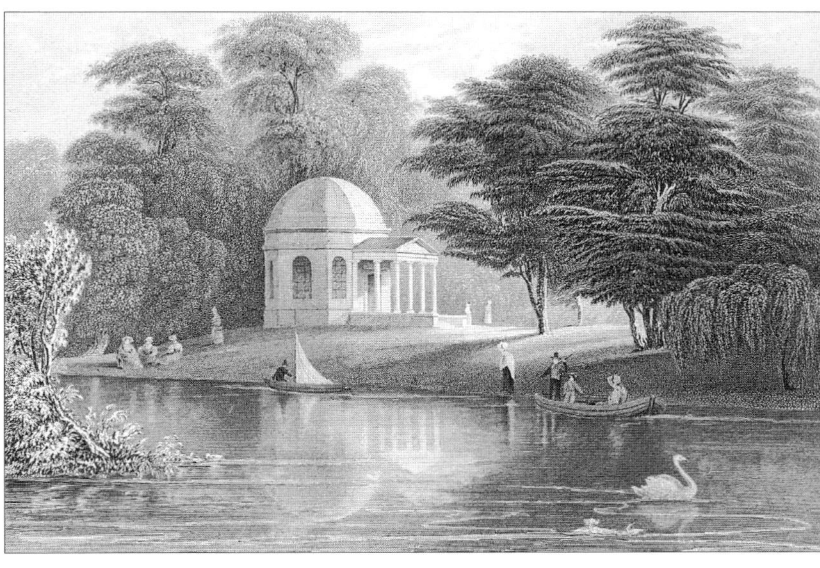

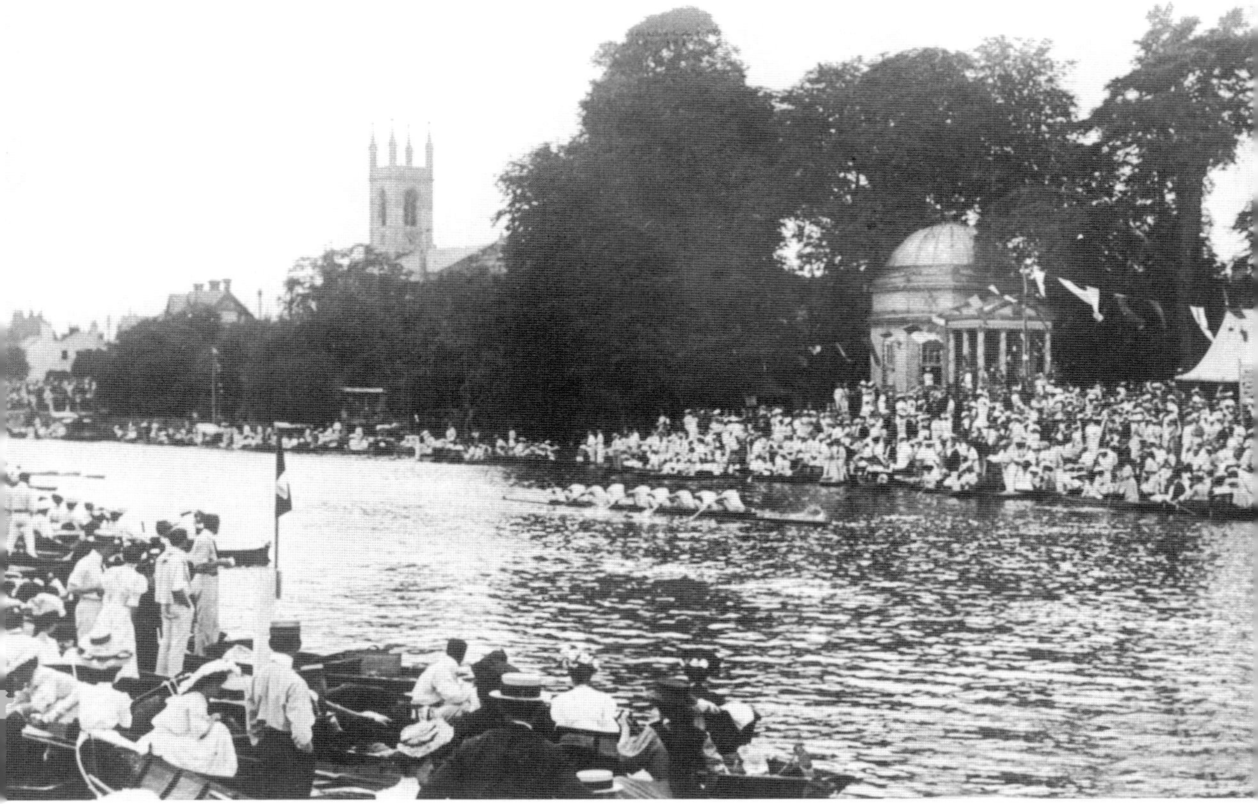

(Above) 147 Both sides of the river were crowded when this photograph of Molesey Regatta was taken in Edwardian times. In the mid-1930s, it was noted in Ward, Lock & Co.'s *The Thames* that Molesey Regatta was 'a first-class fixture and the most important up-river gathering after Henley'.

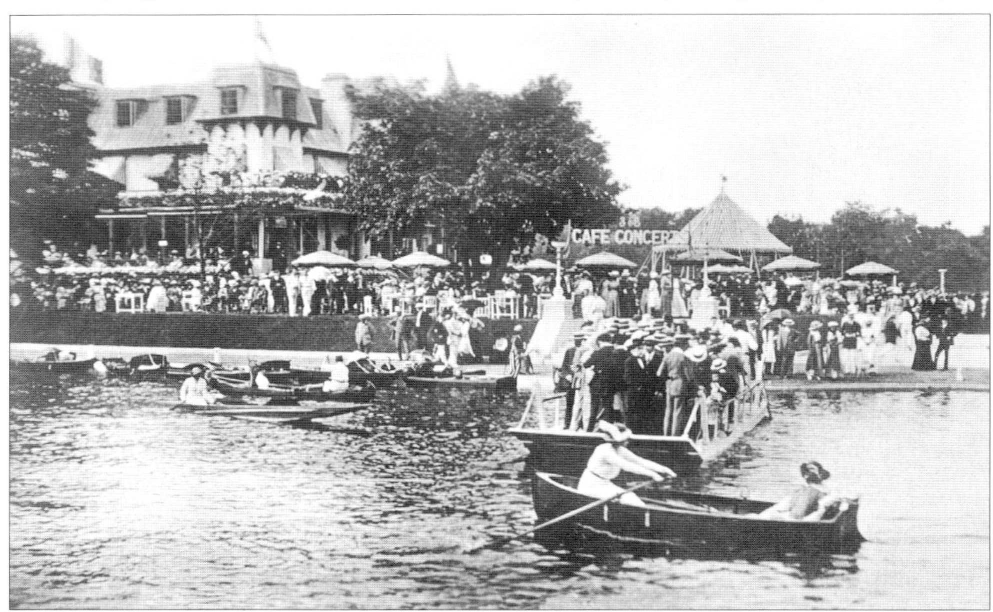

148 The *Karsino* on Tagg's Island at Hampton Court was a sumptuous hotel owned by Fred Karno. This postcard, showing the ferry used to reach the *Karsino*, was postally used on 19 July 1914. The message on the back of it reads, 'Lovely here today. The Scots Guards are playing on the Island ... Enjoying it immensely.'

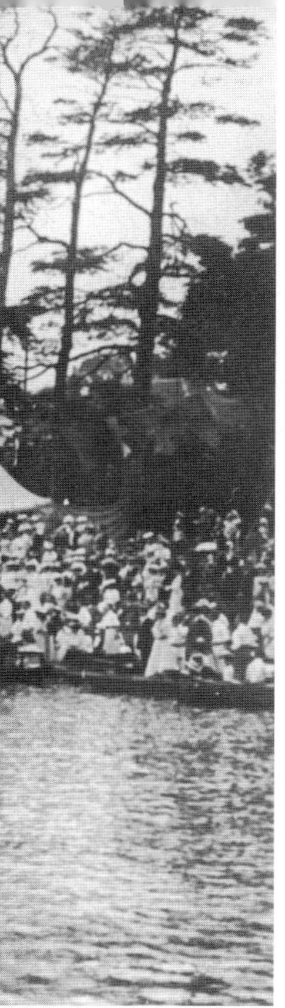

(Below) 149 Molesey Lock was opened for traffic in August 1815 and was rebuilt in 1906. This early 20th-century view of a busy time at the lock shows how popular boating was on this part of the river.

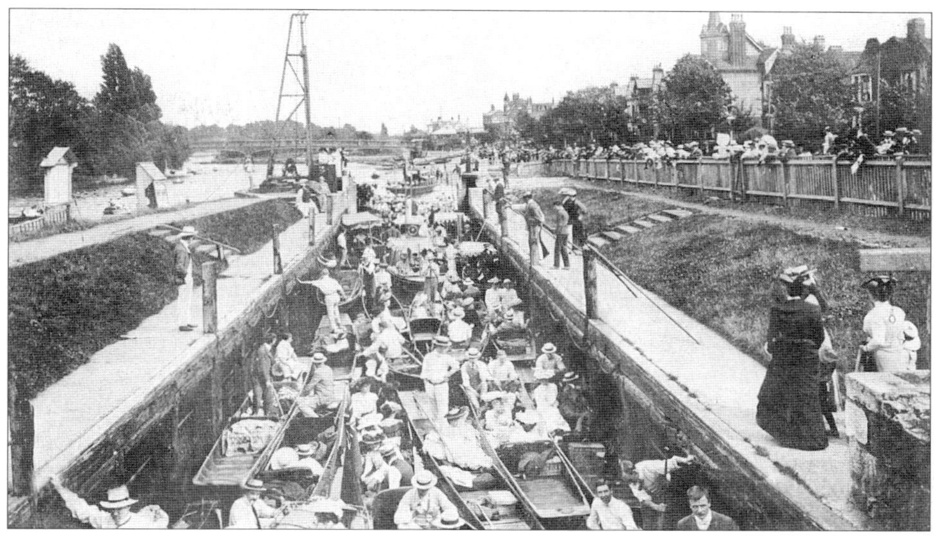

150 Hampton Court Bridge from *Tombleson's Thames*, *c.*1834. Describing the Thames downstream of Garrick's Villa at Hampton, W.G. Fearnside wrote, 'The channel of the river now becomes very confined, until it attains Hampton lock and weir, when the current rushes with considerable impetuosity through Moulsey, commonly called Hampton-Bridge.'

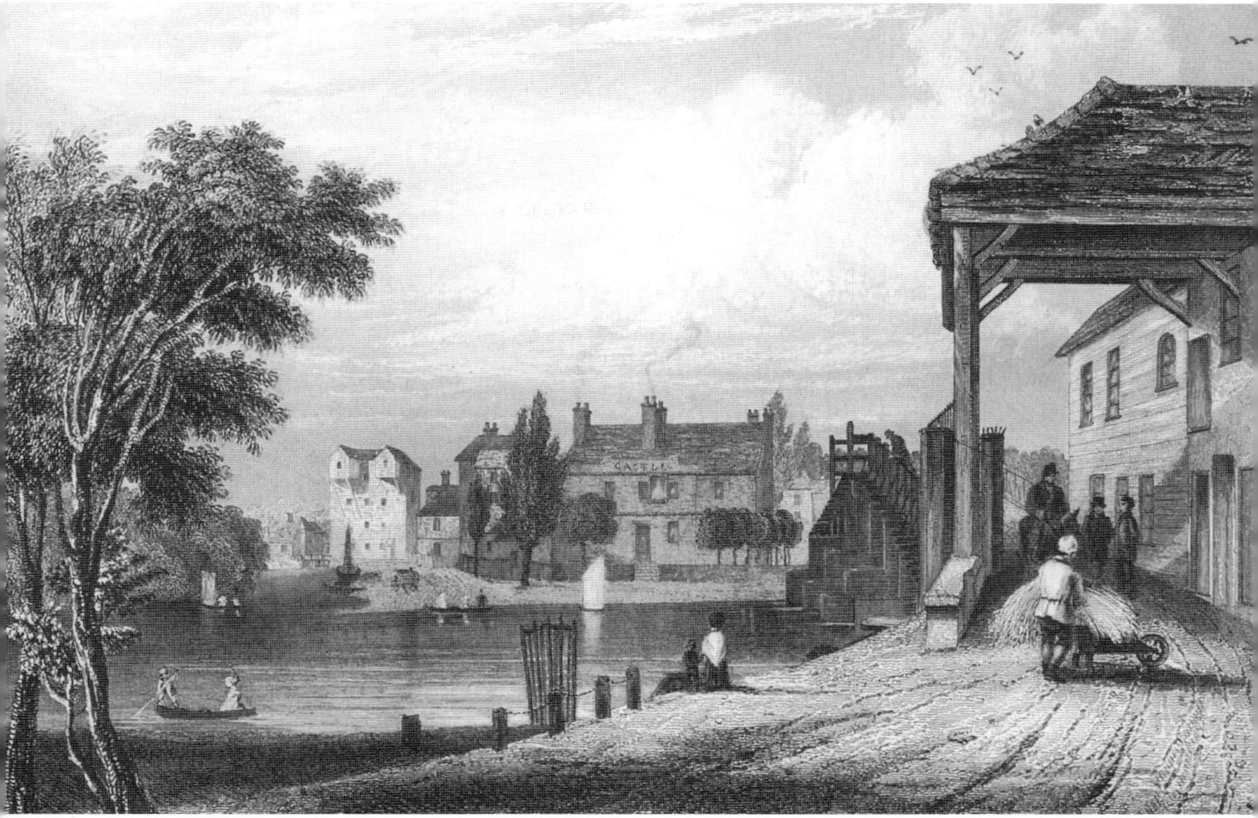

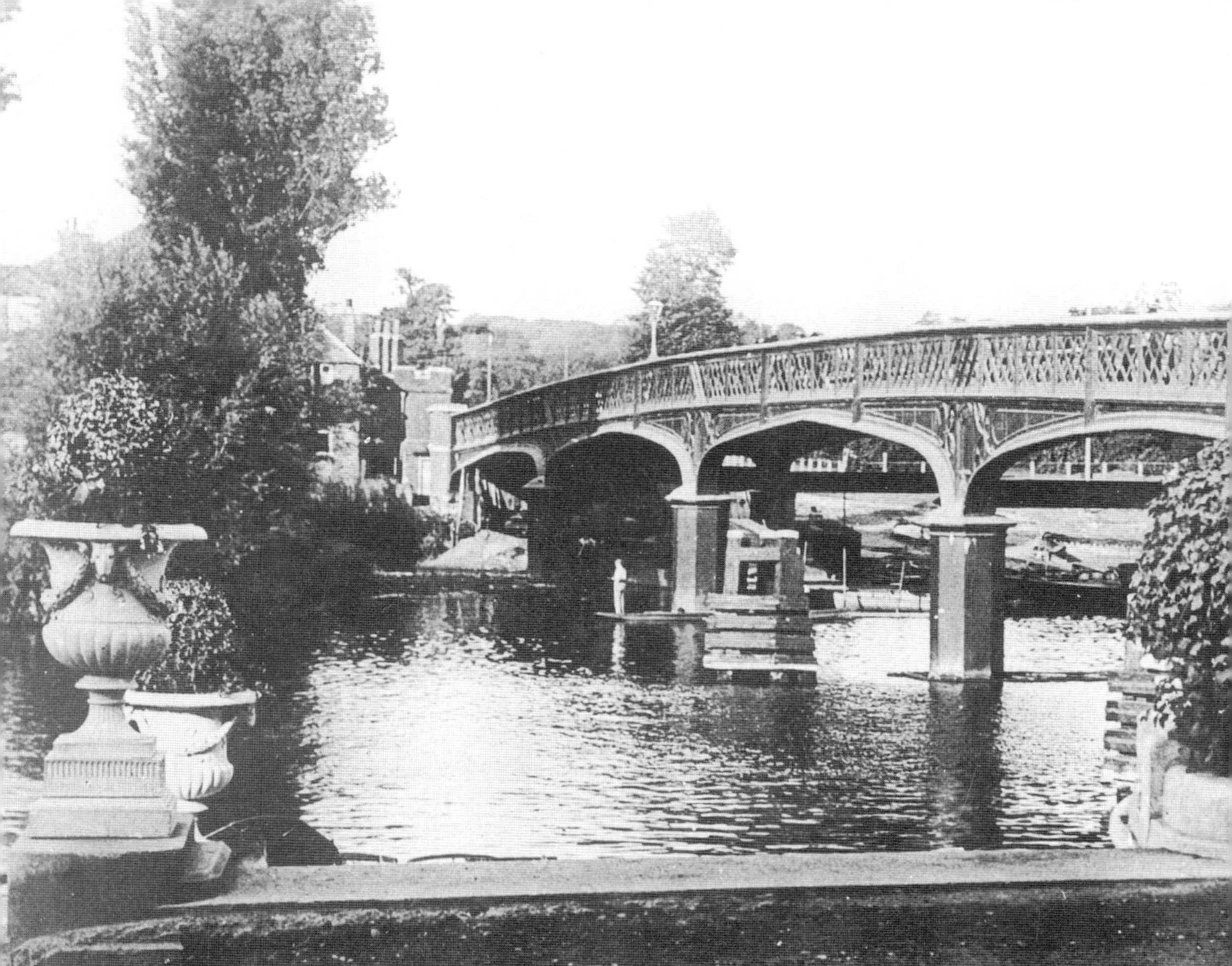

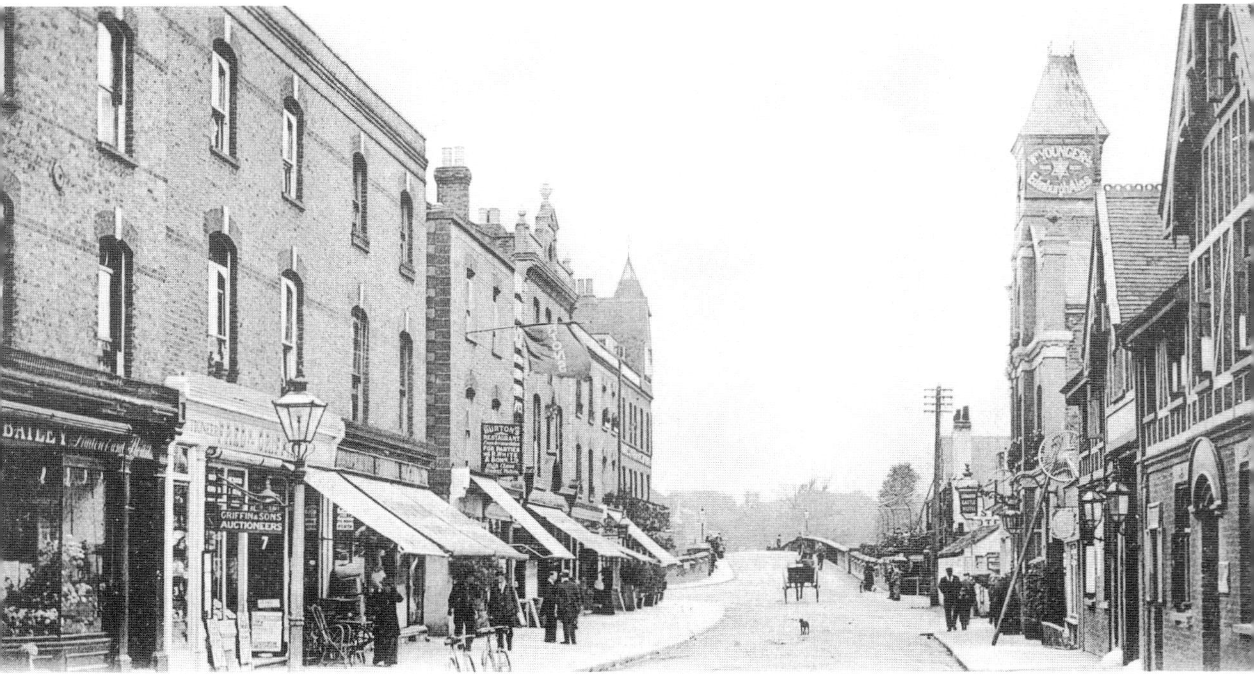

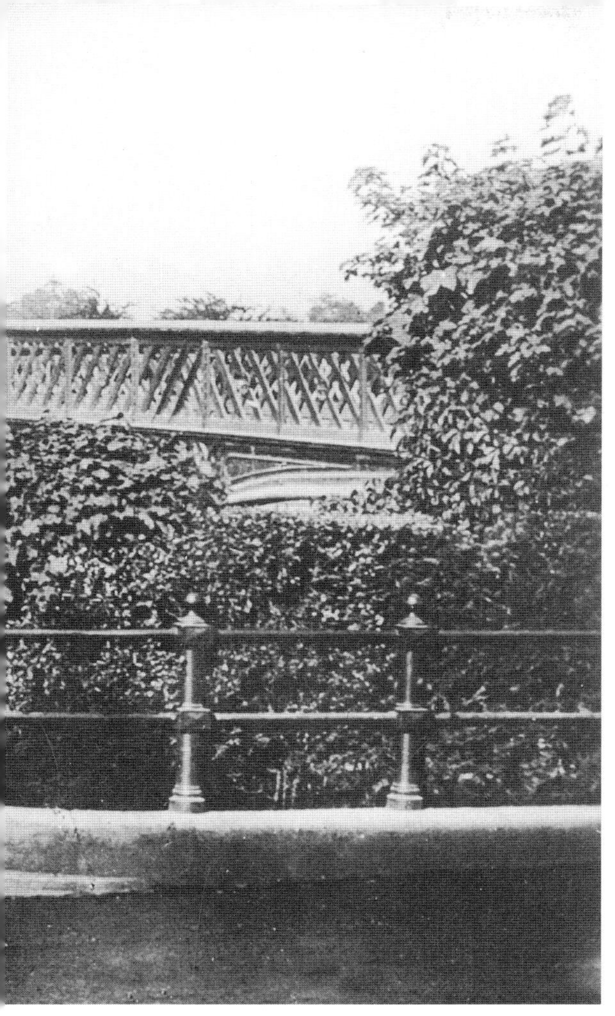

(Left) 151 The iron Hampton Court Bridge, which replaced the 18th-century wooden structure, was completed in 1865. It was replaced by the present bridge in 1933. This postcard of the iron bridge was postally used on 3 December 1910.

(Bottom left) 152 This view of Bridge Road, East Molesey, looks towards Hampton Court Bridge and was postally used on 13 February 1905. The *Castle Hotel* can be seen on the right.

(Bottom right) 153 This Edwardian postcard with the title 'Mixed Bathing at Hampton Court' dates from *c.*1908.

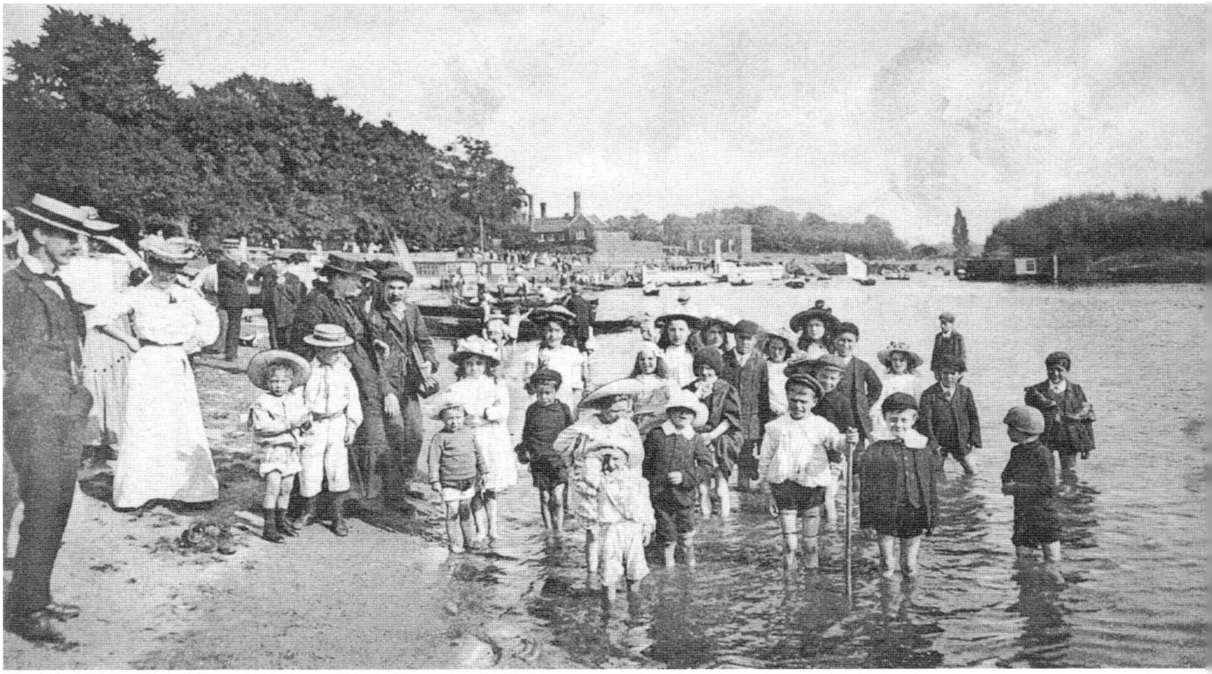

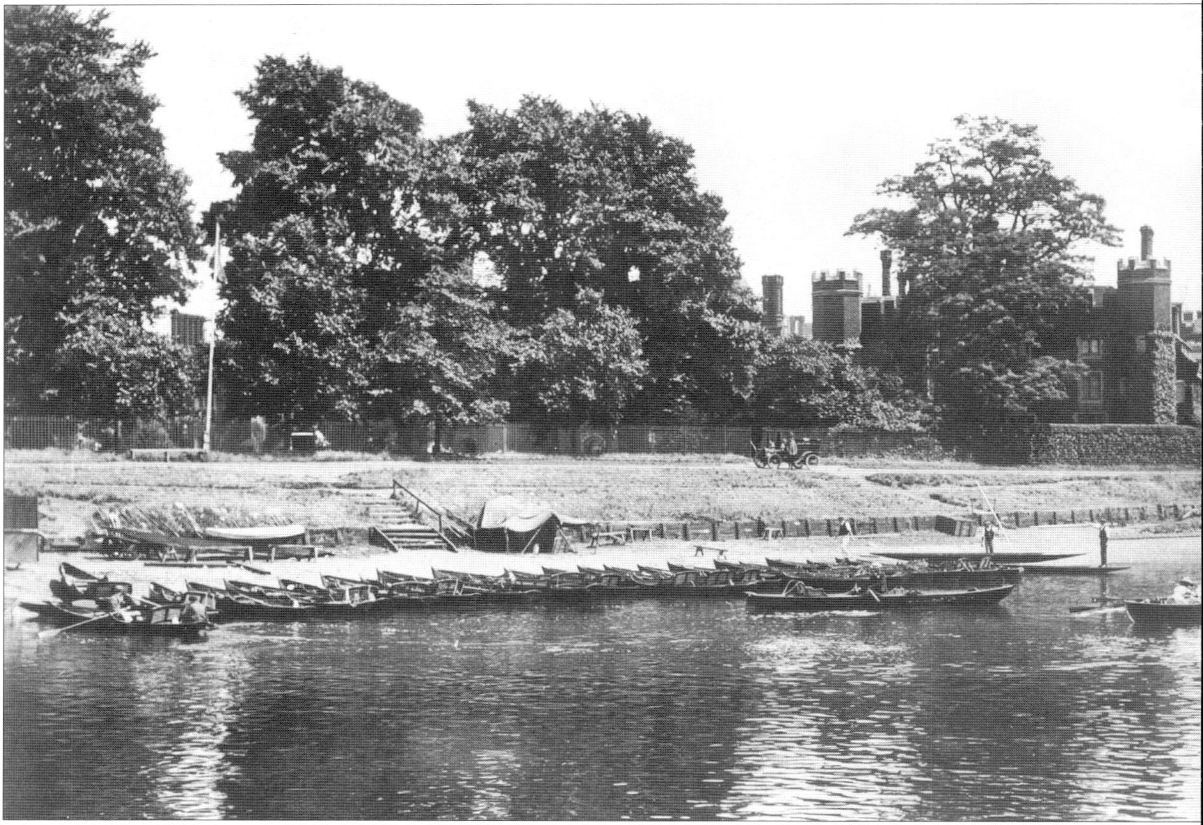

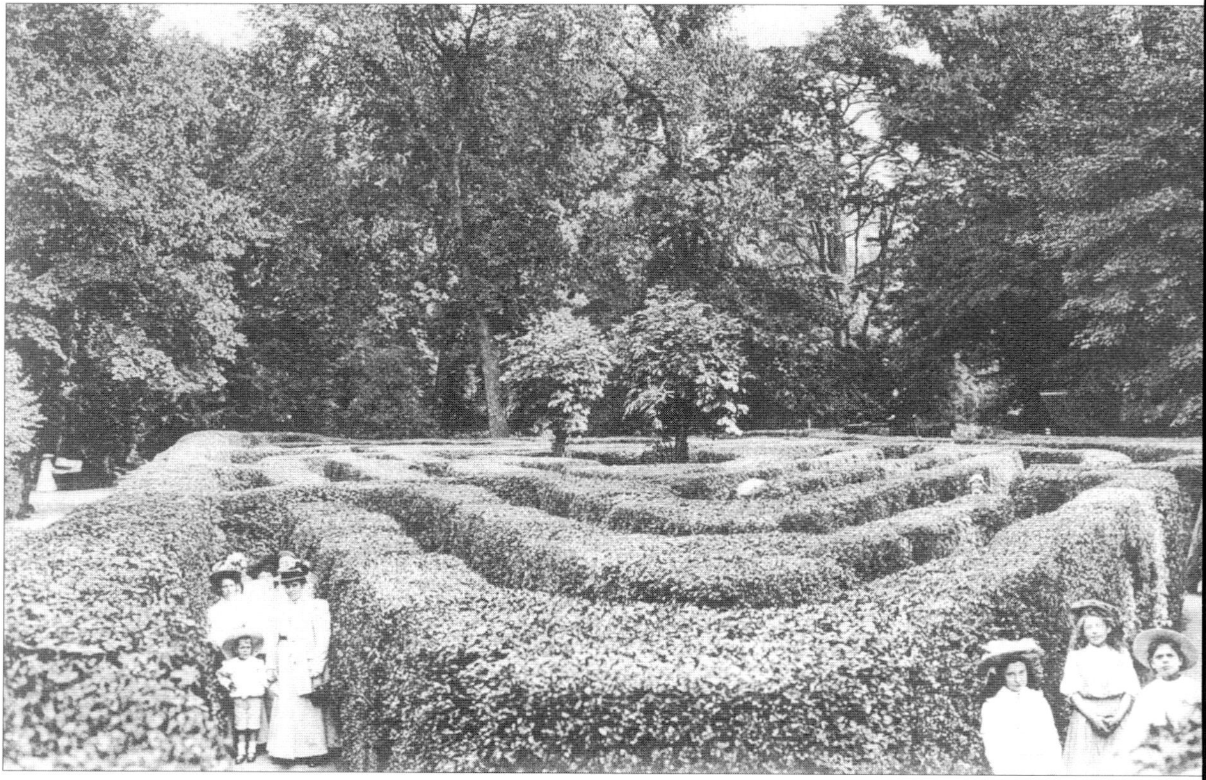

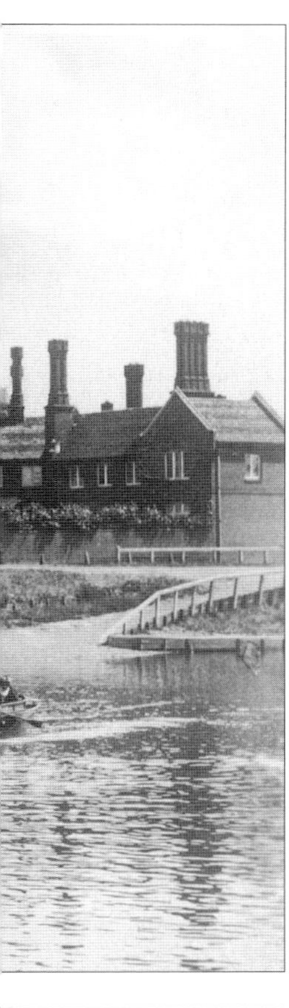

(Left) 154 A postcard of Hampton Court Palace from the Thames. In the late 19th-century and early 20th century, the State Apartments at Hampton Court Palace were open free to the public on every day except on Fridays and Christmas Day. Admission was 10.00 a.m. to 6.00 p.m. from 1 April to 30 September and from 10.00 a.m. to 4.00 p.m. for the rest of the year. The opening time on Sundays was 2.00 p.m. In summer the gardens were open daily until 8.00 p.m. and in other seasons until dusk.

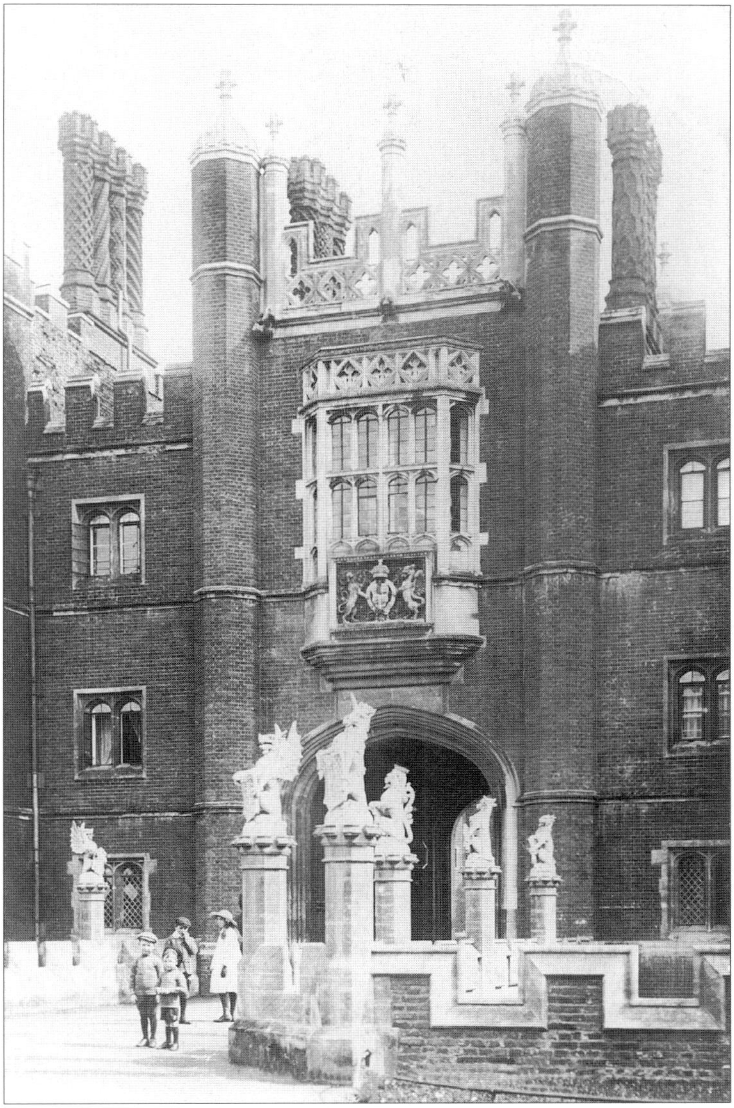

155 The Moat Bridge leads to the main entrance on the west front of Hampton Court Palace. The arms of Henry VIII are on the carved panel over the gateway.

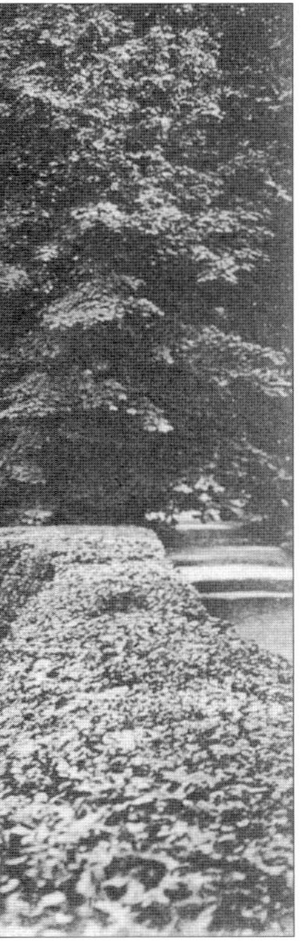

(Left) 156 The maze at Hampton Court Palace was made famous by Jerome K. Jerome in *Three Men in a Boat* in the memorable account of how Harris tried to guide people who were lost out of the maze and ended up becoming lost himself. This postcard of the maze was postally used on 5 October 1908.

Thames Ditton to Teddington Weir

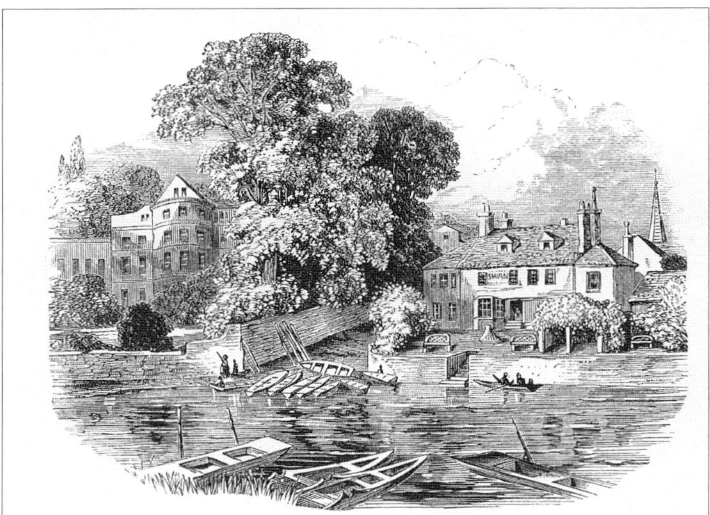

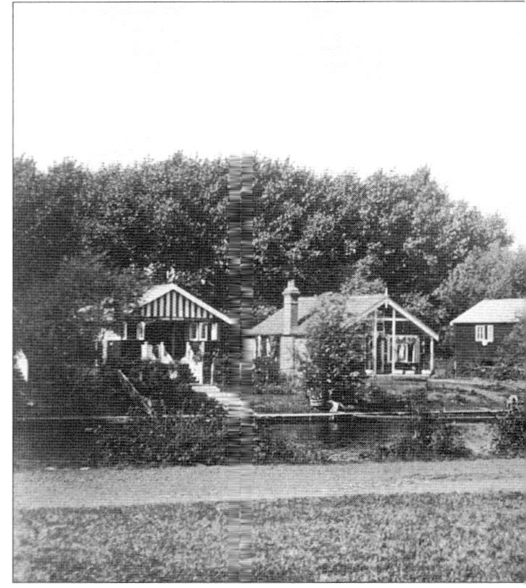

(Top left) 157 An illustration of the *Swan* at Thames Ditton from *The Book of the Thames* by Mr and Mrs S.C. Hall, who wrote, 'Our print exhibits the long-famous inn "THE SWAN;" and the stately mansion — "Boyle Farm" — the residence of Lord St Leonards. "The Swan" is, as we have said, "famous", but only in the records of the angler. Time out of mind, Thames Ditton has been in favour with the punt-fisher'.

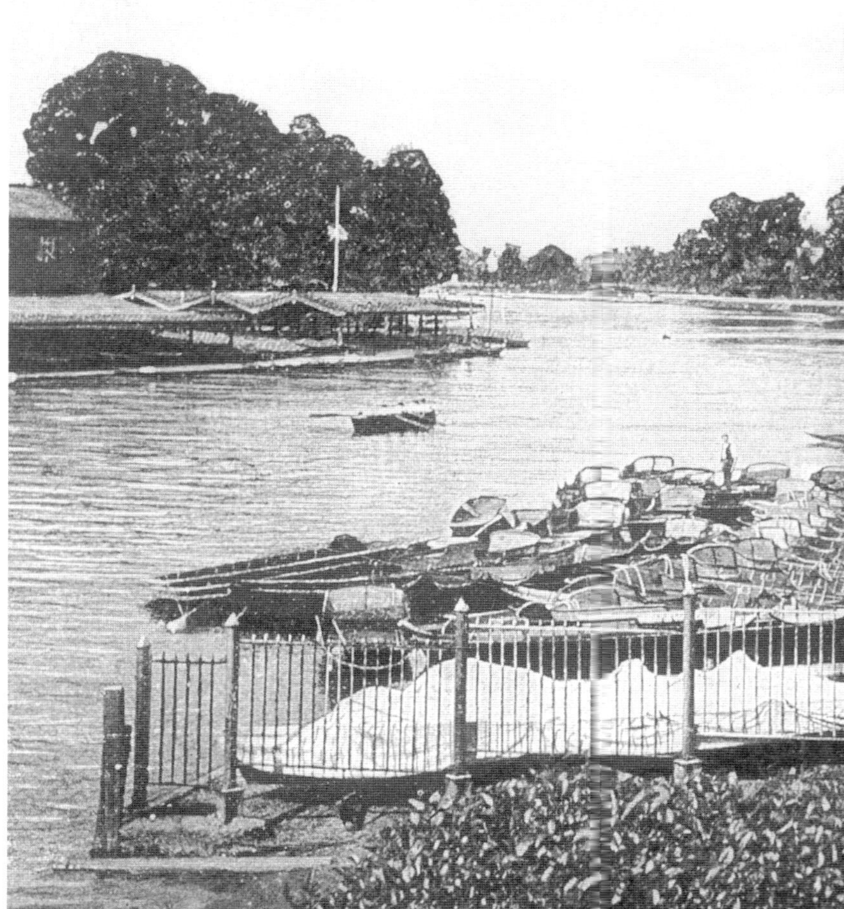

(Centre top) 158 In the early 20th century, the fascination of weekend riverside living in wooden chalets had spread along some parts of the Thames. This postcard view is of the 'The Bungalows' at Thames Ditton.

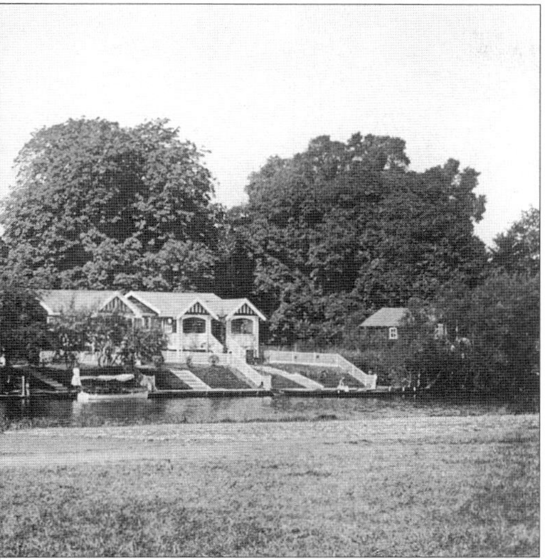

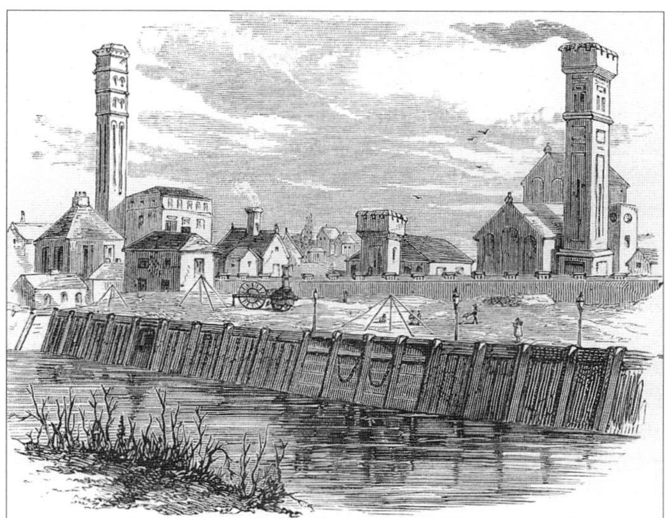

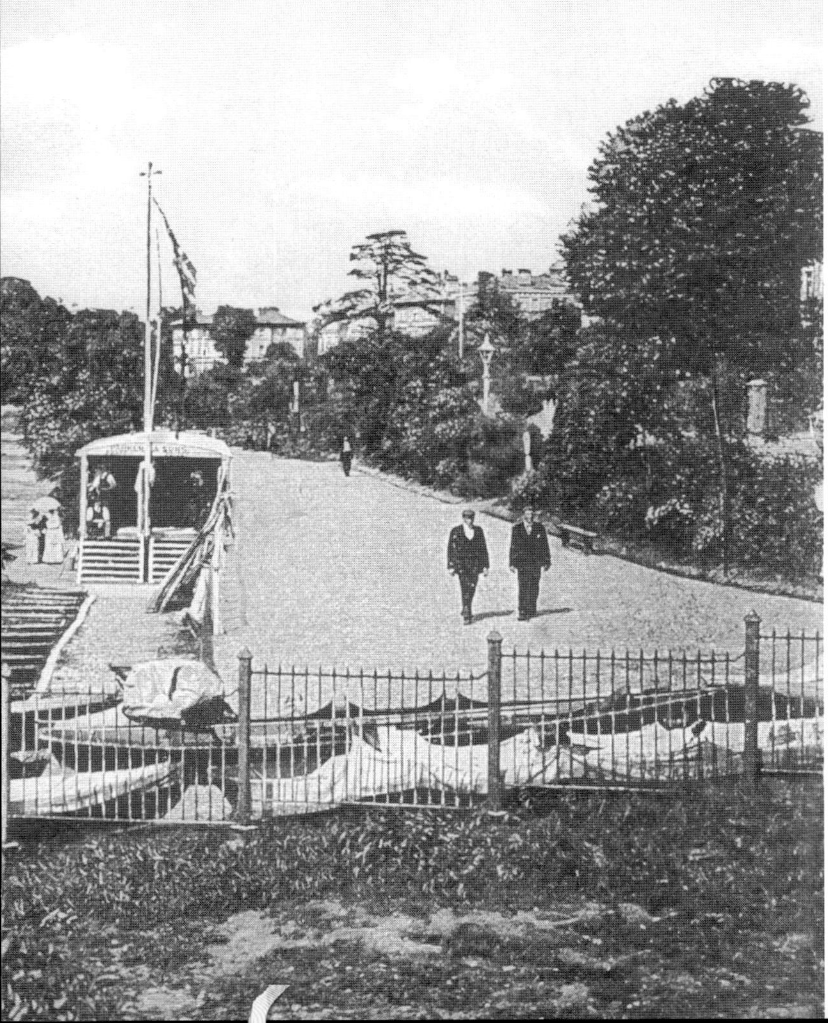

(Top right) 159 This illustration, entitled 'Water-works: Seething Wells', appeared in *The Book of the Thames* by Mr and Mrs S.C. Hall, who noted:

> As we approach Kingston, we pass the new buildings of the company which supplies the Surrey side of London with water. The edifices themselves are by no means picturesque; nevertheless, as objects that cannot fail to attract the eye of all voyagers, we have thought it well to engrave them. The locality in which they are placed is called 'SEETHING WELLS;' and they are the 'Chelsea and Lambeth Water-works'.

(Left) 160 In the early 20th century, small boats were hired out by Parker & Sons at Surbiton.

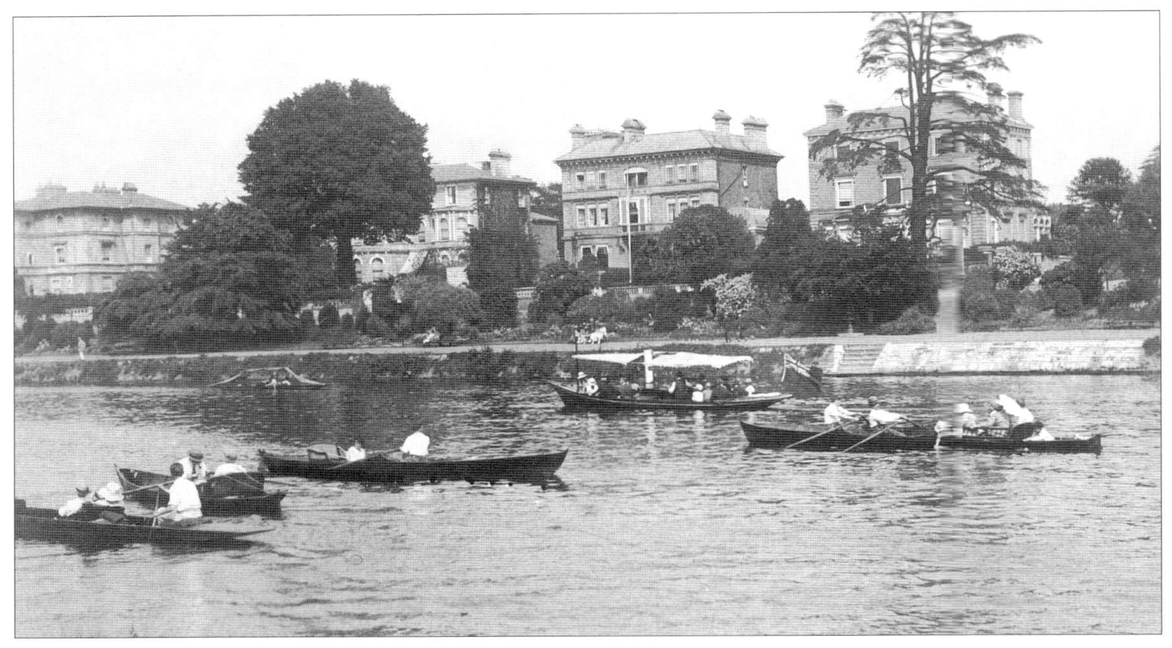

161 Plenty of riverside activity is going on in rowing boats, a small passenger steamer and a camping skiff in this postcard view of the river and promenade at Surbiton, which was postally used on 29 January 1925.

162 St Raphael's Roman Catholic Church, designed by architect Charles Parker and completed in 1848, is a distinctive feature of the riverside in this early 20th-century view of Surbiton's tree-shaded promenade.

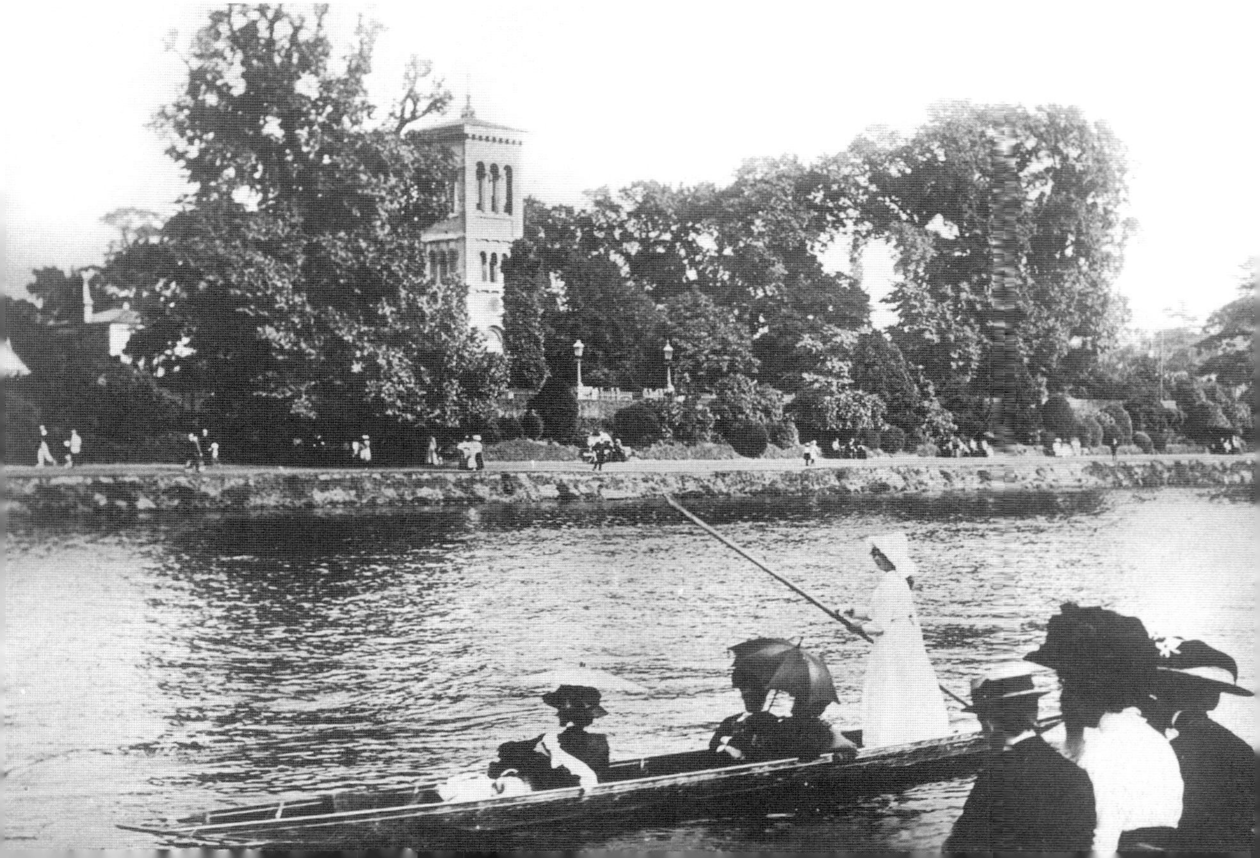

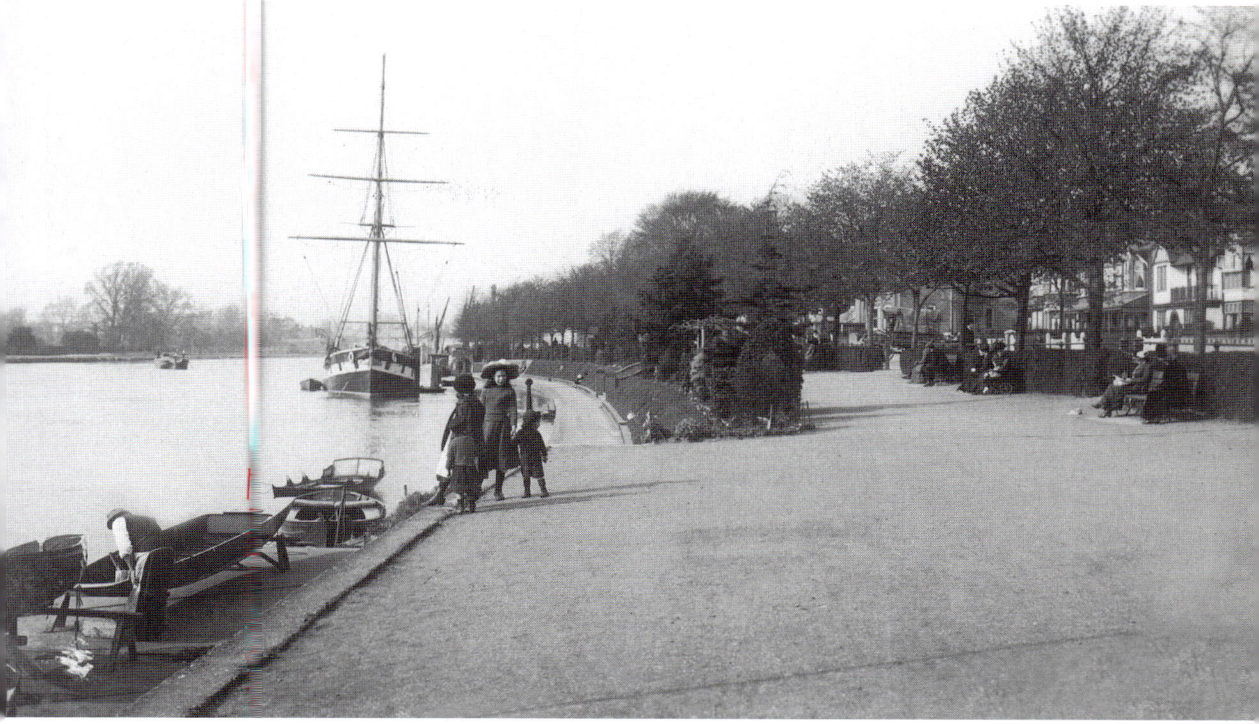

163 Queen's Promenade in Surbiton was created in the reign of Queen Victoria and takes its name from her. The gardens here were opened in 1856. In the early 20th century, a training brig was moored off the lower end of the promenade.

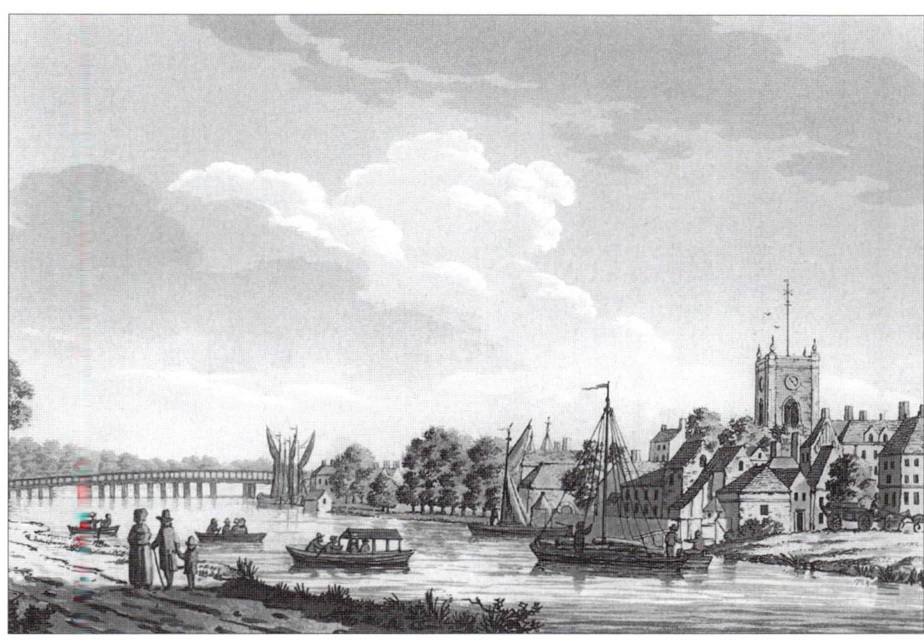

164 An aquatint of Kingston Bridge from Samuel Ireland's *Picturesque Views on the River Thames*. The author stated, 'The old wooden bridge of Kingston consists of twenty arches; it was originally supported by a toll, but in 1567 was endowed with lands amounting to forty pounds per annum, for the repairs, &c. from which time the toll has been taken off.'

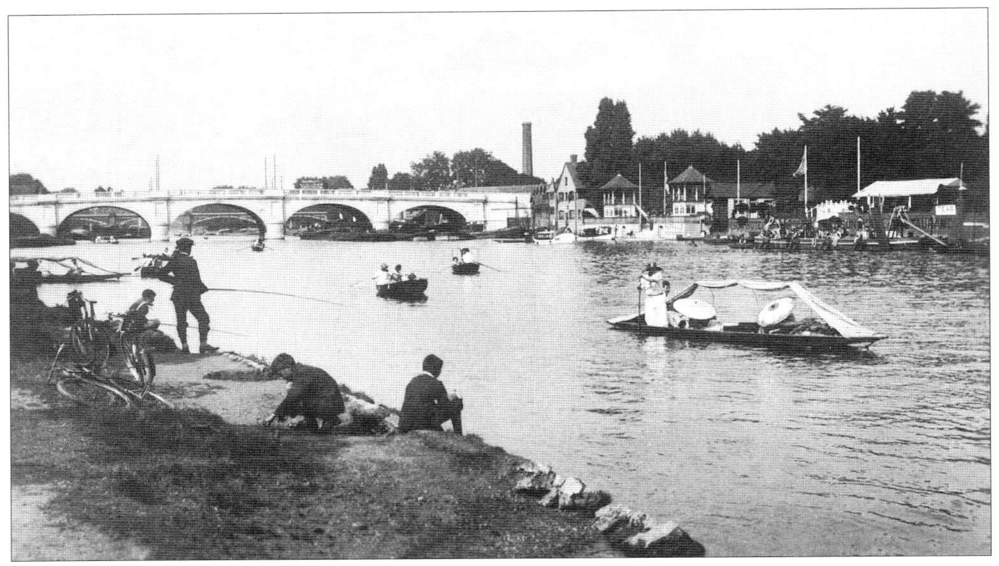

165 This postcard view, which was postally used on 6 November 1925, looks downstream to Kingston Bridge and the railway bridge beyond it. Nuthall's Restaurant, with its gardens, river terrace and landing stage, is on the right of the picture.

166 The Town Hall on the north side of the Market Place at Kingston upon Thames was constructed in brick with stone dressings between 1838 and 1840. The statue at the front of the building is of Queen Anne. To the left of this view, on a granite pedestal, is the Shrubsole memorial, forming a drinking fountain. This was erected to commemorate Henry Shrubsole, the figure of a woman with a child having been carved out of a solid block of marble. This postcard of the Market Square was postally used on 7 October 1925.

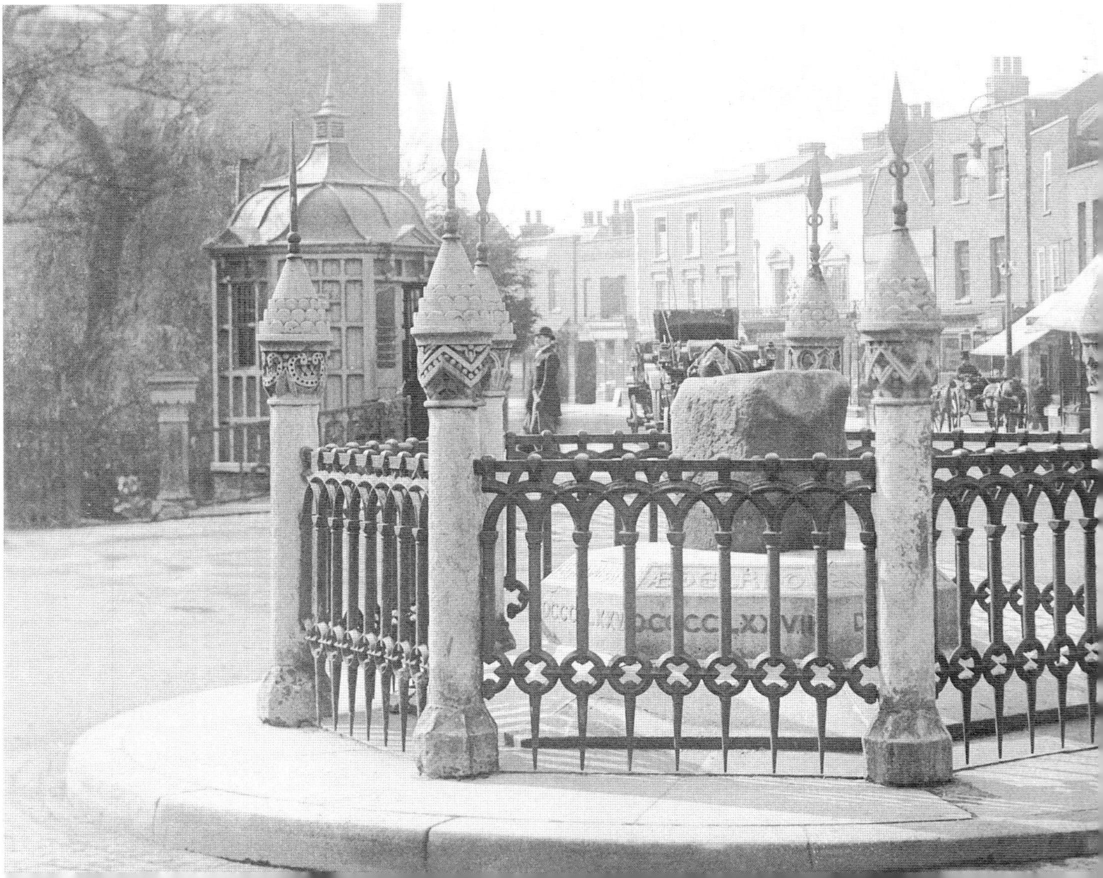

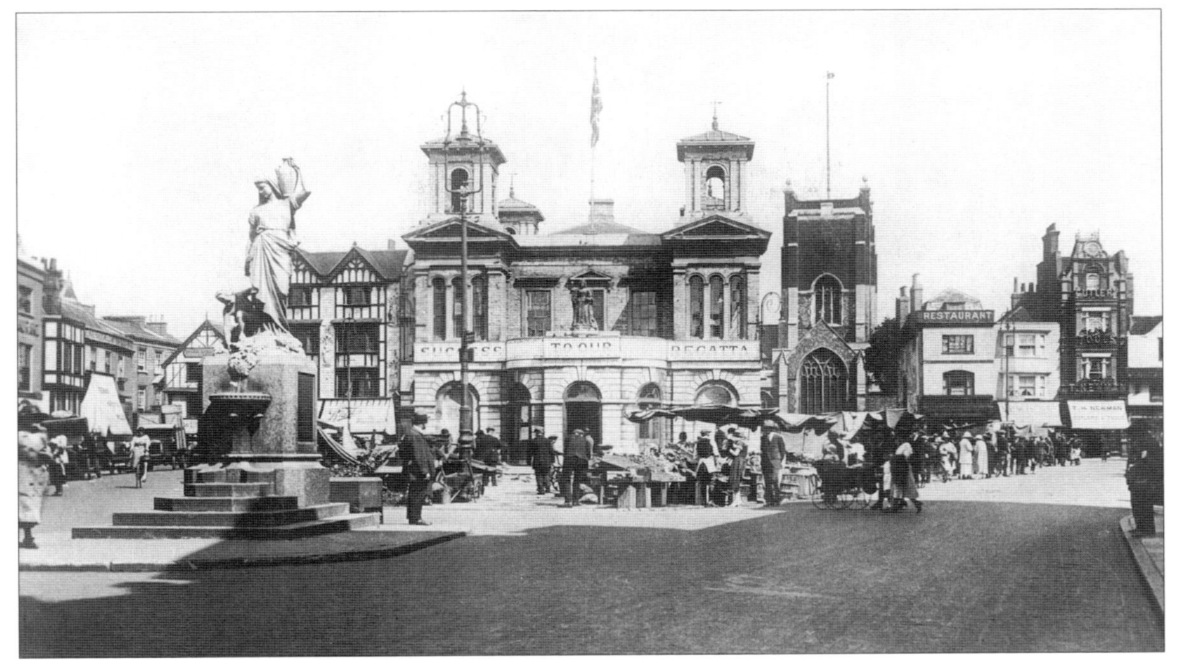

167 The Coronation Stone at Kingston upon Thames is said to have been used at the coronation of seven Saxon kings in the 10th century. Placed on a distinctive base, which had the names of the seven kings written on it, and encircled with decorative railings, the Coronation Stone used to be on the south of the Market Place. This postcard, postally used on 4 March 1910, shows it in this position. Now, the Coronation Stone is situated to the right of the Guildhall in High Street.

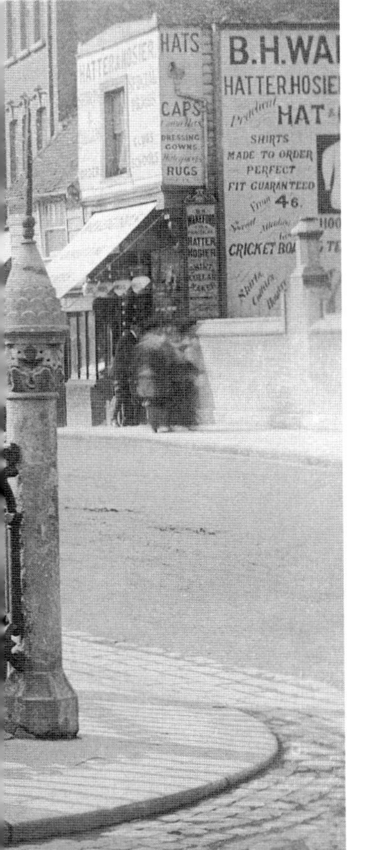

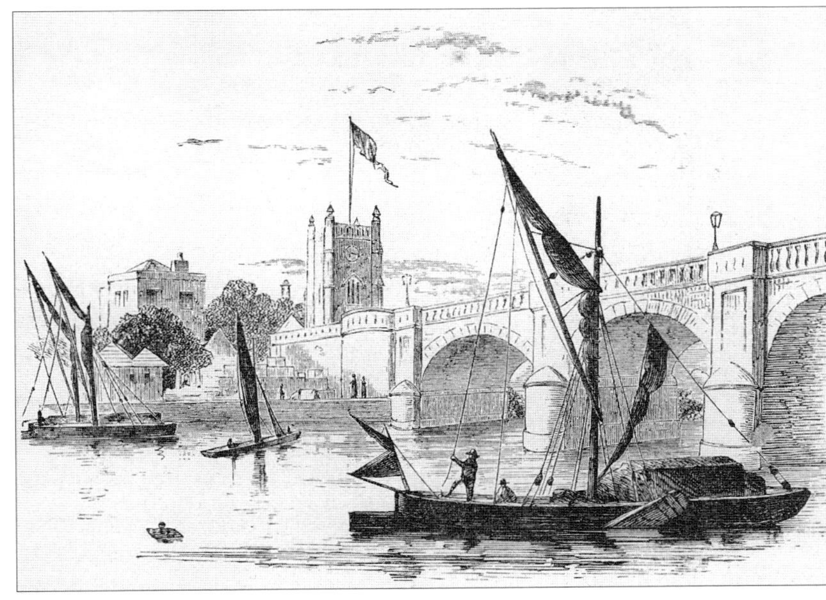

168 Kingston Bridge from *The Book of the Thames* by Mr and Mrs S.C. Hall. Designed by Edward Lapidge, this stone bridge replaced the earlier timber bridge in 1828. The new bridge was opened by the Duchess of Clarence who later, as wife of William IV, became Queen Adelaide. In 1914, the bridge was widened, and further widening and strengthening took place between 1999 and 2001. The Duke of Kent reopened Kingston Bridge on 29 June 2001.

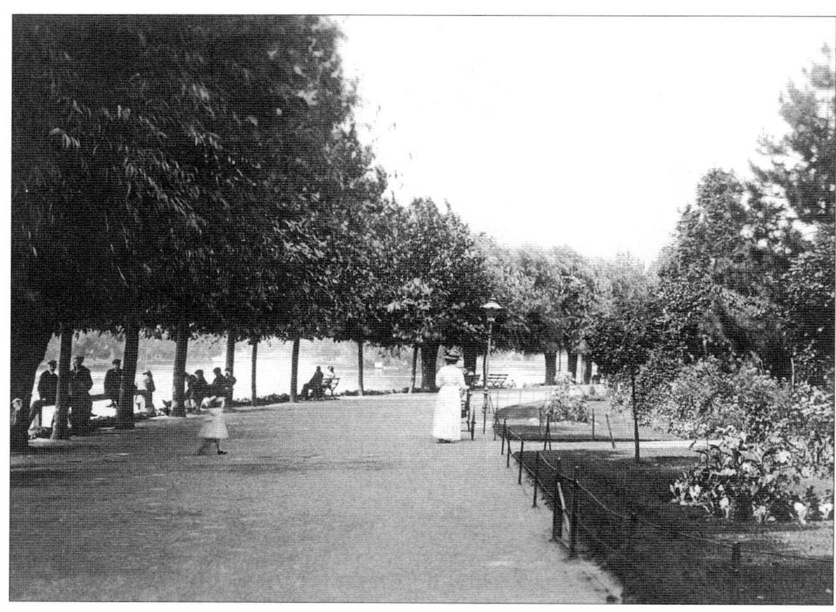

169 Covering over 14 acres, Canbury Gardens are downstream of Kingston Bridge. This postcard view of Canbury Promenade shows a tranquil scene before the First World War. The card was postally used in August 1914.

170 The popular mile-and-a-half stretch of river between Kingston and Teddington was used for racing by sailing craft, canoes and racing skiffs. The message on the back of this old postcard of Teddington Reach notes, 'One X shows Trowlock Island and the other my sailing boat coming up the Reach.'

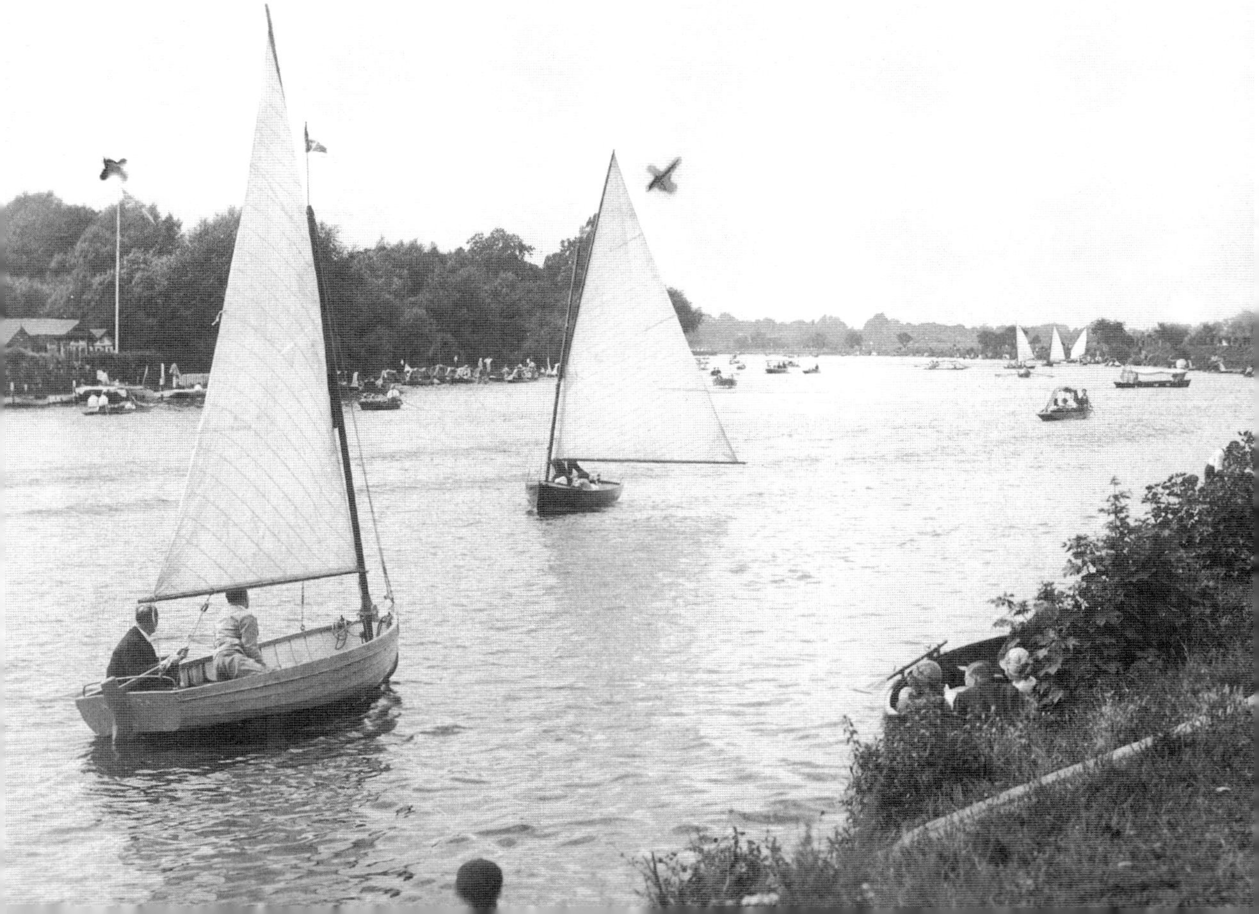

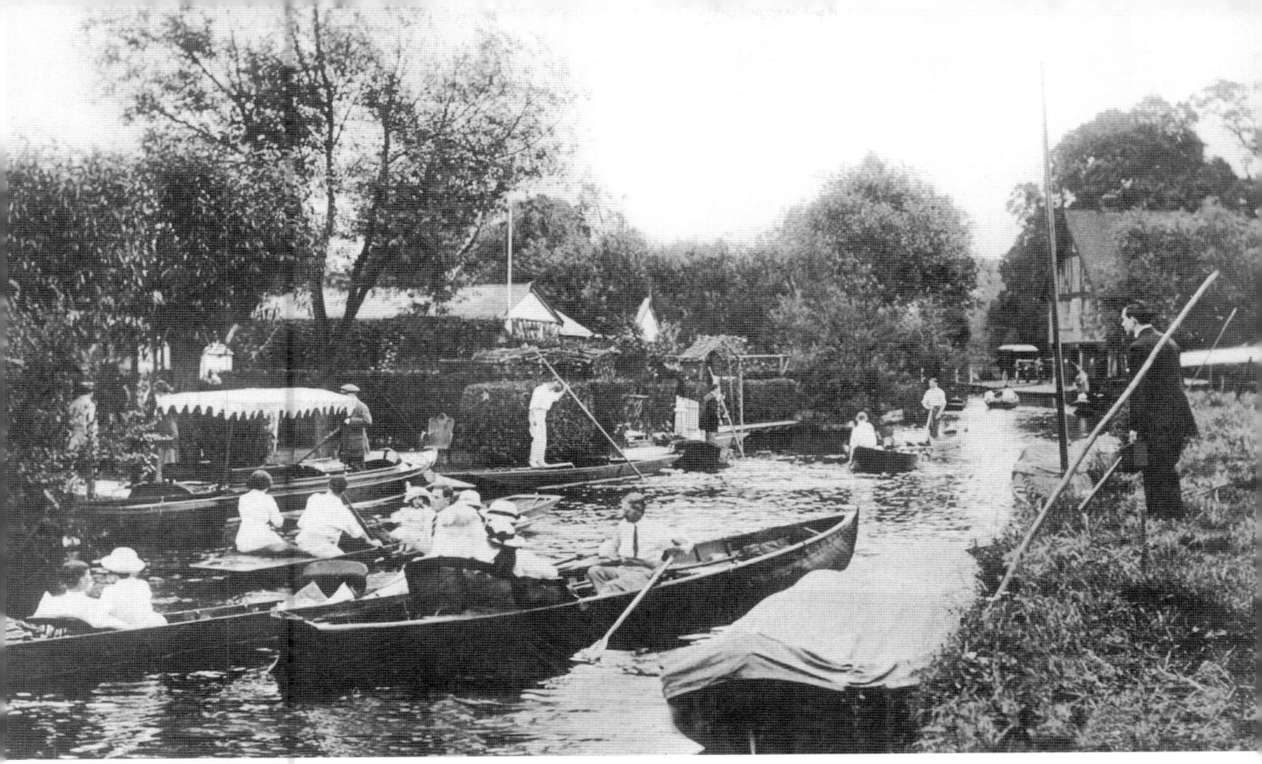

171 The Backwater, Trowlock Island, Teddington. The river in this vicinity could become quite crowded at times, while positions in the backwater around the wooded island were likely to be taken up quickly by small boats as tea time approached.

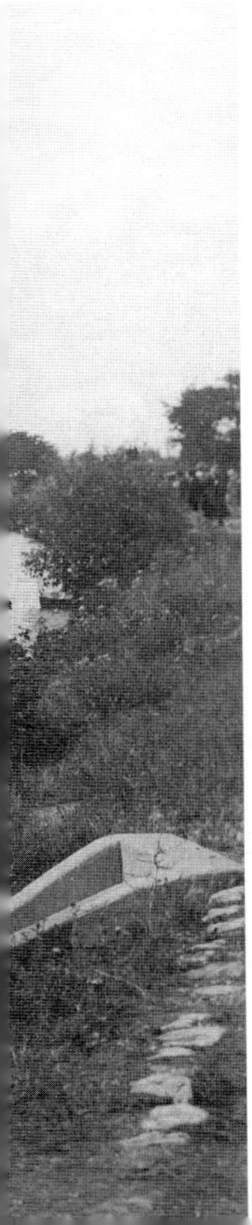

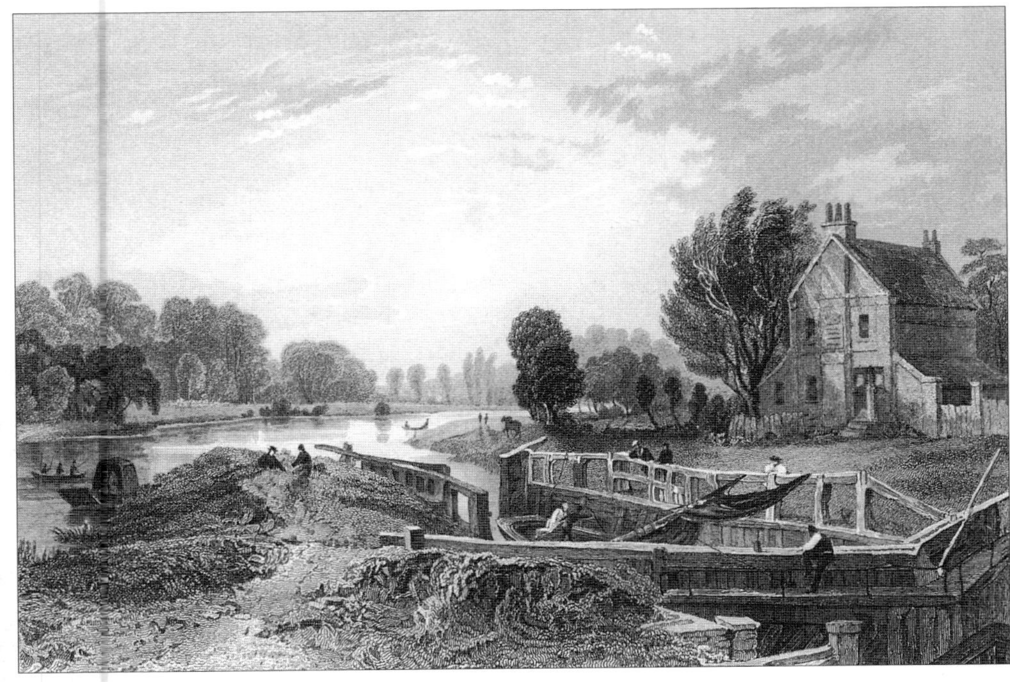

172 Teddington Locks, an engraving from *Tombleson's Thames*, *c*.1834. W.G. Fearnside commented, 'Returning again to the banks of the river, we find the current, with quickened pace, hastening toward Teddington lock and weir, which are the last impediments offered to the free flowing of the stream; and at this place all influence from the diurnal influx of the tide ceases to be experienced.'

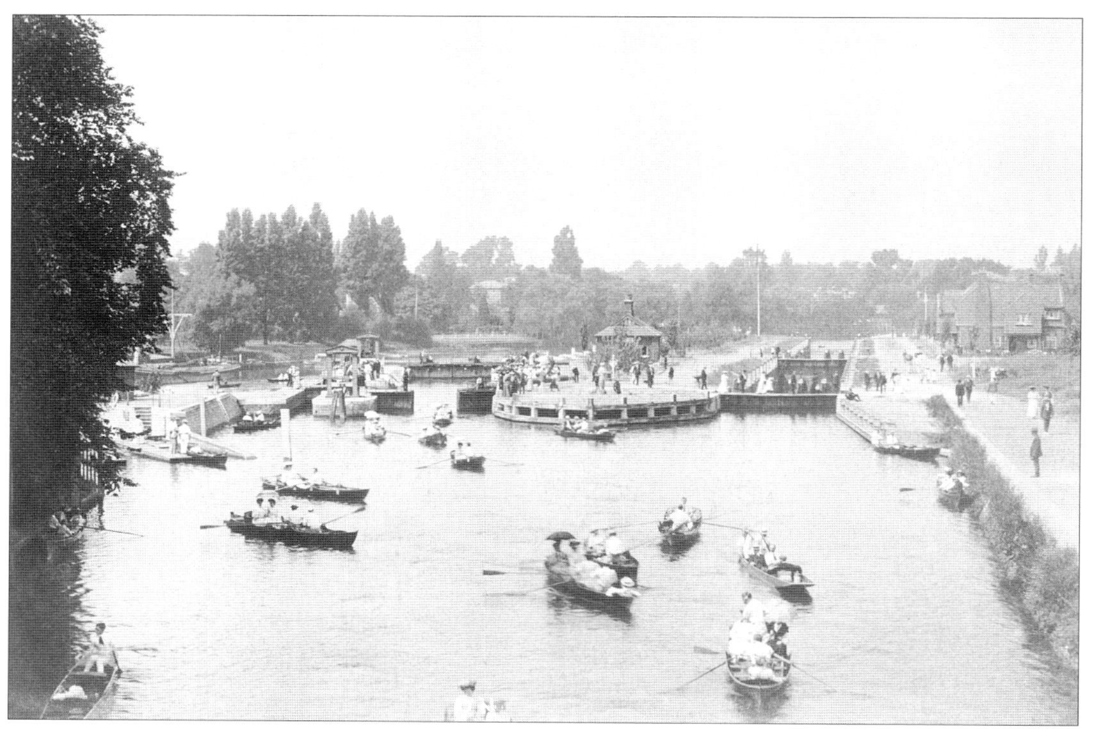

173 At the turn of the 19th century, Teddington Lock had become too small to accommodate all the barges and tugs coming upstream with the tide at the same time. A larger lock, known as the New Lock, was opened on 11 June 1904 at Teddington. It enabled a tug with a string of barges to pass through at one operation.

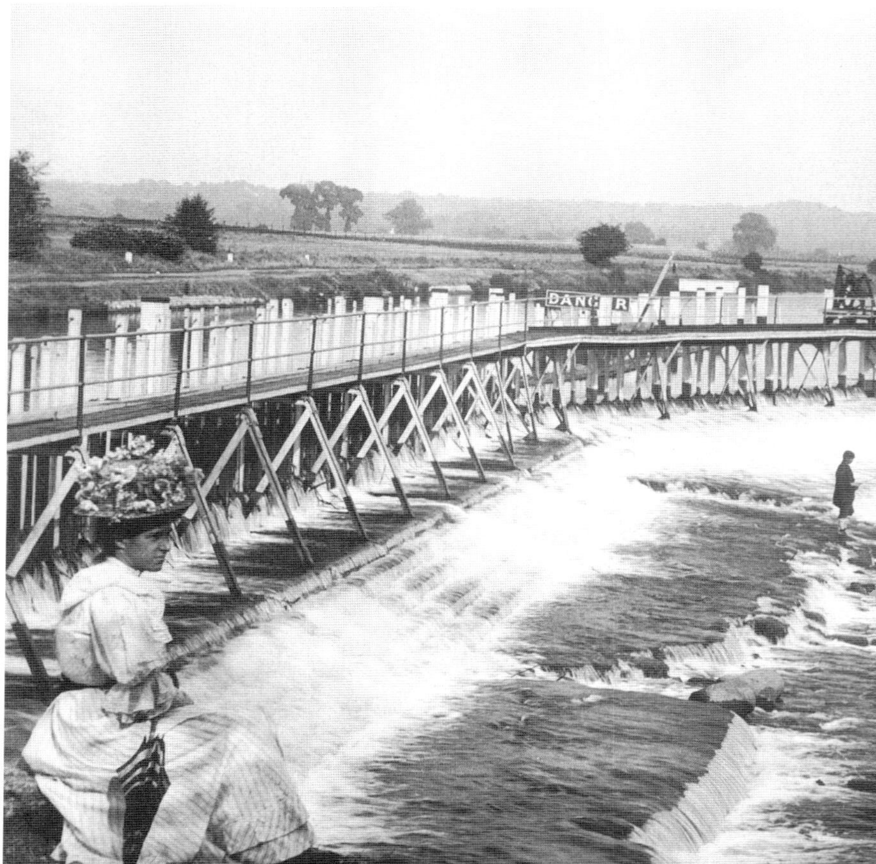

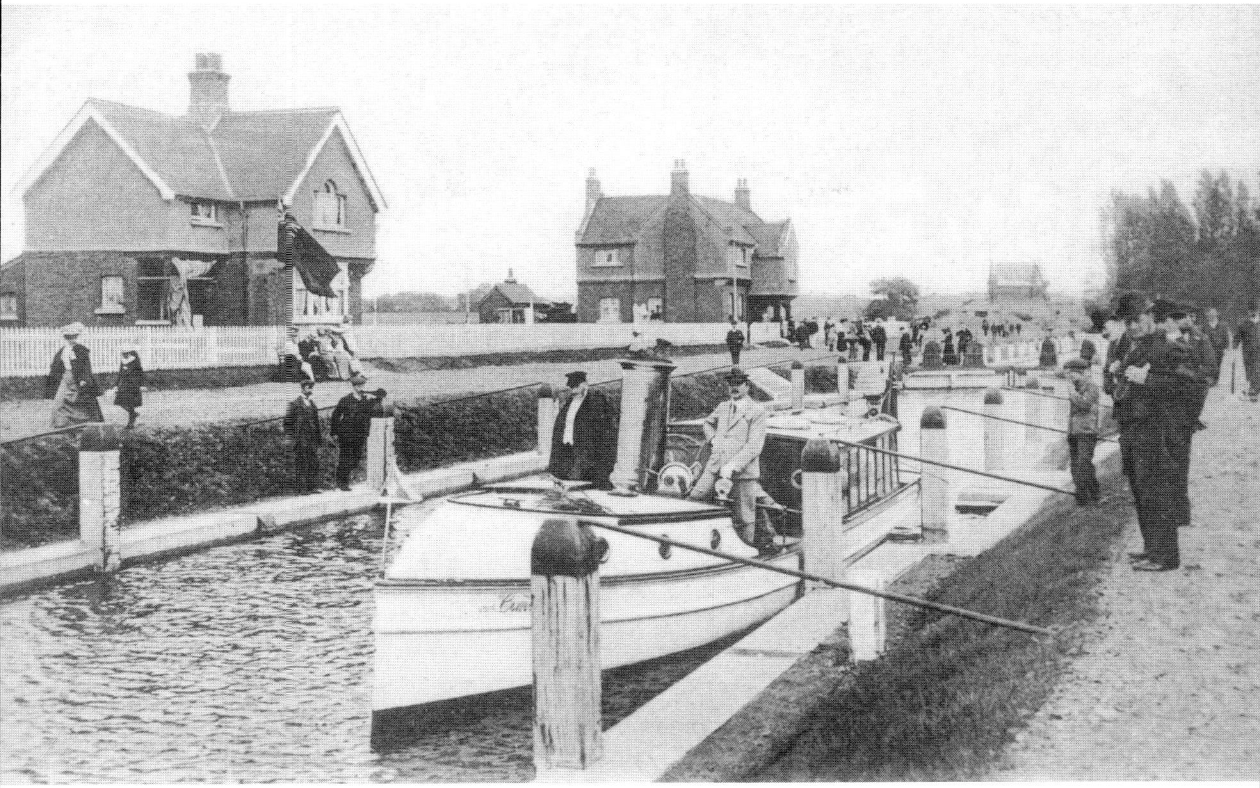

174 An Edwardian view of a steam launch at the New Lock, Teddington.

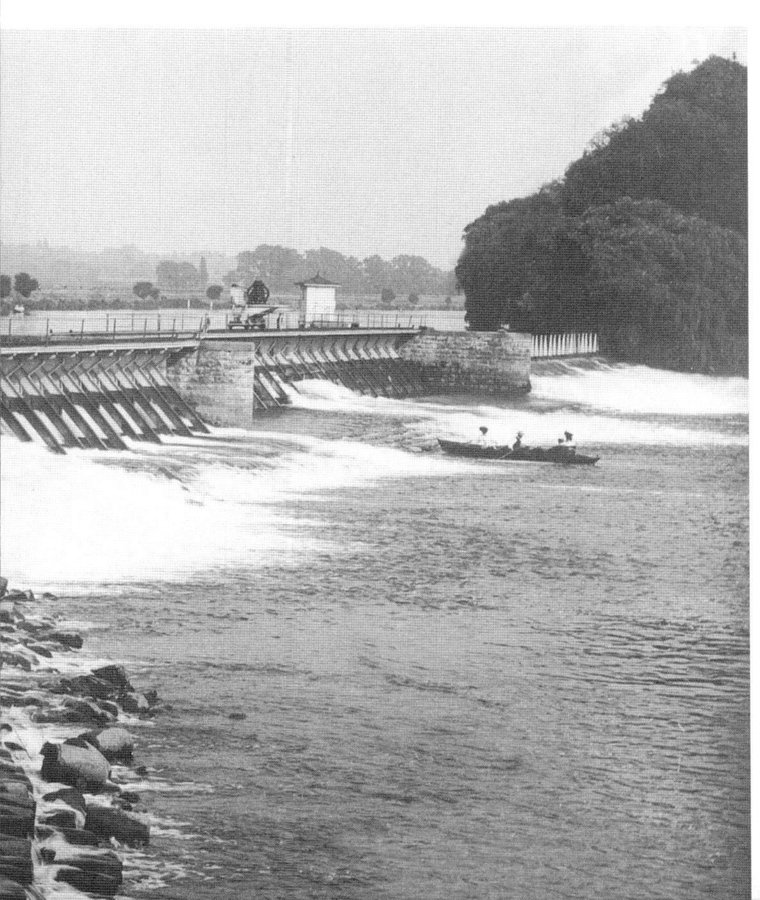

175 In 1869, Teddington Weir was rebuilt by the Thames Conservancy and in 1883 it was made much larger. This postcard of the weir was postally used on 29 August 1910.

Bibliography

Bamford, Horace, *The Old-World Village of Sonning-on-Thames* (nd)
Bowerman, Diana, *Historic Thames Valley Taverns* (1976)
Boydell, John and Joshua, *An History of the River Thames* (1794)
Chaplin, Peter H., *The Thames from source to tideway* (1982)
Cooke, W.B. and Cooke, George, *Views on the Thames* (1822)
Dickens, Charles, *Dickens's Dictionary of the Thames* (1887)
Gedge, Paul, *Thames Journey* (1949)
Hall, Mr and Mrs S.C., *The Book of the Thames* (1859)
Harper, Charles G., *Thames Valley Villages, Vol. II* (1910)
Harrison, Ian, *The Thames from source to sea* (2004)
Hayward, Graham, *Stanford's River Thames: A Companion and Boating Guide* (1988)
Ireland, Samuel, *Picturesque Views on the River Thames* (1792)
Jerome, Jerome K., *Three Men in a Boat* (1889)
Leslie, George D., *Our River* (1888)
Mindell, Ruth and Jonathan, *Bridges over the Thames* (1985)
Nicholson Ordnance Survey Guide to the Thames (1984)
Nicholson Ordnance Survey Guide to the Waterways: Thames, Wey, Kennet & Avon (1997)
Paget-Tomlinson, E., *Britain's Canal and River Craft* (1979)
Pearson, Michael, *Canal Companion: Kennet and Avon, River Thames Oxford-Reading-Brentford* (2007)
Pennell, Joseph & Elizabeth Robins, *The Stream of Pleasure* (1891)
Read, Susan, *The Thames of Henry Taunt* (1989)
Rolt, L.T.C., *The Thames from Mouth to Source* (1951)
Ryan, E.K.W., *The Thames from the Towpath* (1938)
Salter, J.H. and J.A, *Salter's Guide to the Thames* (16th edn 1913)
Taunt, Henry, *A New Map of the Thames from Thames Head to London* (3rd edn 1879)
Thacker, Fred S., *The Thames Highway Volume II: Locks and Weirs* (1920)
Thorne, James, *Rambles by Rivers: The Thames* (1847)
Tombleson's Thames (c.1834)
Ward, Lock & Co., *The Thames* (4th edn)

Index

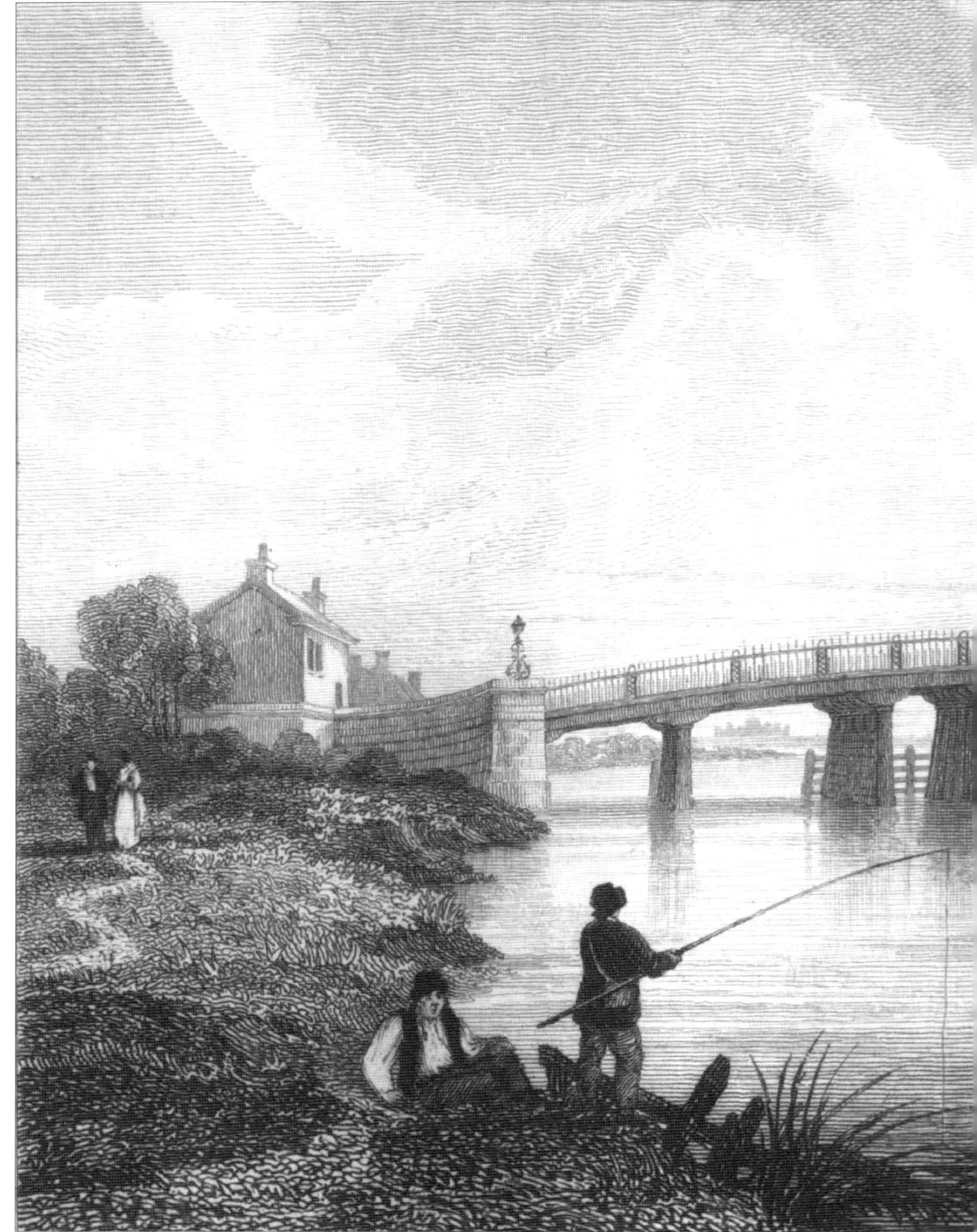